W9-CHP-035

Contours of Canadian Thought

The leaps of knowledge in nineteenth-century science shook the foundations of religious and humanistic values throughout much of the world. The Darwinian Revolution and similar developments presented enormous philosophical challenges to Canadian scientists, philosophers, and men of letters. Their responses, many and varied, form a central theme in this collection of essays by one of Canada's leading intellectual historians.

McKillop explores the thought of a number of English-Canadian thinkers from the 1860s to the 1920s, decades that saw Canada's entry into the modern age. We meet Daniel Wilson, an educator and ethnologist for whom the pursuit of science was a form of poetic engagement, requiring the poet's sensibilities; John Watson, one of the world's leading exponents of objective idealism, whose philosophical premises helped to undermine the very religious tradition he sought to bolster; and William Dawson LeSueur, an apostle of Positivism, whose spirited defence of critical inquiry and evolutionary social ethics led him towards an entirely contradictory position.

In addition to profiles of individuals, McKillop considers the ways in which their ideas operated in the context of Canadian institutions including the universities and the press. From these perspectives emerges a detailed analysis of the life of the mind of English Canada in an age of questioning, of doubt, and of struggle to reorient the intellectual and philosophical positions of a quickly changing society.

A.B. McKILLOP is professor of history at Carleton University. He is the author of *A Disciplined Intelligence: Critical Inquiry and Canadian Thought in the Victorian Era* and *A Critical Spirit: The Thought of William Dawson LeSueur*, and editor of *Contexts of Canada's Past: Selected Essays of W.L. Morton* and W.D. LeSueur's *William Lyon Mackenzie: A Reinterpretation*.

A.B. McKILLOP

Contours of
Canadian Thought

F
1021
.M345

UNIVERSITY OF TORONTO PRESS

Toronto Buffalo London

© University of Toronto Press 1987
Toronto Buffalo London
Printed in Canada

ISBN 0-8020-5740-3 (cloth)
ISBN 0-8020-6652-6 (paper)

Canadian Cataloguing in Publication Data

McKillop, A.B., 1946–
Contours of Canadian thought

Includes index.
ISBN 0-8020-5740-3 (bound) ISBN 0-8020-6652-6 (pbk.)

1. Canada – Intellectual life. I. Title.

FC95.3.M35 1987   971.05   C87-093279-9 F1021.M35 1987

This book has been published with the
assistance of the Canada Council and the
Ontario Arts Council
under their block grant programs.

For Richard A. Swanson

Contents

Preface

It is no longer necessary, as it once was, to be tentative when suggesting that in the colonial Canada of a century or so ago men and women might actually have had a little time to think and to reflect. Life in Canada during the nineteenth century was arduous, certainly enough; but the historical scholarship of the past two decades has demonstrated that the generations of colonial Canadians were generally well aware of what was going on in the larger Anglo-American intellectual world. That we do not yet have the full measure of their response, or of their contributions to it, is less a reflection of a failure of yesterday's Canadians to address the major intellectual problems of their day than it is of the simple fact that later historians have yet to investigate many important elements of their own past. A poorly investigated past can lead, after all, only to a diminished history and an impoverished historical consciousness.

This book consists of a number of explorations I have made in order to outline some – but by no means all – of what I believe to be the formative contours of English-Canadian thought. It is intended to introduce university students to some of the major works of scholarship in the small but lively field of Canadian intellectual history, to indicate problems inherent in the writing of intellectual history, and to suggest possible approaches that might help surmount these problems. The first three chapters address these concerns. In 'Nationalism, Identity, and Canadian Intellectual History,' I sought to survey some of the few major works in the field in the early 1970s, and to demonstrate the way in which most of them emerged from the traditional preoccupation of Canadian historians with political nationality and cultural identity. Commenting at some length on the pioneering work of S.F. Wise, Ramsay Cook, and Carl Berger, among others, it dealt primarily with a level of Canadian thought that stood somewhere between journalistic observation and philosophical system-making. It did so because very little in the way of Canadian historical scholarship suggested otherwise.

By the time 'So Little on the Mind' was written, some six years later, historians had begun to alter this picture in major ways. By the early 1980s, a few books by Carl Berger, S.E.D. Shortt, myself, and others had demonstrated the fact that the thought of Canadian historians, academics, scientists, philosophers, and clergymen held a degree of coherence, substance, thematic continuity, and relationship to 'universal' themes not previously known or understood. 'So Little on the Mind' addressed itself to the nature and implications of some of these new studies and put forward a general approach to intellectual history that would lead intellectual historians to consider a central problem: how to investigate the thought of individuals while not ignoring the complexity of social realities. 'Science, Humanism, and the Ontario University' dealt with the problems of intellectual historians rather more obliquely – this time in the context of the environment in which most of them do their work: the university. It is at least worth considering whether the marginalization of intellectual history within the historical profession (which helps account why relatively little of it is done) is itself a measure of the decreasing weight of humanistic values in a civilization largely preoccupied by, and dependent upon, science and technology.

It is not too much to say that each of the remaining chapters of the book has the relationship between scientific and humanistic values as a central theme. 'Evolution, Ethnology, and Poetic Fancy' focuses on the thought of Daniel Wilson, one of Canada's foremost scientists and educationalists during the early years of the Darwinian Revolution. 'Science, Ethics, and "Modern Thought"' provides a general context by which to measure the orientation of the English-Canadian response to the social and ethical implications of Darwinism, and it fixes on the figure of the most distinguished of Canada's native-born men of letters, William Dawson LeSueur – a veritable apostle of the Victorian 'critical spirit.' 'The Research Ideal and the University of Toronto' examines the institutional context in which Daniel Wilson's career took place, the University of Toronto, and re-examines aspects of his scientific thought (and, inferentially, that of his generation) against that of younger scientists dedicated to divorcing contemporary science from all forms of metaphysical and traditional humanistic claims. It also suggests that academic thought and accomplishment cannot properly be fully understood apart from the specific institutional context in which it takes place.

'The Idealist Legacy' deals with the means by which many Canadians achieved a measure of intellectual accommodation to the seemingly divisive imperatives of late nineteenth-century science and religion. It draws attention to the thought of John Watson of Queen's University, one of the foremost idealist philosophers of this period. For his own generation, Watson was a powerful and persuasive force in Canadian life, and the idealism he preached and wrote about seemed to bridge the widening gulf between science and sentiment. Ultimately, however, the 'idealist alternative' proved inadequate for those who managed to survive that most idealistic of wars, the Great War of 1914–18. 'Science, Authority, and the American Empire' examines the postwar attitudes of a number of members of the English-Canadian intelligentsia, particularly those who wrote for the *Canadian Forum* in the 1920s. It indicates that while, to some, the nineteenth century seemed to have come 'unhinged,' a considerable measure of continuity of intellectual concern remained – not least of which was the preoccupation with the relationship between science and values.

In 1860 Canada was an overwhelmingly rural, largely pre-industrial society, a colonial dependency which, while part of a frontier environment in North America, was nevertheless dependent on Great Britain for many of its intellectual and cultural props. By the conclusion of the Great War, almost as many Canadians lived in cities or towns as on farms, a complex industrial economy existed, and the dependency on 'the old country' was becoming fragile. America, accordingly, now received the kind of earnest Canadian attention in intellectual matters that earlier had been reserved for Great Britain. Accompanying this major demographic, social, and economic transformation was an equally significant yet elusive shift in attitudes, thought, and values that transcended national boundaries: the reorientation of religious belief, Christian and usually Protestant, that took place in the face of the intrusion of evolutionary science into hitherto sacrosanct domains. Religious and secular imperatives met and mixed with ambiguous and disturbing results in the half century after Charles Darwin released his *Origin of Species* for publication in 1859.

That mixture, and the differing forms of personal and institutional accommodation it entailed, lie at the heart of this book. Much of Canada's intellectual past consists of the attempts of people who were moralists of different hues to come to grips with modernity as they understood it. My hope is that in offering this collection of explorations, a measure of understanding will have been gained about the nature of that moral concern and of certain aspects of the modernity they faced.

Most of the pieces in this book were originally given as invited occasional addresses, but together they form a thematically coherent whole. I have tried to excise undue repetition, but to the extent that a degree of repetition remains I can only respond, with Northrop Frye, by saying that one can do worse than to rearticulate one's own central myths and to hope that they reflect significant contours in the intellectual life of the English-Canadian historical reality. I thank the publishers who have been gracious enough to allow me to reprint pieces that first appeared in their pages. I also offer my thanks to Gerald Hallowell, of the University of Toronto Press, for encouraging me to undertake the project, to Rosemary Shipton for her expert and efficient copy editing, and to Gwen Peroni for rendering the resulting text into 'machine-readable' form. Carleton University, in particular Dean Naomi Griffiths of the Faculty of Arts, provided the funding necessary for transcription.

Finally, a word about the person to whom this book is dedicated. Richard A. Swanson, of the Department of History at the University of Manitoba, has opened the minds of many students to the complexities and the joys of intellectual history. I am fortunate to have been one such student. I have not always been wise enough to act upon his astute counsel (on 'Swanson's Second Law,' for example), but I count myself lucky to know him as teacher, colleague, and friend.

Contours of Canadian Thought

1

Nationalism, Identity, and Canadian Intellectual History

This piece was possibly the first attempt in Canada to discuss directly the orientation and characteristics of historical writing on the intellectual history of its English-speaking community. It suggested that the few books and articles that had been written on different facets of intellectual history in Canada tended, on the whole, to be outgrowths of the older concern with national identity and to be preoccupied with nationalism. This article can be seen, in retrospect, as itself an unintentional expression of the themes under investigation. Its concluding call for a broadening of 'intellectual history' into 'cultural history' in order to utilize the imaginative works of novelists and cultural critics as legitimate sources for historical investigation remains as potentially fruitful now as it did when the piece was originally published. It appeared under the same title in Queen's Quarterly *81 (winter 1974): 533–50.*

The late Frank H. Underhill issued a challenge to Canadian historians: 'It strikes me,' he said, 'that, if we are to understand ourselves better, we need to devote a great deal more study to our intellectual history, to the values, to the guiding ideas and ideals, that have influenced the minds of different groups of Canadians at different times.'[1] Underhill wrote prior to the great national awakening that was given its momentum by Expo 67. Since then, there has been intensified debate over the question of American control of Canadian resources and an intoxicating rise in nationalist feeling in almost every facet of Canadian life. Part of this expression of nationalist consciousness resulted in an increased number of people engaged in the academic study and writing of Canadian history, and with this development came a degree of specialization within the discipline unknown prior to the 1960s. By the 1970s nationally organized groups committed to the study and writing of Canadian urban history, western Canadian history, Loyalist studies, and Canadian labour history – among others – had come into existence. No such organization, however, has been formed for the study of Canadian intellectual history. Hence, the editor of a 1972 collection of articles in Canadian history could write: 'The historian of ideas has received practically no attention from students of the Canadian scene.'[2] The first problem of the student of Canadian intellectual history is simply that, relative to other branches of the discipline in Canada, there has been so little of it written.

Before an attempt is made to characterize and to assess some of the intellectual history that *has* been written in Canada, it is first necessary to consider briefly the nature and distinguishing characteristic of 'intellectual history' in general. Described decades ago as an endeavour so methodologically amorphous that practising it was like trying to nail jelly to a wall, intellectual history can perhaps best be understood in terms of its insistence that the value of ideas is derived from the relationship of those ideas to an historical context that is predominantly social in nature. In contrast to exponents of the 'history of ideas,' who assess the significance of ideas in terms of the inner coherence and logic of a particular system of thought, intellectual historians view such significance as coming from an essentially external context. As the American historian John Higham noted in a seminal article entitled 'Intellectual History and its Neighbors,' the intellectual historian presupposes a conception of mind that is primarily functional: mind works in response to environment and 'makes its mark by serving the practical needs of the workaday world.'[3]

But how may this distinction make more clear the work of Canadian historians on the subject of Canadian thought? Perhaps the best way to answer this question is by referring to one of the few extended discussions of the nature and direction of Canadian intellectual history. In an article entitled 'Sermon Literature and Canadian Intellectual History,' S.F. Wise states: 'Canadian intellectual history must be concerned, almost of necessity, with the kinds of ideas that lie between the formal thought of the philosopher or the political theorist and the world of action, and probably closer to the latter. Since (to understate the matter) no connected history of formal thought in Canada is possible, the Canadian intellectual historian must be concerned primarily with the interrelationship between ideas and actions, and therefore the intellectual commonplaces of an age, its root notions, assumptions, and images, will be of more significance to him than the study of coherent bodies of abstract thought.'[4] For Wise, the endeavour of studying ideas in Canada is aided by viewing those ideas – whether political, religious, or literary – as related to, and gaining their significance from, an external context. Ideas must be viewed in their relationship to the actions of men, and these will reflect, as often as not, a thought that is not well articulated: 'notions,' 'assumptions,' 'images,' and 'values.' Here, then, we have an intellectual history which relies as much upon the insights of social psychologists as it does upon those of the practitioners of textual criticism (whether literary or philosophical).

Such a conception of the function of the intellectual historian can indeed bear fruit for the study of much of Canadian thought, as Wise himself shows in his analysis of the social and ideological assumptions reflected in the sermons of Bishops Charles Inglis of Nova Scotia, Jacob Mountain of Lower Canada, and John Strachan of Upper Canada. This, ironically enough, is largely because Canadian thought in general has been characterized by a 'colonial mentality' which imported from external sources – usually British or American – much of its intellectual, as well as its investment, capital. Hence, while the historian of ideas may well lament the failure of Canada to have produced a Bentham or a Burke, a Mill or a Russell, the intellectual historian in Canada has no lack of minds to study that reflect, to use Wise's phrase, 'the commonplaces of political or social language' derived from external authorities. In other words, if the intellectual historian in Canada looks for originality of thought he will find precious little. But having faced this fact, he should not let it serve as an excuse for ignoring the thought which did exist. If he sets as the aim of his endeavour the admittedly more prosaic goal of establishing what it was that Canadians *were* thinking, and what assumptions informed what thought, he will find himself on a fascinating and, in the end, a more productive line of inquiry. To carry out this research is not to celebrate the mediocre or to elevate the second-rate; it is rather to recognize colonial minds as just that, and to view colonialism as a phenomenon indicative of a stage of political, constitutional, and social growth, not as a source of national shame. Colonial minds must be studied not primarily as colonial, but as minds.

Another significant factor has helped to shape studies of Canadian thought. Canadians have been preoccupied throughout their national existence with the twin problems of nationalism and national 'identity.' Hence is asked again and again the answerless question: 'Who are we and what are we?' Such a national obsession (so much so that a leading Canadian historian has declared it to be the Canadian equivalent of Portnoy's complaint[5]) came about, at least in part, because of the long-held assumption that a national 'identity' would somehow inevitably and naturally emerge as the result of the process of political evolution that witnessed the gradual movement of Canada from colony to nation. Not until certain external, 'foreign' restrictions – seen to hinder this evolution to nationhood – were removed would Canada's 'identity' be realized. As applied to the areas of race and religion, and as witnessed in the Manitoba Schools Question or in the early twentieth-century popular novels of Ralph Connor, this nationalist fallacy was further based upon the notion that only when the disruptive influences of diverse languages and cultural attitudes were removed could the 'coming

Canadian' (to use an evolutionary expression current at the time) emerge and, with him, a unique Canadian identity. This was especially true with respect to English-Canadian attitudes towards the French Canadian, whose religion and cultural life were seen largely as the relics of a feudal past outside the mainstream of progress. Not until the 'two solitudes' were one, it was argued, could a truly Canadian identity be achieved.

Although the standard dictionary definition of 'identity' – derived from the terminology of philosophy – rests heavily upon the notion of similarity of kind (which translated into social terms means 'harmony' or 'consensus'), perhaps a more fruitful way of conceiving of an 'identity' for Canada is by expanding the term to incorporate within it the potential for contradiction, diversity, and paradox. The basis for this national (and individual) identity may be provided by the common recognition that part of the constitution of the national-state involves an acknowledgement of the existence of diversity, whether of language, race, region, or ideas. This conception of identity, viewed simply as the nature of social circumstances at any given point in time, allows Canadian intellectual historians to cease doubting the value of their efforts should they be studying thought that is derived from beyond Canada's boundaries. Whether thought in Canada is 'indigenous' or 'derivative' becomes a secondary consideration. The important activity is the assessment of how those ideas, whatever their origins, are handled within the Canadian context. As Wise notes in his discussion of the duties of the Canadian intellectual historian: 'No doubt the stock of Canadian ideas is replenished every generation from European and American sources; and doubtless it should be an important function of the Canadian intellectual historian to perform the sort of operations that will trace Canadian ideas to their ultimate external source. But his major task, surely, is to analyze the manner in which externally-derived ideas have been adapted to a variety of local and regional environments, in such a way that a body of assumptions uniquely Canadian has been built up; and to trace the changing content of such assumptions.'[6]

It is not surprising, therefore, given this traditional quest by Canadians for collective self-definition, that most of the books concerned with ideas in Canada address themselves in one way or another to the question of national identity, and that all must be viewed as 'intellectual history' rather than exercises in the 'history of ideas' because each views the significance of ideas as derived from their relationship to an external, social context. I shall deal here only with those works which seem most provocative and stimulating in this respect: Gordon Stewart and George Rawlyk's *A People Highly Favoured of God* (1972); a series of articles on the subject of Upper Canadian Toryism by S.F. Wise; Carl Berger's *The Sense of Power* (1970); Ramsay Cook's *Canada and the French-Canadian Question* (1966) as well as his *The Maple Leaf Forever* (1972); and D.G. Jones's *Butterfly on*

Rock (1970). It should be added that the books and articles discussed will be looked at primarily in terms of the methods they employ, their commentary (explicit or implicit) upon nationalism and identity, and their implications for the future study of Canadian intellectual history. Any assessment of the validity of their conclusions on the basis of other evidence would serve little purpose in the present context.[7]

The first historical period that has been given extended treatment by Canadian intellectual historians – mainly because of its formidable influence in shaping aspects of the Canadian character – has been the age of the American and French revolutions. If the American national psyche was forged, as some have claimed, in the fires of the revolutionary experience, Canada's has been shaped at least in part by its rejection of the American (and later the French) Revolution. In Upper Canada, the influence of the Loyalist tradition – rooted both in fact and in myth – has indeed been strong in causing aspects of this identity to be articulated, as the work of both Wise and Berger shows. The case of another British North American colony during the American Revolution, Nova Scotia, was, however, more complex.

A substantial proportion of the population of Nova Scotia on the eve of the revolution was in fact not British but Yankee. Nova Scotia had always kept fairly close cultural, social, and economic links with the New England colonies, so close that it has been described by a leading student of the period as 'New England's Outpost.'[8] The question that has always intrigued historians is, given this affinity with New England, why did Nova Scotia not join the American colonies in the rejection of the British imperial tie? What, in short, made 'The Neutral Yankees of Nova Scotia' (to use another J.B. Brebner title) remain neutral? Until recently most answers tended to be drawn largely in social and economic terms: the debt of Halifax merchants to mercantile relationships with England; dependence upon the British navy; the isolation of the outports (caused by geological barriers); and so forth. With the publication of *A People Highly Favoured of God: The Nova Scotia Yankees and the American Revolution* (1972), by Gordon Stewart and George Rawlyk, the psychological and religious dimensions of this 'crisis of identity' have been given a more substantial emphasis and significance. Many of the American settlers who emigrated to Nova Scotia had done so a full decade or so prior to the outbreak of the American Revolution in 1775–6. Because of this, they missed what historians such as Bernard Bailyn have called a crucial decade – a decade which saw the articulation and intellectual justification (in pamphlets, sermons, and newspapers) of a revolutionary stance. For the Nova Scotia Yankees, the result was a profound crisis in their social and individual identities.

It is here that the religious element enters. The decades before the revolution in

America had seen an immensely popular, evangelical, religious revival known as the 'Great Awakening.' Historians have argued persuasively that this phenomenon, democratic in some of its implications, helped to prepare the emotional state of mind necessary for many Americans to accept what essentially was a democratic revolution. Transposed into Nova Scotia, however, the Awakening – led by the popular preacher Henry Alline – had a very different psychological effect. Alline's preaching did indeed give Nova Scotians an identity, but it was one that was apocalyptic and other-worldly, one that allowed those caught up in the movement to become convinced that they had been chosen by God not to throw off a tyrant's shackles but to remain apart from the political sins being committed by both sides. Alline, as Stewart and Rawlyk point out, 'constantly emphasized in his sermons that New England was no longer deserving either of respect or allegiance, [and the result was that the Nova Scotian] Yankees began to extricate themselves from the domination of New England which had placed them in such an awkward situation during the revolutionary war. Instead of being a backward offshoot of New England on the remote, northern fringes of the continent, the Yankees of Nova Scotia could regard themselves as a people with a unique history, a distinct identity and special destiny ... By creating a religious ideology that was specifically geared to conditions in the northern colony, the Great Awakening began to turn the Yankees into Nova Scotians.'[9]

As interesting for our purposes as Stewart and Rawlyk's specific arguments is the type of 'intellectual history' they conceived themselves to have been writing. The influence of the Great Awakening in Nova Scotia was found not in highly articulate pamphlets written by members of an elite group, but in the thought of farmers and fishermen. 'This is an intellectual history,' the authors state, 'of a people "at the bottom" who read but little and whose major preoccupations in life were tilling fields and catching fish.' Indeed, they almost go so far as to take their work out of the area of intellectual history altogether: 'Rather than being intellectual history it is more accurate to regard this volume as an attempt to describe the effect of widely held religious values on a particular society at a crucial period in its development' (x). Their work is best understood, however, despite their disclaimers, as a good example of intellectual history as characterized above: as history that insists upon assessing the influence of ideas according to the social context in which those ideas are found. Indeed, this context is in fact the authors' major interest: their work, like that of John Irving on Social Credit in Alberta, is not so much concerned with tracing the influence of any one idea or cluster of ideas as with analysing social behaviour under certain exceptional environmental circumstances.

One step in time towards the present and in method towards the history of ideas is the work of S.F. Wise on the nature of Loyalism and on the Upper Canadian Tory mind. In attempting to understand both Tory thought and basic assumptions, as well as to establish the extent of electoral and intellectual support, Wise offers what amounts to a critique of the liberal-nationalist bias which dominated English-Canadian historiography from the 1920s through the 1950s – of which more shall be said shortly. It will be remembered that the Family Compact was long represented in many Canadian grade-school history textbooks as all that was anti-democratic, anti-liberal, retrogressive, oligarchic, bigoted, and power-hungry; in short, as a plain hindrance to the coming of responsible government and the movement towards nationhood. While by no means denying or ignoring the many shortcomings and weaknesses of Compact members, Wise attempted to understand various Tories as much as possible from within the framework of their own assumptions. He was able to do this by studying the rhetorical flourishes, the key words and phrases, in their sermons and political speeches – fraught as these often were with intellectual commonplaces and unquestioned assumptions. And it was precisely because their writings, speeches, and sermons were full of such shibboleths that Wise was able to draw from them the social values those Tories so desperately wished to preserve.

Wise chose to study English-Canadian conservative thinkers not only in the context of the circumstances in which they lived, but also in the less tangible context of their sense of the past and the influence of the European heritage from which they drew their ideas and assumptions. Thus he found an evangelical Christian providentialism derived from England strongly informing their thought. He found, too, the influence of eighteenth-century English thinkers such as Bolingbroke and Burke, And together, he notes, the combination of Anglo-conservatism and providentialism served as the basis for what Anglo-Canadians such as Bishop Strachan hoped would become a unifying myth for the nascent Canadian nationality. Such a hope, however, was doomed from the outset. As Wise concludes, in a brilliant essay appropriately entitled 'God's Peculiar Peoples':

Unlike Massachusetts Bay and nineteenth century French Canada, the societies of English-speaking British North America did not discover in the providential theology the materials for a myth that would unite them as a people apart, and supply them with a sense of inner cohesion and direction. Among the frontier folk of the Maritimes, the effect of the idea of a special Providence was to exalt the humble as against the worldly, and ultimately, when given a secular twist, to provide a basis for political dissent ... But in the hands of Strachan and his fellows, the providential sense of mission was too narrowly conceived, too deeply rooted in the defence of a dying order to catch the imagination of the people, and to provide the basis for an emergent Canadian nationalism.[10]

In his studies of Upper Canadian Toryism, Wise was thus investigating a phenomenon similar to that analysed by the authors of *A People Highly Favoured of God*: the felt necessity on the part of certain Nova Scotians in one case and of Upper Canadians in the other to bring into existence what in fact were mythologies that would provide a sense of corporate identity, a sense of community, for two provinces on the fringes of the British empire. 'The foremost function of myth,' Mircea Eliade has written, 'is to reveal the exemplary models for all human rites and all significant human activities ...'[11] In both Nova Scotia and Upper Canada an articulation of such exemplary models was strong indeed, and the insistence of Stewart, Rawlyk, and Wise upon exploring fully the social milieu in which such demands were made goes a long way towards explaining in one case how a sense of social identity more or less came about and in the other how it was thwarted. What is more, the work of these authors shows that one need not have as subject an original or brilliant mind, a Burke or Locke or Rousseau, in order to make the study of intellectual history yield a significant reward.

Wise's conclusions also present us with a paradox with respect to Canadian political nationality itself; the providential, Tory, anti-revolutionary tradition in English-Canadian thought, he notes, failed to produce a unifying myth that could serve as the basis for national consensus and hence identity. Yet the very force to which this Toryism apparently succumbed – nineteenth-century democratic liberalism – has in Wise's view been 'so episodic in character [at least in any radical form] that it may scarcely be said to have existed.'[12] This peculiar circumstance in Canadian political development perhaps makes more understandable how it could come about that Canada's leading liberal-nationalist historian, Frank Underhill, spent much of his intellectual life unsuccessfully (so he claimed) 'in search of Canadian liberalism,' finding the roots of that liberal tradition constantly thwarted by the forces of Toryism, while the dean of Canadian conservative-nationalist historians, Donald Creighton, has portrayed Sir John Macdonald's blueprint for the Canadian nation as having been progressively destroyed at every turn by Canadian liberals during 'Canada's first century.'[13]

Some of the manifestations of this paralytic feature of Canadian political history and historiography are implicitly assessed in the work of two of Canada's leading intellectual historians, Carl Berger and Ramsay Cook. A central feature of the work of both is the common concern with Canadian nationalism – of both liberal-nationalist and imperial-nationalist varieties. Considered together, their writings point to the following: that whereas liberal-nationalists were forced by the dictates of their political assumptions to ignore, if not repudiate, an integral part of Canada's history, imperial-nationalists in Canada were never fully able or willing, given the demands of their assumptions, to accept much of its sociology.

Carl Berger's *The Sense of Power: Studies in the Ideas of Canadian Imperialism* (1970) was an important contribution to Canadian intellectual history. One of the major reasons was that Berger methodically and in abundant detail reconstructed those aspects of Canadian history which liberal-nationalists had virtually ignored. Even more brazenly, he dared to study certain leading Anglo-Canadian imperialists within the larger context of their conceptions of Canadian nationality. To the uninitiated this may sound contradictory, for were not Canada's imperialists those who in fact *hindered* the growth of Canadian nationality through their insistence upon strengthening the imperial tie, in the same way that Upper Canadian Tories had obstructed the growth of constitutional nationality by their obstreperous resistance to responsible government? It is precisely because of his exploration of this seemingly contradictory equation of nationalism with imperialism that Berger makes his most significant contribution to Canadian historiography. Like Wise, he takes opposition to the liberal-nationalist interpretation of Canadian history: 'The conflict between imperialism and nationalism [which was basic to the liberal-nationalist interpretation],' he writes, 'added up to a struggle between the past and the future, the desire to remain a colony and the wish to be a free nation. Once this framework was accepted, it was easy to account for the failure of imperialism: it succumbed to Canadian nationalism.'[14]

Berger took upon himself the task of qualifying what in his view was a fallacious dichotomy. Moreover, he did what liberal-nationalist historians had seldom done: he took the thought of Canadian imperialists seriously and, like Wise and the Upper Canadian Tories, as much as possible looked at that thought from the point of view of their own assumptions. The result was that Berger found that Canadian imperialists, too, had a vision for Canada's 'national' future, a vision which – from their perspective – if carried out might have contributed greatly to 'national' awareness in the largest sense of the word. For Canadian imperialists, nationality did not end at the shores of the Atlantic; it extended over time and space to include within its conception both the land masses of the British empire (especially the imperial heartland, England) and the past existence and present value of a long and rich British political and cultural heritage. 'Canadian imperialism,' Berger concluded, 'was one variety of Canadian nationalism – a type of awareness of nationality which rested upon a certain understanding of history, the national character, and the national mission' (9).

To have taken imperialist thought seriously had scarcely been the major concern of liberal-nationalist historians such as O.D. Skelton, for to have done so would have meant the study of minds that were 'colonial' rather than 'national,' immature rather than mature. Hence, in their view such an endeavour could contribute little to any true understanding of the Canadian national consciousness.

Berger showed that this was emphatically not the case and his work reinforces the point made earlier about the necessity of studying those living in a colonial situation without making that colonial environment into a kind of intellectual skeleton-in-the-closet.

What Carl Berger did in the way of criticizing liberal-nationalists for having failed to recognize the validity of expressions of nationalism other than their own, Ramsay Cook has done for the imperial-nationalists themselves. In both *Canada and the French-Canadian Question* (1966), a series of informal essays written during the 'Quiet Revolution,' and *The Maple Leaf Forever* (1972), a collection of essays written in the period of post-Expo nationalism, Cook stressed – for the instruction of English and French Canadians alike – his claim that 'we have had too much, not too little, nationalism in Canada, and that our various nationalisms are the chief threat to the peace and survival of Canada.'[15]

When Cook writes of the dangers of competing nationalisms it is clear that whether he is speaking of the English- or French-Canadian variety he means the kind of nationalism upon which was based Berger's imperial-nationalists' creed. 'Like nationalists everywhere,' Berger wrote, 'the Canadian imperialists assumed that the people whose ideals they expressed possessed a distinctive national character which was the product of racial inheritance and social training, environment and historical experience' (128). It is precisely this nationalist-state appeal to the inflammable criteria of race – and with it language and religion – as the basis for social consensus, and hence national identity, to which Cook strenuously objects; for the persistence of such an appeal in a traditionally bicultural and demographically multi-ethnic country can only have negative consequences. (The history of schools questions in Manitoba, the North-West Territories – Saskatchewan and Alberta before 1905 – and Ontario in the first two decades in the twentieth century fully illustrates the strength of this claim.) Accordingly, Cook consistently puts forward as an alternate conception of nationality the Actonian 'nation-state' idea, which avoids racial and linguistic appeals by building nationality instead upon such juridical bases as constitutional structure and political boundaries and accepting such conditions as racial and linguistic diversity as part of the Canadian 'identity' itself: as sociological facts and not impediments to nationality.

Hence the very characteristics of Berger's Anglo-Canadian imperial-nationalists which were sources of at least potential national greatness – their deep sense of past racial heritage and their vision of a future grandeur based upon the predominance of that race – are shown by Cook also to have been their greatest weaknesses. The same sentiments which allowed them to believe with George Parkin in 'the immense energy' contained in 'the growing strength of the Empire,' an energy which Parkin believed 'might be turned in directions which would make for the world's good,'[16] also persuaded many of his Anglo-Canadian contemporaries that in order to do so it was necessary to create 'a homogeneous Race' in Canada.[17] At the same time, the very strength of nation-state 'patriots' such as the 'autonomist' J.S. Ewart – their refusal to combine appeals to race and religion as the basis for a sense of nationality – also blinded at least some of them to the fact that for others nationality was more than a purely cognitive experience. During his private studies as a young man, Ewart was once struck by a sentence that he read in Carlyle's work on heroes. The sentence went: 'Their feelings were the parents of their thoughts.' Ewart's response to this, as set forth in his notebook, was that 'Sentiments ought to be a posteriori – If a priori they are prejudices or predilections.'[18] This was precisely the basis of his critique of Canadian imperialist thought.

The result of this intellectual inability on the part of both nationalist-state and nation-state adherents to transcend their own 'nationalist' assumptions was, in a sense, the creation of two political solitudes within English-Canadian thought. This is illustrated, on the one hand, in a rather pathetic essay by one of Berger's imperial-nationalists, Andrew Macphail. No less brilliant for being pathetic, Macphail's essay, 'The Conservative,' puts forward the claim that the Quebec of its author's day is 'the last refuge of civilization upon this continent'; yet Macphail's conception of nationality is such that he can view the French Canadians only from the Anglo-Saxon heritage of which he is a product. French Canadians remain for him a people apart, and Quebec a refuge rather than an integral part of Canada. What is more, he is equally blinded by the near-religious nature of his imperial-nationalist faith to the arguments of those liberal-nationalists which would possibly have helped him to incorporate French Canada within his own sense of nationality.[19] Equally symptomatic, on the other hand, is John Ewart's insistence upon a 'Kingdom of Canada' that would nevertheless strip from the idea of the monarchy all ties based upon 'sentiment' or upon the sense of moral obligation.[20] While for Macphail, to use his own words, ultimately 'only dreams and memories last,' for Ewart no statement or creed could be legitimate or bear any claim to reality unless it could be reduced to a rigidly syllogistic form.[21]

At their two extremes, the competing nationalisms dissolve into mysticism and harden into rationalism; and the thought of Andrew Macphail and J.S. Ewart illustrates both the strengths and the weaknesses of the extreme forms of these major Anglo-Canadian nationalist positions. The major contribution of Berger and Cook lies in the fact that they point with clarity to these strengths and these weaknesses. Both do so by looking to the stock notions, assumptions, and intellectual obligations of Canadians as they have addressed themselves to the question of their nationality. In the end, Cook would undoubtedly agree with Berger's comment on Canadian nationalist thought, for it applies equally to the study and writing of Canadian intellectual history in general: the 'only way in which an account of Canadian nationalist thought can be written is by inquiring into the ideas and ideals which men in the past read into their interpretations of Canada and by exploring the relationships between these conceptions and the environment in which they circulated. Those who require more than this ask more of history than it can ever give.'

Several requirements are therefore necessary to facilitate a successful discovery of the full measure of Canadian intellectual life. First, there is the necessity to view Canada's long-held 'colonial' status as a constitutional phenomenon rather than a source of intellectual shame, and to recognize the equation of that colonial status and 'immaturity' of thought for the fallacious nineteenth-century evolutionary claim that it is.[22] Second, it is necessary to come to an understanding of the thought of Canadians by placing that thought against the social and intellectual contexts in which it is found, and assessing it through the analysis of the meanings of the assumptions, beliefs, and values that may be found, in varying degrees of articulation, within it. Third, it is necessary to recognize (as is evident when the claims of Berger and Cook are viewed in conjunction with one another) that neither the liberal-nationalist nor the imperial-nationalist conception of Canadian nationhood and identity contains the vital ingredients from which can be forged a new Canadian identity.

Identity is a matter of present existence, not a future pattern to be hammered out on the anvils of the national past; and since today's national existence is tomorrow's national history it becomes a requirement of the historian simply to delineate – neither to condemn nor to celebrate – the contours of that past. This may mean, within the Canadian context, outlining the predominantly conservative tone of the Canadian nineteenth century, a tone which S.F. Wise claims then represented 'the mainstream of Canadian opinion.'[23] Yet to do so at a time when one leading Canadian social critic has spoken of 'the impossibility of conservatism as a viable political ideology'[24] is by no means an easy task, for to many students of Canadian history this may seem an exercise in raising to the level of 'historical significance' those aspects of the Canadian past which, from the perspective of the 1970s, seem insignificant. It is far easier to elevate whatever elements of radicalism that have found their rightful place in Canadian history and thought to the level of a continuing political tradition battling against the prevailing orthodoxy than to assume the less pleasant duty of assessing the nature and influence of the particular orthodoxy itself. This point should not be misunderstood. I am not arguing that politically or religiously 'orthodox' thought should be studied at the expense of those currents of dissent and protest which have done so much to shape the course of Canadian history. I am arguing for a Canadian history, and especially a Canadian intellectual history, that is pursued by means of relating Canadian thought to the broadest possible social context – a history, in short, which is willing to take into account what Jacques Barzun once called the *esprit de finesse* that is the result of studying the 'reciprocal dependence of the articulate and inarticulate in life.'[25]

Intellectual history carried out in this manner gradually shades methodologically into the study of cultural history, if 'cultural' is considered in the anthropological sense of the word. And it is this emphasis upon a conception of the Canadian historical experience in broadly cultural terms that may bring about the most fruitful rewards for the future study of Canadian thought. Such an approach would ultimately lead to the recognition that Canadian political, religious, educational, and literary history are in fact products of the same social experience. To deny this, of course, is virtually impossible; yet in terms of the textbook treatment of Canadian history this seems to have almost been the case in the past. For the most part, Canadian historical studies seem to have implicitly assumed that even if 'Canadian history' and 'Canadian literature' are products of the same historical process, to be of 'historical significance' events must somehow be overtly political in nature. Hence historians have studied at length (and rightly, within the solely political context) the ambivalent political career of William Lyon Mackenzie, who in social terms may be observed to have failed to carry out a political rebellion because he failed for various reasons to garner sufficient popular support. Yet nowhere in history textbooks is mentioned the literary career of Susanna Moodie: a career which, no less ambivalent in its own way, nevertheless managed to put into words the terrors and delights, the tragedies and triumphs, of a life which was at once of the frontier and of 'civilization.' How many Canadian women during the first half of the nineteenth century attempted in a similar way to bring a degree of refined, 'civilized' life to the frontier? Surely the publication of Mrs Moodie's *Roughing It in the Bush* is as significant an event in its own way as were the heroics of Laura Secord, whose accomplishments with lantern and cow in the performance of a political act of bravery have long been celebrated.

The list of writings in Canadian literature that can serve, like Mrs Moodie's, as excellent sources by which to gain a sense of the *esprit de finesse* of any given period in Canadian intellectual and cultural life would be a substantial one. Thomas McCulloch's *The Stepsure Letters* (1821–2) and T.C. Haliburton's *The Clockmaker* (1836) are indispensable for an understanding of various aspects of the cultural life of Nova Scotia during the colonial period. Susanna Moodie's *Roughing It in the Bush* (1852) along with Catherine Parr Traill's *The Backwoods of Canada* (1836) are both strong documentations of life in Upper Canada during the second quarter of the nineteenth century. Canadian imperialism between the late nineteenth century and the conclusion of the Great War may be examined in either Sara Jeannette Duncan's novel *The Imperialist* (1904) or Beverley Baxter's *The Parts Men Play* (1920). The role that ethnicity and assimilationism played in the settlement of the 'last, best West' is reflected in a number of novels, ranging from those of Ralph Connor, such as *The Foreigner* (1909), to those by Robert E. Knowles, whose *The Undertow* (1906) is similar to Connor's fictional work in both theme and format. That life on the prairies during the first half of 'Canada's Century' was by no means as happy as romanticists of the West would have one believe is reflected in Frederick Philip Grove's *Fruits of the Earth* (1933), Sinclair Ross's *As For Me and My House* (1941), and John Marlyn's *Under the Ribs of Death* (1957). Finally, life in the Canada described by George Grant in *Lament for a Nation* (1965) and *Technology and Empire* (1969) is fictionalized in Richard Wright's *The Weekend Man* (1970) and by Harry J. Boyle in *The Great Canadian Novel* (1972).

The utilization of Canadian literature by Canadian historians as a means of examining various facets of the Canadian imaginative response to the environment is growing. Carl Berger and Ramsay Cook have recently published essays which utilize the study of fiction to assess the social and personal assumptions of a man and his age. In both cases the subject is Stephen Leacock. And what Berger and Cook have done for Leacock, J.L. and J.H. Thompson have done for Ralph Connor and A.G. Bailey for Sara Jeannette Duncan.[26]

One needs only to mention briefly two literary works which also make strong contributions to Canadian historical studies to give more credence to the claim that the study of Canadian literature is moving closer towards that of cultural history – and hence also towards intellectual history. The first, Eli Mandel's edited collection of essays, appropriately entitled *Contexts of Canadian Criticism* (1971), is organized into three sections: 'The Social and Historical Context,' 'The Theoretical Context,' and 'Patterns of Criticism.' There is scarcely an essay in this collection (which draws from the work of Canadian historians, philosophers, and literary critics) that cannot be described as in some measure an exercise in intellectual history.

The second book that must be mentioned in this regard is D.G. Jones's *Butterfly on Rock: A Study of Themes and Images in Canadian Literature* (1970). Jones's interpretive synthesis of much of Canadian literature, heavily influenced by the critical theory of Northrop Frye, was explicitly designed to employ a cultural approach to its subject. Such an approach, Jones admitted, is not without its difficulties: It 'assumes a relationship between literature and life that can never be defined with precision.' Nevertheless, it also allows him to isolate themes and images in a way that reveals how Canadian authors have 'participat[ed] in and help[ed] ... to articulate a larger imaginative world, a supreme fiction of the kind that embodies the dreams and nightmares of a people, shapes their imaginative vision of the world, and defines, as it evolves, their cultural identity.'[27]

We thus return once again to the question of identity. Canadian literary critics, it is obvious, are reaching back into the Canadian cultural past to an increasing extent in their attempt to articulate the assumptions and ideas that have informed the Canadian literary imagination. As they do so, they reach by necessity towards the methods of historical analysis, particularly towards those of the intellectual historian. It is to be hoped that those Canadian historians whose primary interest is also with the Canadian mind – be it political or literary – will make a similar attempt to bridge the narrowing gap between 'history' and 'literature' since politics and literature, like religion and education, are in the end simply different manifestations of a diverse, yet shared cultural experience that must transcend any consideration of nationalism. Jones expresses this point of view well:

Quite apart from the fact that the spirit of nineteenth century nationalism is by no means dead, in Canada as in other parts of the world, the question of a national identity is not to be equated with simple chauvinistic pride, political independence, or some inevitably chauvinistic self-assertion. For Canadians, as for others, it is a question of recognizing and articulating a view of life within which they can live with some assurance, or at least with some conviction. That is, it is less a question of nationalism than of an imaginative stance towards the world, towards nature and culture, past and present, the life of the body and the life of the mind ... It is a question of finding a satisfying interpretation of these fundamental elements in human life so that one can take a stand, act with definitive convictions, have an identity. As John Newlove puts it, it is a question of feeling at home (4–5).

Should students of Canadian intellectual history – as they take up Frank Underhill's challenge – predicate their work on a basis such as this, they may perhaps come to feel 'at home' in their work and their country in a way that Mr Underhill himself never did.

2

So Little on the Mind

'So Little on the Mind' was solicited by the Royal Society of Canada as a means of evaluating the past, present, and possible future directions of Canadian intellectual history. It evaluated Canadian writing in the context of the development of international scholarship, but sought also to move beyond commentary on existing work in order to indicate future approaches that practitioners ought seriously to consider. Major aims of the modern intellectual historian, it was suggested, should be to affirm the inherent value of ideas, to discern patterns of structure (whether in the mental or social worlds), and to search for coherence. The article reflects a major problem of intellectual history in the 1980s: to take the new social history seriously into account while remaining a discernible and viable subdiscipline. It was published under the same title in Transactions of the Royal Society of Canada, 4th series, 19 (1981): 183–200.

What are the prospects of studying the intellectual history of English Canadians today? If we were to judge from what has recently been said in other national contexts we would be forced to conclude that they are not good. Particularly in the United States, intellectual history as a subdiscipline is in a state of crisis. Robert Darnton begins his chapter on 'Intellectual and Cultural History' in *The Past before Us: Contemporary Historical Writing in the United States* (1980) with these encouraging words: 'A malaise is spreading among intellectual historians in the United States. Twenty years ago, they saw their discipline as the queen of the historical sciences. Today she seems humbled. No dramatic dethronement has occurred; but after a realignment of research during the past two decades, she now sits below the salt, surrounded by rude new varieties of sociocultural history and bewildering language – *mentalité, épisteme*, hermeneutics, semiotics, hegemony, deconstruction, and thick description.'[1] For similar reasons the essays in a recent collection called *New Directions in American Intellectual History* amount to a great deal of anxious intellectual hand-wringing.[2]

To date, Canadian intellectual historians have shown little inclination to engage in this kind of morbid introspection. There has not yet been any requiem for the decaying body of a once-vigorous historical approach to ideas in Canada because, quite simply, it has not yet been established (at least to the satisfaction of all concerned) whether there was ever a body in the first place. One of the most time-worn clichés concerning intellectual history is that to be engaged in it is 'like trying to nail jelly to a wall.' The task in Canada is especially difficult because if – to extend the metaphor – the jelly has a quivering and precarious form, the wall itself is, at first glance, not in sight. Elsewhere, intellectual history is in a state of crisis because, unlike other subdisciplines that comprise historical scholarship, it has failed to develop a rigorous methodology. Its approach to the study of thought has in fact been gelatinous in its eclecticism. Canadian intellectual historians, while aware of these difficulties, have so far been spared this sense of crisis because, few in number, they have until now necessarily been less concerned with methodological rigour as such than with the prior task of delineating the major contours of Canadian thought. Their work, as a result, has been marked neither by defensiveness nor despair, but by enthusiasm.

Most of those in English Canada who were drawn to intellectual history in the 1960s were significantly influenced by the scholarship of those golden years of Anglo-American work on the life of the mind. They were drawn largely because no serious and sustained study of Canadian intellectual life then existed. In contrast, there existed a rich range of American and European studies. Among the American works, one could draw upon the books of Perry Miller, Merle Curti, Henry May, Morton White, and Richard Hofstadter.[3] And in British and European history there existed the influential studies of A.O. Lovejoy, Crane Brinton, Basil Willey, Gertrude Himmelfarb, and Walter Houghton.[4] The books of such authors were inspirational not only because of their brilliance of execution but also because many of them had provoked heated and complex historiographical debate in the review pages of learned journals. In contrast, Canadian scholarship until the 1960s scarcely carried with it anything resembling a historiographical tradition, that is to say, a tradition of historical writing whose subject-matter was the contour, the rifts, and the nuances of historical interpretation. English-Canadian historical scholarship was seldom drawn, even in presidential addresses of the Canadian Historical Association, to philosophical speculation about the nature of the craft; instead, it rested content with a common-sense empiricism. The occasional historiographical forays of a Morton or a Careless were seldom placed on the same plane as the multitude of straightforward empirical studies.[5] The 'facts' of Canadian history were regarded as the proper concern of the historian and they were divorced from the anxieties of speculative historiographical debate to the extent that it was possible to do so. The idea that, given a choice, a scholar might wish to examine, for example, evolving interpretations of the meaning of the National Policy rather than the policy itself was, for some professors, a matter of no little scorn. In some quarters it still is.

The gradual acceptance of historiography as a legitimate realm of inquiry by the historian was of major importance, for it had the effect of suggesting the significant, if obvious, fact that the nation's understanding of its past and the writing of its history involved matters of mind as well as of fact, of intellectual substance as well as empirical data. In the absence of any substantial record of historical scholarship on the life of the mind in Canada, this simple discovery revealed a new dimension in areas of inquiry that were often thought to have long been settled. If Canadian historians were uncertain of the natural subject-matter of the country's intellectual life, they could, at least, turn to the record of historical writing itself. They did so, and it is significant that, for example, some of Ramsay Cook's best essays in intellectual history have been examinations of English- and French-Canadian historians' conceptions of the past and its place in the present, while Carl Berger's two books also hinge on the matter of historical consciousness and interpretation.[6] For both, 'historiography' – in its broadest sense – provided a point of entry into hitherto uncharted realms of Canadian thought. But perhaps more indicative of this revisioning of Canadian history by the early seventies was a review of Donald Creighton's *Canada's First Century* by William Westfall, entitled 'Creighton's Tragic Vision.' Ostensibly examining Creighton's book, the review also made a substantial contribution to an understanding of Creighton's way of thinking by focusing on the structural dynamics of his thought. The piece concluded that, when all was said and done, Creighton was a historian who would rather have written *Hamlet* than history; and anyone who recalls that in the last few pages of *The Commercial Empire of the Saint Lawrence* Creighton stressed the 'fatal flaw' in the character of the river system cannot help but conclude that by focusing on the author as well as on the book Westfall had turned a modest book review into a significant contribution to intellectual history.[7]

Even while this legitimation of 'historiography' as an area of historical study was being achieved in Canada, helping in so doing to uncover certain features of the country's intellectual life, methodological battle-lines were being drawn elsewhere among historians of the mind. The allegiances then being solidified in fact already had a long history. As early as the 1940s those who derived their inspiration and method either from A.O. Lovejoy's seminal book, *The Great Chain of Being*, or from Perry Miller's brilliant examination of *The New England Mind* were coming to be called 'internalists' because they spoke of 'unit ideas' such as 'romanticism' or because they gave aggregations the characteristics of an individual mind, as indicated by the title of Miller's book. They were inclined, said their critics, to view ideas as autonomous entities capable in themselves of generating social as well as intellectual change. Demographic or economic imperatives were at times conceived as mere adjuncts to the life of the mind, at best entertained, at worst entirely ignored.[8]

Criticism of the 'internalists,' whose major forum was *The Journal of the History of Ideas*,[9] came from those who viewed thought largely in functional terms, as responding to the dictates of physical environment. If exponents of the first camp were deemed 'internalists' it was inevitable – given the moth-like propensity of intellectual historians to fly towards dualities – that those of the second group would be called 'externalists.' The American historian John Higham led the criticism of 'internalist' intellectual history in a series of historiographical articles,[10] and his pleas for a more broadly contextual approach were bolstered by brilliant example in the work of Henry Nash Smith, who pioneered the 'myth and symbol' approach to American thought, and of Richard Hofstadter, who wove American political culture firmly into the fabric of the country's intellectual life.[11] The 'externalists,' too, came to have a journal as its major forum: *American Quarterly*.[12] Two divergent methodological paths had now been cleared. One led towards the history of philosophy and linguistic analysis; the other towards theories of symbolic action and social psychology.

This wealth of American scholarship emerged at a time when North Americans were largely searching for ways of articulating the consensus of values that were seen to transcend the divisiveness of ideology. The 'consensus' school of American historiography that emerged in the 1950s, ranging from Richard Hofstadter's brilliant series of essays, *The American Political Tradition*, through Louis Hartz's hermetically sealed examination of liberal hegemony in *The Liberal Tradition in America*,[13] were very much part of the intellectual life of the Cold War years in the United States. But the 1960s broke down the consensualism that allowed the search for a 'national mind' to be viewed by historians as the apex of inquiry. A vital part of this process was the critique of conventional historiography by the New Left during the years of the Vietnam War, and related to it was the advent of new forms of social history. Since that time, American historiography has never been the same. Intellectual history found itself accused of ignoring social conflict, cultural pluralism, and the common man. To date, as a subdiscipline, it has proved unable to address itself adequately to this major challenge.[14]

It is ironic, if characteristic, that intellectual history in Canada began to emerge precisely when it was beginning to be seriously challenged in America. Whatever misgivings Americans may have been voicing about the weaknesses of the various kinds of intellectual history by the 1960s, the fact is that what they *had* produced was of significant value in aiding the reconception of a Canadian past that had itself not, as yet, inspired a single sustained study of its thought. This is perhaps best illustrated by dwelling briefly upon three items published in Canada between 1968 and 1970, for, apart from the occasional challenge by Frank Underhill for Canadians to get to know their intellectual history,[15] they were of necessity the starting-points for those who wished to do intellectual history in this country. The first item is S.F. Wise's article, 'Sermon Literature and Canadian Intellectual History,' published in 1968; the second is Peter Waite's presidential address to the Canadian Historical Association, 'The Edge of the Forest,' given in 1969; the third is Carl Berger's book, *The Sense of Power*, published in 1970. Taken together, they say a great deal about the problems faced by the Canadian intellectual historian-in-the-making.

Consider, first, the effect upon the aspiring intellectual historian of a statement with which Wise began his influential essay:

Canadian intellectual history must be concerned, almost of necessity, with the kinds of ideas that lie between the formal thought of the philosopher or the political theorist and the world of action, and probably closer to the latter. Since (to understate the matter) no connected history of formal thought in Canada is possible, the Canadian intellectual historian must be concerned primarily with the interrelationship between ideas and actions, and therefore the intellectual commonplaces of an age, its root notions, assumptions, and images, will be of more significance to him than the study of the coherent bodies of abstract thought.[16]

In his article, Wise had used the sermons of Bishops John Strachan and Charles Inglis in order to examine a declining tradition of British and Protestant providentialism. It was coherent thought, of a kind. Moreover, for the first time a major Canadian historian had set forth the Canadian intellectual historian's objectives. But essentially, Wise seemed to conclude, he had better settle for studying elevated public opinion and social images. This was a powerful and persuasive argument in 1968, for there existed in Canadian historiography no evidence of the coherent and the abstract in Canadian thought and – so it seemed – a great deal of the commonplace.

A year later came Peter Waite's presidential address. Behind the disarming, puckish humour of a beautifully delivered speech there was a clear, if implicit, message for the student of the life of the mind in Canada, and it bolstered that of Wise. It began with Waite's homage to his colleague and mentor, George Wilson. 'He taught me,' said Waite, 'to distrust theories and look for the man instead.' And a little later: 'I suppose he reinforced the distrust of theory that is alleged to be

[the] inheritance of the Anglo-Saxon mind. Bentham's question, ''What use is it?'' makes the point and serves as introduction to my theme this evening. This can be construed broadly as a materialist view of history, or if you prefer it metaphorically, the edge of the forest ... For in the beginning was the forest.'[17] Given the arduous demands of clearing the forest, Waite seemed to say, how could we expect Canadians to have thought coherently about anything other than the sources of their next meal? Moreover, we were clearly being told that, as English-Canadian historians whose inheritance derives from Anglo-Saxon traditions, we would only be true to ourselves and our calling if we held to a common-sense empiricism that distrusted theoretical speculation about the nature of historical change. As Waite was to write, in his contribution to a festschrift for Donald Creighton: 'The Anglo-Saxon mind has always been reductionist in character. Explanation, in philosophy and in history, has usually been sought, not through metaphysical conceptions, but rather by bringing these down to earth. Thus the complex is reduced to the simple, the mysterious to the obvious, and the grand to the humdrum.'[18]

By 1970 intellectual historians looking for direction from Canadian scholarship had been left, in effect, with two calling-cards: the commonplace and the humdrum. Neither had the effect of encouraging romantic attachment. Yet given the fact that these were among the only suitors to call upon the innocent maidens of intellectual history, they were scarcely to be ignored. Then came the publication of *The Sense of Power*.

There can be no doubt that, together with the essays of S.F. Wise and Ramsay Cook in the 1960s,[19] Carl Berger's first book helped to establish intellectual history as a legitimate and fruitful area of inquiry in Canada. Yet if today we look at *The Sense of Power* as an artifact of the profession, it seems warranted to suggest that it essentially affirmed the declared truths of Wise and Waite. Its fundamental contribution rested less in elucidating the place of ideas in Canadian life than in addressing certain central problems in Canadian political historiography. Indeed, the book had taken the most time-worn, seemingly settled area of Canadian historiography – the whole debate between imperialists and nationalist – and had given it new life. It constituted, as Sarah Binks might say, a summerfallow of the mind.[20]

Yet *The Sense of Power* did not alter what was beginning to emerge as the general understanding of the nature and dynamic of English-Canadian thought. However important the historiographical reorientation aided by Berger's book, there still existed the hegemony of the commonplace and the humdrum, and none of the ideas of Charles Mair, Colonel Denison, or even Stephen Leacock seemed to suggest otherwise. Berger was less concerned with the methodological implications of his approach than he was with shifting our understanding of English-Canadian political assumptions. The result was a book that inspired because it was unique[21] but there was, in its pages, no explicitly expressed statement of just how the intellectual historian might go about his task. It suggested to others the merits of 'group biography,' but it did not point directly to the location of ideas elsewhere in the Canadian public or private record worthy of study. When Berger's second book, *The Writing of Canadian History*, appeared six years later, it affirmed by example the fact that much else could yet be done.[22]

For whatever reasons, few practitioners of intellectual history in Canada have felt impelled to speak or to write about the nature of their subdiscipline in the way that social historians, for example, have long done. Perhaps this simply is evidence of the hold of the Anglo-Saxon's distrust of the speculative, an ambiguous triumph at best. Whatever the reasons, the search for Canadian thought proceeds at present largely by serendipity. Even less than in the United States is the field a coherent one, and as a result students are often left confused when they attempt to distinguish between works whose manifest intention is to address themselves to ideas and those that may be brimming with ideas but which have other purposes. How, for example, should we classify André Siegfried's classic book, *The Race Question in Canada*, written early in the century, or Frank Underhill's collection of essays, *In Search of Canadian Liberalism*?[23] Should they be seen as early examples of intellectual history, for they *do* deal with ideas? Or are they simply works of some brilliance which only seem to be intellectual history by the sheer force of intellect manifested by their authors?

Such questions are important ones to raise, for they point to the difficulty of constructing principles of exclusion by which the subfield of intellectual history can be defined. Since almost any book touches upon the domain of ideas at some point – and this is certainly the case of books written by intellectuals – the task of drawing up a reading list of works of intellectual history becomes a frustrating one. Certain authors come immediately to mind in the Canadian context since their work is self-declared intellectual history. In this category are Carl Berger, Ramsay Cook, Richard Allen, Michiel Horn, William Westfall, Allan Smith, S.E.D. Shortt, and Douglas Owram, among others.[24] But how should we categorize the work of Michael Bliss, whose book, *A Living Profit*, analyses the social assumptions of late-nineteenth-century businessmen? And what of literary critics such as Eli Mandel or D.G. Jones, when they make forays of a historical nature?[25] One easy answer to such questions is simply to state that at times even historians or critics who are not manifestly engaged in writing intellectual history nevertheless do it as they go about their other tasks. When, for example, John English dealt with the role of intellectuals in his book on early-twentieth-century national politics, *The Decline of Politics*, should we conclude that he was, for a chapter at least, doing intellectual history? The same question may be asked of Eli Mandel's essay on the prairie as a region of the mind or Frank Underhill's essay on Goldwin Smith. Each, after all, was at that point dealing with ideas.[26]

Yet if this is all that can be said of our ability to give Canadian intellectual history some sense of direction, its prospects are clearly, as our American colleagues suggest, not very good. The essential problem is not one of subject-matter, for the scholarship of the 1970s has pointed to numerous facets of Canadian thought that merit examination. The problem resides, rather, in finding ways to suggest how such studies can be executed so that intellectual history remains a discernible sub-discipline rather than the bastard child of cultural criticism or social history. Is it, in short, possible to establish a range of focus for intellectual history so that it takes social reality into account while remaining distinct from a social history that views ideas as of only secondary importance?

Perhaps this task can be initiated by suggesting that the aims of the intellectual historian should essentially be threefold: first, to affirm the inherent value – what, for short, we might call the 'integrity' of ideas; second, to discern patterns of structure; third, to search for coherence. Needless to say, these three requirements can by no means be seen as mutually exclusive activities: on the contrary, they are interdependent and mutually reinforcing. Together, however, they serve to give the student of ideas a general program, a sense of direction, if not a specific method.

To suggest that the first task of the intellectual historian is to assume that ideas have an inherent value, and 'integrity,' is *not* to equate the notion with some unstated imperative to maintain that ideas are autonomous entities, independent of or superior to experience. The matter is one of focus, of the need for the student of intellectual history to concentrate relentlessly on the origin, character, and ramifications of thought *in itself* as the centre of study. Even if our ultimate objective is to place certain ideas or assumptions fully into the social context in which they arose, our initial task must be to examine the ideas themselves. In this undertaking, it does not matter whether we are examining loosely ratiocinated 'images' one step removed from emotional response, articulate rejoinders to issues of the day (that is to say, 'public opinion'), or systematic expressions of organically related clusters of ideas. The location of attention is, after all, simply a matter of the historian's particular interest in a given topic. Whatever the locale, or the degree of 'sophistication,' of the thought under examination, it still remains necessary to keep a tight focus on the nature and the form of the manifestation of thought itself. For this reason, the core of any research project in intellectual history must, at least in the first instance, be the thought of an individual or individuals, and this is so even if the form of the study is not ultimately to be biographical. Carl Berger's book, *The Sense of Power*, was tightly focused thematically precisely because it was preceded by a dissertation that was constructed around a series of biographical studies. The book itself did not take that form, but it benefited greatly from his detailed earlier attention to the thought of individuals *qua* individuals.[27]

The discovery of patterns of structure has been placed second in my list of tasks not because it is secondary in importance but because it is central to the whole endeavour. And the term 'structure' should be allowed to operate at several levels. In the first place, the historian examining ideas must necessarily come to grips with the structure of mind itself, with relationships of intellect, affection, and will. Here, ironically, the very term 'intellectual history' is somewhat problematic, for it implies a preoccupation with the first of these qualities of mind, possibly at the expense of others. Yet thought, like conduct, is scarcely the product of intellect alone. In this sense, the phrase 'intellectual history' is something of a conceit, the product of intellect turned upon itself, a scholarly snake devouring its tail. My own book, *A Disciplined Intelligence*, had something of this characteristic, for it was a study of the structure and rise to dominance (in Canada) of the intellect, a course of historical events that helped to bring about the very conditions that gave a phrase like 'intellectual history' a discernible meaning and thereby made possible the existence of the subdiscipline of which the book was an example.[28] It is instructive to recall that early in the nineteenth century the word 'intellectual' was an adjective, and when later it became a noun it was for the purpose of describing an individual of unbalanced mind.[29]

Beyond the need to examine mental structures there is also the need for the intellectual historian to concern himself with social and ideological structures. Needless to say, this can take many forms. If, as has been suggested, thought must first be studied at the level of the individual, the fact remains that such thought cannot be understood with the individual as sole referent. The categories of intellection, affection, and will are essentially categories of form that are capable of being examined quite apart from the world of social experience. If it is assumed, however, that an essential task of the intellectual historian is to relate mental structures to those of social experience, it follows that he is necessarily led to an assessment of the relationship between forms of knowledge and of social experience. In an article entitled 'On the Concept of Region in Canadian History and Literature,' William Westfall notes that much of W.L. Morton's work involved his attempt to 'resolve the discrepancies that had existed in his mind between the locality he knew and the ''unreal'' world he had assimilated from a different literary culture.' Westfall goes on to say that such a search, in the mind of an historian, can have the salutary effect of replacing 'the single factor rigidity of environmentalism with a dynamic approach that emphasizes a dialectical tension between experience and form.'[30]

Two points should be observed here. The first is that in stressing the 'dialectical tension between experience and form' within Morton's mind, Westfall provides us with a structural approach to a study of Morton's thought (just as he had, earlier, for that of Donald Creighton) that fixes its focus on ideational forms while not discounting the influence or importance of material factors. Such an approach may well be more fruitful than one that seeks to establish, for example, whether or not Morton was a 'Red Tory,' for the clear implication is that such a tension is inherent in the nature of thought in its relation to social experience.[31] Perhaps here is one way of stepping beyond the functionalist view of mind that has so characterized the corpus of Canadian historiography on the life of the mind while not falling into the obverse trap of ignoring the impact of environment on mental life.

Speaking of the inclination of western Canadian literary critics to view the literature of the region as deriving somehow from prairie gumbo or scrubby bushland, Westfall states: 'In assuming that all aspects of the literary process can be derived from the environment, these literary critics have also assumed that the form that a writer gives to his words can be explained environmentally. The categories of literature, however, like the lines on a map, are abstractions, they are applied by many to give order and meaning to his artistic representation. They do not originate in the land itself. This theoretical consideration brings into the concept of literary regions questions of form, mythology, and identity.'[32] Westfall casts his words here in the context of prairie literature and its savants, yet they are equally applicable to Canadian history and historians since something universal is involved: the tridimensional interaction of mental structures, social experience, and forms of knowledge. Taken together, they shift our attention beyond 'thought' to the matter of consciousness. Recognizing the legitimacy of such a shift involves broadening the intellectual historian's task, yet it also serves to sharpen his focus. It would take into account theories of man's purpose (his definitions of human nature), but it would also search for the means and mechanisms by which man comes to have 'knowledge' of 'society' at all.[33] Furthermore, it includes as part of the natural compass of intellectual history such general considerations as the 'character of individual and group dominance, the sources of social cohesion, [and[the nature and function of religious sentiment.'[34] By necessity, it would involve a closer alliance with the social sciences and social theory.

Related to this examination of the nature and forms of consciousness is the third major task of the intellectual historian: the search for coherence. At a certain point, in fact, the two words – 'consciousness' and 'coherence' – blend in meaning, for both involve rationality, congruity, and intelligible meaning. Hence, attached to the examination of the series of relations that together constitute consciousness must necessarily be the search for coherence. Yet this association, in turn, introduces a potential problem of major proportions.

The past itself flows both ways, and is marked by order and disorder, congruence and dissonance, pattern and chaos. It is, in a sense, a 'seamless web.' The practice of intellectual history, however, tends to have a certain one-directional quality about it. Intellectual historians tend to search for order in disorder, congruence in dissonance, pattern in chaos; in short, for the lines of juncture within that web. For this reason, much of the intellectual history that has sought to examine ideas within a broad social context has been concerned as much with social character as with social conflict. This was certainly true of American historiography during the 'golden years' of intellectual history in the 1950s and early 1960s,[35] and it has no less been the case with Canadian scholarship in the 1970s.

The easiest organizational form for this search for consensual values to take has, of course, been the one that worked within existing historiographical categories. Hence both American and Canadian intellectual history have examined in the first instance the various forms of national consciousness. Berger's book, *The Sense of Power*, is specifically organized around the notion of nationality, and it deals with competing definitions of it. *The Writing of Canadian History* takes these competing forms of national consciousness into a later period and into a specific profession: Canada's national historians. The essays of Ramsay Cook, especially those in *The Maple Leaf Forever* and *Canada and the French-Canadian Question*, may be seen as inverted variations on this nationalist theme: forms of national consciousness are still the major preoccupation but they are portrayed as essentially destructive urges. Nevertheless, Cook is still concerned with elucidating national character.

Similarly, most other Canadian books in English-Canadian intellectual history have also been preoccupied with the consensual values that comprise aspects of national consciousness. Richard Allen's study of the Social Gospel in Canada, *The Social Passion*, had as its subject Canada's self-proclaimed 'national' church – the United Church of Canada – in its formative phase. Doug Owram's book, *The Promise of Eden: The Canadian Expansionist Movement and the Idea of the West 1856–1900*, while sensitive to the discrepancies between social value and social fact, was largely a study of the transcontinental nationalist aspirations of late-nineteenth-century Ontarians. And *A Disciplined Intelligence* claimed the existence of a 'moral imperative' that helped shape the contours of the modern Anglo-Canadian sensibility.[36]

This tendency to enjoin the search for coherence with nationalist aspirations represents both potential strength and present weakness. One Canadian historian has claimed that, given the extraordinary specialization of the discipline of history and the discovery of the complex, regional nature of Canadian social experience, the task of synthesizing the new scholarship in a way that achieves unity of vision while reflecting diversity of experience may well fall to the intellectual historian.[37] Given the recent attention to regional and class dimensions of Canadian history, Donald Swainson adds: 'Are we then left without historians of the nation? Has the history of disintegration taken control? Perhaps not, even if only because a pendulum cannot forever swing in a single direction.'[38] Needless to say, this is an important challenge and, if met, could result in a major achievement. But it is fraught with a pitfall to which intellectual history is especially prone. Allan Smith pointed to it when he concluded a review of *A Disciplined Intelligence* by saying that the book 'joins Berger and Shortt's work in suggesting that there is, as Hayden White observed some years ago, a close relationship between the first move a society makes towards writing its intellectual history and a conservative yearning to celebrate a fixed and settled body of ideas.'[39]

Smith's point deserves attention, for there can be little question that the search for the central features of a nation's experience (especially, perhaps, its major intellectual constructs) fosters the inclination towards unity and celebration. This is as true of present writing on Canadian intellectual history as it once was of American. But at the moment it is less a pressing historiographical problem than it is a source of future difficulties. For once the historian sees unity rather than coherence, uniformity rather than congruity, as his essential aim, the gap between intellectual history and social history can only widen. The general corpus of Canadian intellectual history at present may be characterized, if rather crudely, as having so far been reasonably sensitive to the diversity and coherence of patterns of ideas in Canada. At the same time, however, it has been less successful in dealing with the 'integrity' of the ideas themselves and has virtually ignored the structural character and determinants of thought, knowledge, and society.

Such an assertion forces us to return to the centrality of the need for the intellectual historian to discern patterns of structure, whether in thought, social assumption, or society. Without it, his other tasks can be more problematic than constructive. Without this emphasis the necessity of examining the nature of ideas in themselves can lead to a crude textualism conducted without adequate attention to problems of motive, intention, or causation. Moreover, the search for coherence can lead to the kind of comfortable trap outlined by Smith, one in which a scholarly work becomes an extension rather than an examination of the manifestation of thought under investigation. The study of ideas in relation to both ideational and social structures would, in contrast, serve to keep the intellectual historian more directly in contact with the complexity of the historical record. His search must, ultimately, be for coherence, not unity; it must not be undertaken at the expense of negating or ignoring the reality of discord, discontinuity, tension, and contradiction. And it is precisely these factors that an attention to ideas in relation to structure affords. It fosters an awareness of the discrepancies between conscious intention and actual accomplishment; the discordance of intellectual statement and social practice; the disjunction of ideological affirmation and economic trends.[40] Perhaps it is not too much to say that if a basic construct of the social historian is conflict, the equivalent for the intellectual historian is irony.

The notion of 'irony,' however, is a means of understanding the discrepancy between profession and practice, not in itself a mode of historical analysis. It may help us understand the many ways by which men reconcile their manifest intentions with their practical actions, but it alone will not provide the basis of systematic understanding of the relationship between ideas and social change. This can only be accomplished if the intellectual historian goes about his threefold task while constantly examining ideas and their social context within the general context of causation.

The unresolved nature of this relationship between ideas and causation is perhaps at the heart of the current crisis in American intellectual history, for American historians of thought have belatedly come to realize that they have seldom given sufficient attention to the matter and they have found themselves, as a result, profoundly threatened by the new social history. At present they are grasping eclectically at what may prove to be conceptual straws, adding to their essays on method a pinch of Geertzian anthropology here and a smidgen of Kuhnian paradigm there[41] (never in sufficient amounts to alter the troubled taste of the dish). Unlike their social historian colleagues, they have seldom considered that the problem may lie with the nature of the cuisine itself. Until now, they have stood stoically within a generally voluntarist historical tradition when examining the relation of ideas to the matter of social causation,[42] and the result has been a great deal of conceptual confusion. A good example of this middle way is exemplified by Gordon S. Wood's contribution to the book *New Directions in American Intellectual History*, an essay entitled 'Intellectual History and the Social Sciences.' After noting at length the threat posed by the new social history to his own subdiscipline, he addresses the matter of causation – after a fashion. 'If ideas are not just inseparable parts of the social reality,' he says, following Clifford Geertz, 'but indeed give that reality its existence, then it makes no sense to treat ideas mechanically as detached ''causes'' or ''effects'' of social events and behavior. We no longer have to be locked into the endless see-sawing fluctuations between idea and the social environment that pervades much of our writing of intellectual history, with ideas in the casual ascendancy at one moment and the social factors at another and with their reciprocal ups and downs somehow accounting for historical changes.'[43]

We may well sympathize with Wood's wish to transcend the 'internalist' / 'externalist' nexus on the matter of ideas as causal agents, but this should not prevent us from questioning his means of resolving the problem. First, it seems, he urges us to reject 'the futile dichotomy of ideas or beliefs as causes or effects of social forces' in favour of 'treating ideas functionally and instrumentally.' Second (and related) he seemed to counsel what can only be regarded as a retreat into the traditional American pattern of voluntaristic compromise as if in the hope that an epistemological 'vital center' will continue to hold. His essay concludes, as a result, with these words: 'Only by being able and willing to move between these two worlds – the small world of free will, moral purpose, and individual intention and the large world of deterministic aggregate culture – can the historian write an intellectual history that will satisfy both his humanistic instincts and the demands of social science.'[44]

This removal of ideas from the realm of causation in fact marks a serious retreat from a full understanding of their nature and function, just as the implied antipathy of 'humanistic instincts' and 'demands of social science' serves only to mystify. Wood is of the view that by adopting Geertz's notion of ideas as 'templates for the organization of social and psychological processes,' they can be regarded 'not just as inseparable parts of the social reality' but in fact as giving 'that reality its existence.'[45] Yet if this is so, how can they then be separated from the question of causation that alone will help us understand the central dynamic of history: the matter of social change?

The retreat by intellectual historians into such essentially ahistorical formulations does little to further our comprehension of the ongoing place of consciousness in society. It marks a seeming admission, however reluctantly given, that the intellectual historian has no business trying to demonstrate that forms of consciousness are central to an understanding of the nature and origins of social transformation. The analysis of such transformation, they seem to suggest, is the preserve of economic determinists, especially social historians. Yet the practitioner of intellectual history does not need to retreat into definitions of ideas as Geertzian 'templates' or into idealist categories that make ideas into determining historical forces in order to preserve a central position within his craft. It may well be that the intellectual historian's most important contribution to the profession is yet to come, and that when it does come it will be out of a general acceptance of the framework of historical materialism.

It has long been recognized that a major weakness of the canon of Marx and Engels – and therefore of much Marxist critical theory – has been its failure to elucidate clearly the place of consciousness and ideas in the general relationship of 'base' and 'superstructure.' A great deal of crude reductionism has been the result, and, with the notable exception of Antonio Gramsci, few sustained attempts to formulate a materialist theory of culture were made until recent years.[46] Yet there was no reason why this should necessarily have been so, for neither Marx nor Engels (according to the latter) meant to suggest a *rigid* distinction between base and superstructure in the process of social change. As Engels wrote to a friend in 1890:

According to the materialist conception of history, the *ultimately* determining element in history is the production and reproduction of real life. More than this neither Marx nor I have ever asserted. Hence if somebody twists this into saying that the economic element is the *only* determining one, he transforms that proposition into a meaningless, abstract, senseless phrase. The economic situation is the basis, but the various elements of the superstructure – political forms of the class struggle and its results, to wit: constitutions established by the victorious class after a successful battle, etc. in the brains of the participants, political, juristic, philosophical theories, religious views and their further development into systems of dogma – also exercise their influence upon the course of the historical struggles and in many cases preponderate in determining their *form*. There is an interaction of all these elements in which, amid all the endless host of accidents (that is, of things and events whose inner interconnection is so remote or so impossible of proof that we can regard it as non-existent, as negligible), the economic movement finally asserts itself as necessary. Otherwise the application of the theory to any period of history would be easier than the solution of a simple equation of the first degree.[47]

This passage contains a number of signposts that point to the kind of intellectual history that perhaps alone can synthesize the scholarship of Canada in the past decade or so. It would continue to focus firmly on thought, and it would search for coherence and congruence; yet it would do so by examining ideas against the nature and the imperatives of past and present social and economic structures. The main point to make here, however, is that the confusion lamented by Engels is not a reflection of the insignificance of ideational structures in a material world but rather of the failure of critical theorists and historians alike – at least those in Canada – to place those structures firmly in a social framework. As Raymond Williams has recently stated, in reference to the 'classical' period of Marxist theory: 'What is fundamentally lacking, in the theoretical formulations of this important period, is any adequate recognition of the indissoluble connections between material production, political and cultural institutions and activity, and consciousness.'[48]

In the absence of any such serious reflection about the way ideas come about or operate, and about their ideological functions, the Canadian intellectual historian can only urge that his colleagues go about these tasks or, better still, undertake them himself. It is not a sufficient excuse to say that the historian should first try to find the location and the size of the subject-matter that is the 'wall' of Canadian intellectual history before he attempts to handle the theoretical 'jelly.' Enough has been done in the field over the past decade to suggest that the subject can be a rewarding one, and anyone who has delved into primary sources will have discovered that further evidence of Canadians-in-thought is abundant to the point of being overwhelming. The problem at hand is to establish the means by which intellectual history may be practised in ways that make it something other than a mere adjunct of idiosyncracy, a feat of intellectual legerdemain rather than an exercise that is vitally related to other forms of historical scholarship.

In this respect the prospects are indeed great, even if they are also fraught with difficulty. As we pursue our objectives we will probably, and quite often, find ourselves concluding with Oscar Wilde that 'the basis of optimism is sheer terror.' But I would rather take a deep breath, head for my study, and take comfort with the words of Dean Swift. 'I must complain the cards are ill-shuffled,' he groused, 'till I have a good hand.'

3

Science, Humanism, and the Ontario University

In September 1984 the Ontario Historical Studies Series and McMaster University jointly sponsored a conference on 'New Directions for the Study of Ontario's Past.' My own contribution to it was to participate in a session on 'pure and applied science,' chaired by Gerald Killan of King's College, University of Western Ontario. Papers were to be brief, to facilitate discussion, and the session began with a provocative one by Richard A. Jarrell of the Department of Natural Science, York University, entitled 'Technology and Social Change in Ontario History.' Professor Jarrell stressed the determinative role of technology throughout history in general; my duty, as I saw it, was to suggest the place of values in such an epistemological universe, to question the validity of Jarrell's thesis, and to place 'science' and 'values' into the general context of higher education in Ontario. In the present context, the piece suggests that the historiography of higher education in Ontario has, thus far, contributed relatively little to an understanding of the intellectual history of the province; it also sets a general thematic environment in which to place several of the essays that follow. The essay is published here for the first time.

As with the study of the role of technology in shaping Ontario's past and its present, there exists little scholarly examination of the place and function of science and humanistic learning in the universities of the province.[1] But the state of scholarship in higher education is such that a point of departure seems clearly to have been reached. Institutional history has reached its zenith – the way is cleared for new directions to be taken.

In the last decade most of the older universities have had major histories written of them. The late Hilda Neatby and her colleague, Frederick Gibson, wrote a two-volume history of Queen's University; Charles Johnston has completed his own two-volume study of McMaster; J.R.W. Gwynne-Timothy has written a massive one-volume history of the University of Western Ontario; and for a number of years now Robin Harris and Gerald M. Craig have been labouring on a two-volume study of the University of Toronto.[2] Any historian of higher education in the province, whatever his or her own approach to the subject, must be profoundly grateful to have the products of their labours near at hand. Each of these volumes varies, of course, in quality; but for the most part they are of a high calibre indeed, and make possible, by their fidelity to detail and to institutional uniqueness, a measure of generalization about patterns of institutional development that would otherwise be impossible.

They remain, nevertheless, institutional histories. Each has attempted to place its subject in a broader social and, at times, intellectual context, and again they have succeeded (or failed) in varying degrees. But for the most part they have built upon the work of earlier chroniclers of their own institutions and, while they have utilized archival sources in a much more sophisticated fashion than did their predecessors, they have produced historical accounts that remain part of the 'institutional' genre. Though less antiquarian, thematically broader, and conceptually more acute than earlier works, they nevertheless mark no departures in conceptual approach or methodology. Such studies are the necessary foundation-stones for the pursuit of other themes in the history of higher education, just as the constitutional and political history of Canada had necessarily to be written before the social, cultural, and intellectual history of the country could be undertaken. These new institutional biographies are, then, also cap-stones to a certain kind of history. It is now time to turn to other forms of approach to the history of higher education in Ontario.

In such broad accounts of a given university, the history of individual faculties is necessarily given relatively brief treatment. Individual scientists or humanists are occasionally singled out, of course, to add a 'human face' to the story of institutional development, but it is fair to say that for the most part the fundamental place of 'science' or 'the humanities' tends to get lost, or at least subordinated to the perceived necessity of accounting for what was happening in the president's or principal's office. Moreover, as with Gwynne-Timothy's biography of Western, it sometimes proves easier to deal with the emergence of professional faculties such as law or medicine than with what the American historian Laurence Veysey has called 'the plural organized worlds of the humanities.'[3] In part this is due to problems of organization as the historian faces the chaos of evidence available from university archives or calendars. It proves demonstrably easier to discuss the history of academic units such as law or medicine than it is those of the faculties of arts and science. 'Professional' faculties, sometimes autonomous in governance, have a clearer sense of vocational role; their relation to both university and state is often more clearly defined; and their operating assumptions, their disciplinary *locus* or intellectual centres of gravity are relatively easy to establish. For these reasons, even the best of institutional histories of Ontario higher education have a certain hollowness at the centre. The new histories of Queen's and McMaster are splendid examples of what can be done with the institution as the essential subject of concern. Yet at times one senses that certain questions have remained unasked. Quite apart from knowing just who were the students who attended the universities concerned, a difficult enough question,[4] we seldom discover just what it was they learned, or why they were expected to acquire certain forms of knowledge yet not others. What remains untaught, but could have been, can provide vital glimpses into the contexts of culture.[5]

There was a time when Ontario university students could walk from one classroom to another, regardless of discipline or faculty, and receive instruction from professors who shared a fundamentally similar view of the world, generally Christian, idealist, and monistic. Until the 1870s a student could walk from class to class for four years and not be bludgeoned by fundamental differences in epistemology, ethics, or ideology. With knowledge, as with religion, the monistic centre still held – at least in mid-Victorian Ontario. From the 1870s through 1914, ethical relativism, the gradual emergence of the social sciences, and the challenge of technological and professional imperatives derived from a burgeoning industrial economy grew apace. So did the commoditization of knowledge as the college-turned-university accommodated itself to the state and to the marketplace. By 1920 the shape of higher education in the province, as elsewhere, had been fundamentally altered.

At present we have little scholarship that can help us understand just how this transformation took place. We do not know what its social, religious, or intellectual consequences were, much less the parts played by the sciences or the humanities during this period of profound structural and functional change. My own book, *A Disciplined Intelligence* (1979), made certain general suggestions along these lines, and in an article called 'Science, Values, and the American Empire: The *Canadian Forum* in the 1920s' I attempted to outline the response of academic humanists to changes in science and technology.[6] But, to my knowledge, not much else has been done on the subject – and certainly nothing on a comprehensive scale. We need to know how knowledge – whether in science or the humanities – is generated, and of its relationship to political, economic, and social structures and change. Yet it is such knowledge, not administrative units such as 'faculties' or 'departments' created to regulate its production, that poses by far the greatest conceptual problems for the historian of higher education. For this reason it is understandable that not many scholars in Ontario have made the attempt. Some, however, have begun to do so.

In the field of science, Vittorio de Vecchi has completed a pioneering study of the relationship of the Canadian scientific community to government in the late nineteenth and early twentieth centuries. Mel Thistle and Peter Oliver have examined the ways in which the state, both federal and provincial, has pioneered in scientific research, thereby undermining at times the claims of the universities as leaders in the field. More recently, Paul Axelrod has studied the ambiguous relationship of the university to the state in the period after 1945, and Philip Enros has examined the dynamics of industrial research in the university setting for the earlier period. At a more general level, Richard Jarrell, Trevor Levere, and others have heroicly attempted to document the place of science and technology in Canadian history.[7]

At the level of contemporary research on the place and function of the humanities in Ontario university life, the results are even more fragmented. Various scholars have treated the humanities by attempting to define their essential assumptions or goals, but no one has attempted to assess their collective significance in a fully historical context, or to delineate changing social or ideological significance over time. Carl Berger has written with telling effect about the intellectual and cultural significance of the writing of Canadian history in the twentieth century; Margerie Fee has completed an insightful dissertation on the ways in which English-Canadian literary critics attempted to define and establish a national literature between 1890 and 1950; Leslie Armour and Elizabeth Trott have published a major work on the development of Canadian philosophical thought in the century after 1850.[8] But no one has examined the assumptions of any one discipline within the humanities against the assumptions of another. The closest approximation to such a greatly needed study lies in biographical treatments of individual humanists and proto-social scientists, such as S.E.D. Shortt's pioneering book *The Search for an Ideal* (1976) and unpublished dissertations by Alan Bowker and Bruce Bowden.[9] Two theses undertaken at the University of Manitoba, one completed and another in preparation, have begun to broaden the context. Erna Buffie's study attempted to examine the phenomenon of cultural nationalism, largely in Ontario, by studying the academic humanists' response to the Massey Commission; and Pat Jasen is currently writing what may become an important contribution, with the tentative title: ' "Knowledge for What?" The Liberal Arts in the English-Canadian University since World War II.'[10] Canadian Scholarship requires more such attempts at synthesis.

In 1960 the National Council of Colleges and Universities sponsored a symposium based on the controversy surrounding the recent publication of C.P. Snow's Rede Lectures, *The Two Cultures*. The title of the symposium was scarcely innovative: 'The Humanities and Modern Science; Two Cultures or One?' Needless to say, the resulting papers and debate did not resolve the question. Dr D.K.C.

MacDonald of the Division of Pure Science in the National Research Council insisted that scientists were, after all, human, and concluded with a plea derived from John Erskine's essay, 'The Moral Obligation to be Intelligent.' George Whalley of the Department of English at Queen's University insisted that the 'two cultures' were the outward projections of 'the two complementary functions of mind – to be or to do; to look or to command; to value or to control,' and insisted that it was 'up to humanists to educate and civilise scientists; and it is up to scientists to let this happen.' Dean P.R. Gendron of the Faculty of Science at the University of Ottawa concluded that while in theory Snow's critics may have been right, in practice Snow was 'absolutely correct.' Finally, Professor F.M. Salter placed the debate into perspective by beginning his address with an anecdote: 'Two Irishmen' he said, 'once lay in wait to murder their landlord. He regularly passed a certain corner at 11 PM. They waited behind the hedge, one with an ancestral blunderbus loaded with nails and spikes, the other with a repeating rifle which had done good service during the "troubles." Eleven o'clock came and passed – eleven fifteen – eleven thirty – a quarter to twelve – twelve o'clock, and still no landlord. At last one of them said to the other, "I hope to God nothing has happened to the poor man."' Accordingly, Salter looked forward to a day when science and humanism would be found in equal measure, and when it would not be necessary to conjure enemies in order to create food for thought.[11]

The audience that day, it must be said, was not impressed. Dean of arts at McGill, H.N. Fieldhouse, dismissed the subject under discussion by saying that it was 'a silly squabble between the scientists and humanists, both of which would be better off without this nonsense about two cultures'; and his colleague at McGill, dean of science H.G. Dion, in what may have been a rare display of collegial unanimity, insisted that the topic was 'not really worthy of discussion by serious and mature people.'[12] In retrospect, we can conclude that perhaps the 'Two Cultures' debate, in Canada as elsewhere, produced more heat than light. It would be unfortunate if we were to pit two abstractions – 'technology' and 'humanism' – in some sort of cosmic, dialectical struggle. Nevertheless, it is the responsibility of the historian of science, or of the humanities, to measure the extent to which scientific and humanistic forms of understanding intersect and to determine to what extent such intersections have been determining factors in the advances of the knowledge produced by both.

To argue in such a fashion is to differ from the approach to the history of science which places fundamental emphasis on advancement, theoretical or technical, and which tends to be dismissive of social and ideological context. Yet the social historian of science in the university must clearly take both approaches into account. Advancements in the university laboratory are clearly important; yet so is the pedagogical element of university science, especially when professors lecture on such topics as the cranial capacity of Indians compared with whites, eugenics, IQ testing, sociobiology, or recombinant DNA. For the social historian of science it is as important to examine the assumptions and procedures of those on the losing side of scientific controversy as it is the winners, for yesterday's science can become today's pseudoscience. Nor can social, cultural, demographic, economic, ideological, or public policy factors be avoided – with either science or the humanities in the institutional context. David F. Noble's book, *America by Design: Science, Technology and the Rise of Corporate Capitalism* (1977), and Paul Starr's study, *The Social Transformation of American Medicine* (1983), have amply demonstrated the depth of insight that can be obtained by such an approach.[13]

The social approach to the sciences or the humanities has one further advantage: it may help to avoid the reification of both. The whole Snow/Leavis debate was to some extent a sustained demonstration of the extent to which well-meaning scholars could engage in this. What the sociologist of religion, Bryan R. Wilson, has said of his own field is, however, equally true of historical inquiry: 'The types that sociologists construct are reifications. Their inherent danger is that, instead of being useful short-hand summaries of crucial elements in the empirical cases they are meant to epitomise, they become caricatures remote from empirical phenomena. The fact that they are not meant to mirror reality can become the excuse for their never again being exposed to scrutiny in the light of increasing knowledge of the empirical. They may then be manipulated on a stage projected by the sociological imagination: the supposed model of the outworking of social processes would thus become a puppet show operated by principles not to be discovered in the real world, but with all the seductive attractiveness of comprehensibility and inherent natural order. Sociology in such a condition [and one could equally say history] ceases to provide explanations, and becomes the ready vehicle for ideologies and ready-made formulae that do not explain the world, but rather obscure its richness and diversity.'[14] Many would agree that words and phrases such as 'church' and 'sect,' 'working class' and 'class struggle,' 'supply and demand' and 'middle class' seem tailor-made for the process of reification as scholars and journalists attempt to bring order to the chaos of experience. It is difficult not also to add other words, such as 'science,' 'technology,' and 'humanism' to the list, for they seem particularly susceptible of being rendered into monolithic categories that explain away rather than explain.

Let me be rather more specific. Take the case of the nineteenth-century 'debate' between capital-S science and capital-R religion. There can be no question of the fact that the debate took place, or that it was acrimonious: the vocabulary of religious warfare was used by the combatants for more than a generation. Yet when the phenomenon is examined in minute detail, and the thought of individuals closely scrutinized, the rigidity of the dichotomy begins to crumble. We see religious assumptions operating within the minds of certain scientists and shaping their science, the acceptance of Darwinian evolution by humanists altering their understanding of historical causation and change as it gradually blended with Christian and philosophical beliefs. In Canada we find scientists such as Daniel Wilson at Toronto, whose accommodation to evolution was made much easier by his essentially poetic sensibility, and humanists such as the idealist philosopher John Watson of Queen's whose very Hegelian view of the world made him accept Darwinian evolution with an almost audible sigh of relief. Once reified, science and religion imply forms of epistemological divergence that were, at times, much more apparent than real.[15]

Until recently, scientists in the Ontario university setting held a distinctly 'humanistic' stance, for teaching rather than research was often seen as the science professor's fundamental obligation. In fact, a suspicion of the specialization inherent in research based on the German model was widespread, especially among the humanities. To be sure, scientists at times pronounced the preoccupations of humanists as irrelevant, but more often than not they chose to be silent when metaphysical or religious questions arose. At other times, as in the 1920s, scientist and humanists alike, writing in the *Canadian Forum*, sought to justify scientific research on the grounds that its aims were at one with the poet – both were searching for 'truth' – rather than on the grounds of practical utility. Until after the Second World War, Ontario's academic humanists were generally ambivalent about the relation of science and technology to traditional values, while its scientists held no fear that the two were incompatible.[16]

After the war, however, the latter stance was less acceptable. With the great increase in American domination of Canadian life, the relationship of science and values assumed a specific form unprecedented since Darwin's lifetime. The United States of America, and the questions of nationality and domination, became central to the dialogue between scientists and humanists. Whereas the 1947 report on *The Humanities in Canada* by Watson Kirkconnell and A.S.P. Woodhouse, sponsored by the Humanities Research Council of Canada, had been content to document the mere existence of humanistic research in Canada and to argue that the spirit of Arnoldian culture could best be maintained by state financial aid, the 1951 Massey Commission made the enemy's nationality perfectly clear. So, in its own way, did the Symons Report of a quarter century later.[17] The most important humanists in Ontario universities since the Second World War have invariably been concerned with the relations of science, technology, and values, and with Canada's place in North America as it attempts to mediate these relations. The writings of Harold Innis, Donald Creighton, Marshall McLuhan,

George Grant, and Northrop Frye bear eloquent and profound testimony to this orientation.[18]

In the absence of any sustained scholarship on most of these matters, it can only be hoped that the history of both the sciences and the humanities in the Ontario university will fully reflect the particularities of social context. By no means will this be an easy task, especially in the case of the humanities; in Canada as in the United States, as Laurence Veysey has reminded us, they have become increasingly characterized by 'a sense of burgeoning variety' and of 'intellectual segmentation' as they have established their niches within the academy. In fact, Veysey surmises, 'We are left with the possibility that the grouping of the fields of history, English, classical and modern languages, philosophy, art, and music may at bottom be nothing more than a growing convenience – perhaps especially for deans and university presidents in neatly structuring their organizations.'[19] In short, is it possible for the social history of 'the humanities' (or for that matter 'the sciences') to be written at all, as those entities exist within the university setting? What, after all, can be a theme that will allow integrated historical treatment of geology as well as particle physics, or of the German language and music, apart from the idea of the advancement of knowledge itself? It is not difficult to examine each discipline by itself, but can each be treated as an integral element of the sciences or the humanities seen as a whole?

Possibly one approach to this problem is to measure the disciplines of the arts and the sciences against certain fundamental categories of human organization – such as time, space, and memory. J. David Bolter, in his provocative book *Turing's Man: Western Culture in the Computer Age* (1984), has suggested that the current revolution in computer technology is fundamentally altering the ways in which both humanists and scientists think about such categories. It is at least arguable that post-Baconian Western science has little use for the notion of 'memory,' because the tools that it has produced point inexorably towards, and help determine, the future. Technology, in this view, is no longer the handmaiden of science; it is co-equal with it and may even be the determining factor in scientific discovery. 'In short,' wrote the eminent American historian of science Derek J. deSolla Price, 'the scientific revolution, as we call it, was largely the improvement and invention and use of a series of instruments of revelation that expanded the reach of science in innumerable directions.'[20] Needless to say, Price's assertions are currently the subject of much debate within the community of the historians of science. Technology and its new handmaiden, science, can be portrayed in such a view as relatively autonomous from politics, economics, or ideology. As Professor Jarrell asserts, in a deliberately overstated way: 'scientific or technological change is the heart, the centre, of historical processes in the modern world, not politics, not economics, not business practices, not religion or social movements.' To some historians, probably most, those are fighting words indeed. If technology, and the 'historical processes' that are its consequences, have no need of such entities, neither do they need the forms of social memory required by each (if only to conjure up reasons for departing from tradition). To deliberately overstate this case, it is possible that a world given over to technological advance is also one of social amnesia, a world where progress can be measured by the size of the graveyards of discarded machines and tools. And dead machines, like dead men, tell no tales.

Yet is the telling of tales, the preservation of a sense of collective memory, not a notion that unites the seemingly disparate humanities in a profound sense? Whether in art, language, philosophy, literature, music – even history – a tale *is* being told, even if it is an overlapping and at times contradictory one. '*Humanitas*,' as E.H. Gombrich has recently reminded us, 'meant to the ancient world roughly anything that distinguished man from beast, and so the notion became identified with what we might call civilized values. Since nobody doubted that these values had first been realized and established by classical culture, it was the memory of this culture which the humanities were expected to keep alive.'[21]

To suggest that science represents the party of futures to be gained and the humanities represent a party of pasts to be preserved requires no necessary choice of sides. The humanist does not, like the protagonist in John Metcalf's academic novel *General Ludd*, need to become a modern-day Luddite and steal the department's typewriter in order to gain some measure of peace of mind.[22] The modern university is necessarily the fundamental meeting-ground of future and past, and such battles as may exist on their behalf will doubtless continue to witness the sciences and the humanities, like Napoleon and Wellington, staring silently at each other from opposing elevations while on the battlefield the pawns, the social sciences, do battle. One might well disagree as to which units should be engaged in the combat, or even whether such combat is necessary, but there should surely be no fundamental disagreement about the site – the university – as an essential forum where the basic reciprocities of human experience, peaceful or not, can take place. We need to know much more about the dynamics of that exchange.

4
Evolution, Ethnology, and Poetic Fancy

The intellectual history of modern Canada was profoundly affected by the Darwinian Revolution, and Daniel Wilson, scientist, historian, artist, and educator, was one of the first in the country to respond to its implications. Wilson's particular reaction to Darwinism was in one sense unique, but it also revealed the ways in which science and sentiment were vitally entwined within mid-Victorian middle-class culture. Religion came, in the eyes of many, to be threatened by, and antagonistic to, the cause of science. Wilson's response, however, suggests that the orthodox science of the day cannot fully be understood unless the pattern of essentially religious assumptions that existed within it is also examined and evaluated by the historian. The paper was given at a conference on 'Science, Pseudo-Science, and Society' held at the University of Calgary. It was published as 'Evolution, Ethnology, and Poetic Fancy: Sir Daniel Wilson and Mid-Victorian Science,' in Margaret J. Osler and others, eds., Science, Pseudo-Science, and Society *(Calgary 1980), 193–214.*

In September 1859 Albert, prince consort, delivered a speech to a distinguished body of British gentlemen in Aberdeen, Scotland. Itself, this was scarcely a remarkable event. Albert gave many speeches during his lifetime, and many Victorian gentlemen listened patiently to such addresses. Yet this occasion was somewhat singular. The gathering to which Albert spoke comprised the elite of the British scientific community, the British Association for the Advancement of Science. Albert was its president for that year. A friend of British science throughout his life in England, and one of the architects of the Great Exhibition of 1851, he began his address with a general discussion of the nature of science – a review which has been described as one 'that summarized prevailing philosophical views and did not break new ground.'[1] It was, all in all, a concise reflection of the prevailing consensus about the nature of mid-Victorian science.

Early the next year the prince consort's presidential address found its way into the *Canadian Journal*, the main publication of the central Canadian scientific community. Those who read Albert's remarks were treated first to some grand generalizations. 'To me,' they read, 'Science, in its most general and comprehensive acceptation, means the knowledge of what I know, the consciousness of human knowledge. Hence, to know, is the object of all Science; and all special knowledge, if brought to our consciousness in its separate distinctiveness from, and yet in its recognised relation to the totality of our knowledge, is scientific knowledge.' The primary activities of the scientist, Albert continued, are those of analysis and synthesis, the reconstruction of 'a unity in our consciousness,' a new understanding of that aspect of the natural world under observation. 'The labours of the man of Science are therefore at once the most humble and the loftiest which man can undertake,' for the process of organized and purposive observation of phenomena which relates the observed object to 'the general universe of knowledge' – through arrangement and classification – has as its end nothing less than the discovery of 'the internal connexion which the Almighty has implanted' in previously incongruous elements of nature.[2]

Hence, the central concern of the different sciences is to establish the essential unity of all nature. But this, Albert warned, is an onerous task because it is also an endless one: 'for God's world is infinite.' Onerous or not, he added, it is the duty of the scientist to remain conscious of the 'unity which must pervade the whole of science,' and the major way this can be done is 'in the combination of men of science representing all the specialities, and working together for the common object of preserving that unity and presiding over that general direction.' The true science, the best science, he concluded, must 'proceed ... by the inductive process, taking nothing on trust, nothing for granted, but reasoning upwards from the meanest fact established, and making every step sure before going one beyond it ... This road has been shown to us by the great Bacon, and who can contemplate the prospects which it opens, without almost falling into a trance similar to that in which he allowed his imagination to wander over future ages of discovery.'[3]

Albert's declaration points to the important fact that on the eve of the Darwinian revolution, in English-speaking countries the scientific enterprise was still conducted along lines laid down by Bacon.[4] This was certainly the case in British North America, where 'Bacon,' like ''Reid' and 'Paley,' was a surname that bore the stamp of final authority. Baconian science, with the Scottish 'Common Sense' philosophy and a Paleyite natural theology, completed the triumvirate of intellectual orthodoxy that dominated many educated Anglo-Canadian minds for the first three-quarters of the nineteenth century.[5]

The Baconian method was rationalistic and empirical, deduction after observation, but it did not exclude the Almighty. 'And all depends,' Bacon had written in the introduction to *The Great Instauration*, his blueprint for the new science, 'on keeping the eye steadily fixed upon the facts of nature and so receiving their images simply as they are. For God forbid that we should give out a dream of our own imagination for a pattern of the world; rather may it be graciously granted to us to write an apocalypse or true vision of the footsteps of the Creator imprinted on his creatures.'[6] Albert's recapitulation of the commonplaces of mid-Victorian British Baconian science had not overtly equated the cause of science with that of religion, except, perhaps, for its almost gratuitous mention of the Almighty. But there were many individuals, both in Albert's learned audience and among his later readers, for whom his articulation of the assumptions of that science was little less than royal approval of just such an equation.

Not a few such readers were to be found at the time among those who practised science in British North America. While men of religion in Canada sought to lay the appropriate religious foundations for the study of nature through the teaching of their own adaptations of natural theology, some of the leading scientists in the colony sought, in their lectures and writings, to build, upon the edifice so carefully constructed by their colleagues, a science in accordance with the orthodox Christianity of their day. 'Let us remember this at least,' concluded the president of the Canadian Institute, Daniel Wilson, early in January of 1860, 'that that great ocean of truth does lie before us, and even those pebbles which our puerile labours gather on its shore, may include here and there a gem of purest ray; and meanwhile the search for truth ... will bring to each one of us his own exceeding great reward.'[7]

Daniel Wilson was, by 1860, one of Canada's leading scientists and educators. A native of Edinburgh, the forty-four-year-old Scot had only been in British North America for a half-dozen years. But by then he had already acquired a respectable international reputation in the field of science. Wilson had come to science after first considering careers in art (he studied for a time with William Turner and had considerable talent as an artist) and in popular literature (he had written reviews and essays for magazines such as *Chambers' Journal*, and had published anonymously a *History of Oliver Cromwell* and a *History of the Puritans* with the firm of his lifelong friend Thomas Nelson).[8] By the early 1840s, however, his mind had turned to antiquarian and ethnological concerns. In 1847, while secretary of the Scottish Antiquarian Society, he published the massive *Memorials of Edinburgh in the Olden Time*, with illustrations executed by himself. Four years later appeared *The Archaeology and Prehistoric Annals of Scotland*, which earned for its author an honorary Doctorate of Laws from St Andrew's University and gave to the world the word 'prehistory.' The impressively researched volumes which made up this latter work also marked a substantial attempt by the author to effect, in the words of the preface to the first edition, 'the transition from profitless dilettantism to the intelligent spirit of scientific investigation.'[9] In 1853 Wilson immigrated to Canada with his wife to accept a position at the University of Toronto as professor of history and English literature. By 1859 he had established himself in the newly built University College, was an active member of the Canadian Institute, and had become editor of the *Canadian Journal*.

The peroration of Wilson's 1860 presidential address to the Canadian Institute had closely paraphrased a famous example of Sir Isaac Newton's sense of humility in the face of the seeming boundlessness of nature and the unity of its laws. But as put forward by the president of the Canadian Institute, that truth and unity were given their essential meaning by the fact that they were, and could only be, a Christian truth and a Christian unity. 'The experience of the past shows how frequently men have contended for their own blundering interpretations,' Wilson concluded, 'while all the while believing themselves the champions and the martyrs of truth.' Such self-delusion would not occur if one was careful to remember the religious nature of truth, for 'all truth is of God, alike in relation to the natural and the moral law, and of the former, as truly as of the latter may we say: "if this counsel or this work be of men, it will come to nought; but if it be of God, ye cannot overthrow it; lest haply ye be found even to fight against God."'[10] A year later Professor Wilson, still president of the Canadian Institute, reiterated the same theme. The aim of the institute, he said, should be to investigate the laws of nature and to uncover 'new truths in every department of human knowledge.'

A sonnet from a volume of Daniel Wilson's poems published in the mid-1870s strikes to the heart of this theme:

> I stood upon the world's thronged thoroughfare,
> And saw her crowds pass by in eager chase
> Of bubbles glistening in the morning rays;
> While overhead, methought God's angels were
> With golden crowns of which all unaware
> They heedless crowded on in folly's race.
> But yet methought a few were given grace,
> With heavenward gaze, to aspire for treasures there,
> All trustfully as an expectant heir;
> Through whomme [*sic*] the soul shone, as the body were
> But a veil, wherein it did abide,
> Waiting till God's own hand shall it uncover.
> O God! that such a prize in vain hover
> O'er souls in nature to Thyself allied![11]

At one level Wilson's sonnet expresses the common Christian desire to transcend his finiteness through the pursuit of the eternal; at another it is a gesture of thanks for the existence of a scientific elect, those 'few [who] were given grace,/With heavenward gaze, to aspire for treasures there, / All trustfully as an expectant heir.' Science thus could serve as a means of grace for the select few to whom were given both the ability and the duty to lift the veil with which God had obscured the presence of His hand in nature. This view also finds close parallels in Wilson's scientific work. To the individual, Wilson wrote in *Prehistoric Man* (1863), 'The drift of the Maker is dark, an Isis hid by the veil!'; but with the aid of the inspiration and guidance of religion, such darkness is dispelled, for 'Christianity ... lifts for us the veil of Isis, tells of the Righter of all the wrongs of ages.'[12]

The dictates of Christian piety were not, then, confined only to the pew on Sundays, not just to the notebooks of philosophy students, nor to lectures on natural theology. They also found their place in the field trips taken by professors of science, and they took their hold as well upon the minds of anyone, academic or layman alike, who looked to science as a source of religious inspiration and affirmation. The inductive, Baconian science extolled by Prince Albert required no abstract 'hypotheses' unprovable by simple observation and induction, no ingenious theories. The Canadian natural theologian James Bovell, in fact, had warned his students of the dangers of such unwarranted extensions of the scientific imagination. 'While false systems of philosophy may tantalize and fret the mind,' he said, 'the calm and reflecting reasoner on revealed truth is content to curb his imagination, and to accept the creator as He has thought fit to shew himself.'[13] The main requirement was simply a 'child-like heart' and the humility that must necessarily accompany the thought of any Christian who, aware of the limitations of his own reason, nevertheless yearns for a measure of unity with the Divine.

Those of like mind who read Prince Albert's address to the British Association for the Advancement of Science might well have placed such an interpretation on his remark that the man of science 'only does what every little child does from its first awakening into life, and must do every moment of its existence; and yet he aims at the gradual approximation to divine truth itself.' He might well have concluded that by the simple inductive process of observation in the Baconian tradition, 'we thus gain a roadway, a ladder by which even a child may almost without knowing it, ascend to the summit of truth.'[14] Such lessons were not lost on Canadian students only a few years removed from childhood. Writing in the initial volume of the *Dalhousie Gazette*, the first Canadian university newspaper, one anonymous student declared that 'the great object of science is the ascertainment of causes – the search after the ultimate – the making of generalizations – the resolution of plurality into unity.' Its 'indirect (although equally great) object,' he concluded, 'is the cultivation of all those qualities which dignify and adorn the moral nature of man.' Science could therefore come to the aid of the nineteenth-century moral philosopher and his insistence on the reality of the 'moral nature.' It should come as no surprise to find editorials in Canadian student newspapers such as the one that wondered: 'What can have a greater influence in purifying and elevating the mind of man than the study of the beautiful and yet wonderful works of Nature around him! What could raise our thoughts more towards the Supreme Being than the contemplation of Nature, and a knowledge of its wonderful laws.'[15]

But such a conception of the methods and aims of science was possible only as long as the essentially static, mechanistic universe of Newton's physics and Paley's physico-theology remained intact. From the late eighteenth century on, however, the idea of the immutability of nature's design had been constantly undermined: by Kant, Buffon, Laplace, Herschel, Cuvier, Lyell, and others. Work in astronomy, geology, and paleontology, in particular, pointed to the fact that nature itself was mutable, changing. By 1859 the *fact* of organic change was well known; there was lacking only a theory of the *mechanism* by which such change took place. 'In this development,' John C. Greene has observed, 'Darwin played a last-minute but decisive role.'[16] It was Darwin, more than anyone else in the nineteenth century, who helped to lift the corner of the veil of Isis. And as with Bluebeard's last wife, impelled to unlock the last door in the castle, many were aghast at their first glimpse of what hitherto had been shrouded in darkness.

Daniel Wilson's 1860 presidential address to the Canadian Institute, published in the *Canadian Journal* early that year, was largely a review of Darwin's *Origin*. For Wilson, science was largely Baconian in method, but it also marked the hazy frontier which links science to the religious and poetic sensibility. The science of William Dawson at McGill clearly bore the Hebraic legacy of his Calvinism (as may be observed by reading Dawson on biblical cosmology); that of Wilson was equally informed and shaped by Wilson the artist and poet. 'In some respects, and perhaps with truth,' the journalist G. Mercer Adam observed near the end of Wilson's life, 'it may be said that Dr. Wilson would have done more justice to himself if he had made a choice in his life's work between literature and science rather than, as he has done, given the prose side of his mind to archaeological studies and reserved its poetical side for literature.'[17] There is a significant measure of truth in this statement. But it is rather too artificial and clear-cut. Just as there was no absolutely rigid 'scientific' or 'religious' side, nor two equal commitments to the different sources of authority implied by these words, there was likewise not, in Wilson's mind, any clearly defined 'prose' or 'poetic' side.

In fact, Wilson's poetic sensibility was always a present and determining factor in his thought, including his science. One of his students at University College in the early 1870s took down the following lecture notes: 'Poetry precedes prose ... As *Rhetoric* has its own forms etc. distinct from Logic, so poetry has its own ... So like pulpit-preaching or pleading – *Poetry aims at giving pleasure by exciting and influencing the Emotions* – and the *license* allowed is only limited by the object the poet has in view ... Poetry addresses the *taste* or aesthetic faculty.' Or again: 'Rhetoric is the art of speaking (and writing) well and persuasively the language of Emotion ... It employs an elaborateness of structure inadmissible in Logic ... In Rhetoric – There must be *continuous emotion*, springing from the subject itself, and *true feeling*.'[18] The aesthetic bent of Wilson's mind must constantly be recalled when considering his scientific as well as his literary work; so should the function of rhetoric, thus defined, when assessing the scientific writings of Wilson (and others) in the nineteenth century.

When Wilson spoke of rhetoric, it is obvious that he did not exclude writing upon scientific subjects from its scope. Scientific writing of the Victorian period was very much an art of persuasion. Parts of Wilson's review of Darwin's *Origin* could have served as blackboard examples of that art. Canadian science, he admitted, had necessarily to be in large measure a practical one. Yet any science of true worth must also transcend purely utilitarian concerns. 'In the Canadian Institute,' he therefore concluded, 'it may be presumed that we pursue science for the discovery of its secret truths; that we climb the steps of knowledge, as the traveller ascends the mountain's unexplored cliffs, gladdened at every pause in his ascent with new grandeur and beauty in the widening horizon which opens on his delighted gaze.'[19] Here is the rhetoric of romantic aesthetics under the guise of the aims of science. In Wilson's view, science was of value insofar as it excited the aesthetic faculty. Wilson's science, in short, owed much to the tradition of which Edmund Burke's essay *The Sublime and the Beautiful* was an integral part. The secret of the veils of Isis, as with all veils, lay in the mystery maintained, not in the actual object hidden.

Wilson's reaction to Darwin's theory of the origin of species was one characteristic of the day, especially on two of the basic issues raised in the *Origin*: first, that there is in nature no absolute distinction between species and varieties because all organic creation is descended from a common primordial stock; second, that the survival or extinction of species rests primarily upon a process, which Darwin chose to call 'natural selection,' that led to the 'survival of the fittest' (a term which Darwin borrowed from Thomas Malthus and lived to regret).[20] Wilson's commitment to an inductive, Baconian science based upon observation meant the rejection, as a consequence, of the notion of a science which set forth 'hypotheses' unproven by such observation and resting mainly upon an evidential basis of statistical probability extrapolated from a mass of evidence.[21]

Wilson's scientific judgments were also shaped largely by his essentially moral outlook. As much a man of religion as he was of science (Wilson was a broad-church Anglican), his scientific works were profoundly affected by the demands of his religious conscience. And in this mixture of religious and scientific assumptions can be seen the problem of determining the ultimate sources of conviction. Daniel Wilson was drawn to science because for him it held the means by which he hoped to penetrate the veils behind which was what Augustine had called the 'great and hidden good.'

His basic objection to Darwin was simply that Darwin had put forward conclusions not supported (though not contradicted) by his evidence, substantial though that may have been. Furthermore, like William Dawson, he believed that these conclusions went beyond the scope of legitimate scientific inquiry. 'Nothing is more humbling to the scientific enquirer,' Dawson began his review of Darwin's *Origin*, 'than to find that he has arrived in the progress of his investigations at a point beyond which inductive science fails to carry him.' Science, he went on, was an endeavour that rested upon an insoluble contradiction. 'True science is always humble, for it knows itself to be surrounded by mysteries – mysteries which only widen as the sphere of its knowledge extends. Yet it is the ambition of science to solve mysteries, to add one domain after another to its conquests, though certain to find new and greater difficulties beyond.'[22] Paradoxical as it may now seem, Dawson's science satisfied, rather than frustrated, him. On the one hand, an inductive Baconian science helped to establish authoritatively the 'truths' of the natural world; yet, on the other, the very boundlessness and seamlessness of the web of nature meant the perpetual revelation of more mysteries of life. Since these were those of God, the endless search for their solution became, for Dawson, a kind of scientific counterpart of the Christian's quest – even in the knowledge that his fallen nature makes the mission impossible except through salvation – for unity with the mind of God, for an insight, however limited and inadequate, into the Divine will. It was for him the ultimate form of piety.

From this point of view, the benefit of Baconian empiricism was that since it was based upon a finite number of observations, limiting itself to observations of 'secondary causes' operating in nature, and insisting that no conclusions be drawn beyond the evidence provided by such observations, speculations of a cosmological sort were beyond its scope. This conception of science therefore dictated a separation of scientific conclusions from metaphysical speculation. Such a science could come in handy to those, like Dawson, who owed much to the 'twin theologies' tradition. In violating the canons of Baconian method by engaging in unwarranted speculation, Darwin (Dawson and Wilson alike believed) had not only transcended the bounds of proper science, but had obliterated the distinction between science and cosmology. As will be shown, however, Wilson himself (and, for that matter, Dawson) violated the requirements of that Baconian tradition in order to engage in his own cosmological speculations.

Like Dawson, Daniel Wilson was clearly disturbed by the events that were then shaking modern science. The problem with Darwin's challenge to the supremacy of Baconian induction by his use of an hypothetico-deductive method (which has since served as the methodological basis of modern evolutionary biology) was that it threatened the very sense of mystery that provided the science of Wilson with its religious and aesthetic dynamics. Not content to describe nature as it appeared after the uncovering of each successive veil, Darwin had dared to assess the natural world as if no veils existed. His discovery of natural selection, an astute observer of the Darwinian method has noted, 'was, above all else, a triumph of reason. If banishing intuition from our conception of the process of discovery deprives us of a sense of mystery, it nonetheless permits us to analyze that process in a far more satisfying manner than did the mythological accounts.'[23] Such a method may have been satisfying for the Darwinian, or may still be for the modern biologist, but not for Dawson or Wilson. The Darwinian hypothesis, said Wilson, appears to have had as its immediate result 'the removal of many old land-marks of scientific faith, whereby we witness some of the conditions of ruin, which mark all transitional eras – whether of thought or action. The old has been shaken, or thrown down, the new is still to build.'[24]

'In this light,' Wilson's review of Darwin's *Origin* began, 'we must look upon that comprehensive question which now challenges revision ... *What is Species?*' Comprehensive and important because it 'forces us back to first principles,' and has equal effect upon paleontology, zoology, and the relations of science and theology, the species question, as resolved by Darwin, stood as a challenge above all because of its bearings upon Wilson's own major interest, ethnology. It involved not only the question 'In what forms has creative power been manifested in the succession of organic life?' but also another, more central to Wilson's particular scientific concern: 'Under what conditions has man been introduced into the most diverse and widely separated provinces of the animal world?' It is clear that to Wilson, the ethnologist, the former question was in fact subsumed within the latter: 'It is to the comprehensive bearings of the latter indeed, that the former owes its origin; for what is the use of entertaining the question, prematurely forced upon us: Are all men of one and the same species? While authorities in science are still so much at variance as to what species really is; and writers who turn with incredulous contempt from the idea that all men are descended from Adam, can nevertheless look with complacency on their probable descent from apes!'[25]

Much of Wilson's review of *Origin* dwelt upon what most observers agree to have been the fundamental challenge posed by Darwin and he was able to summarize the essence of that challenge with admirable brevity: 'He has arrived at the conclusion that there is in reality no essential distinction between individual difference, varieties, and species. The well-marked variety is an incipient species; and by the operation of various simple physical causes and comparatively slight organic changes, producing a tendency towards increase in one direction of variation, and arrestment, and ultimate extinction in another, the law of *natural selection*, as Darwin terms it, results, which leads to his "preservation of favoured races in the struggle for life."'[26]

When he rejected the 'transmutation' theory of evolution through 'the tendency of species to an infinite multiplication of intermediate links,' Wilson also rejected the notion of natural selection. He noted that the evidence of paleontology afforded no positive evidence to affirm the idea of transmutation. 'We look in vain,' he said, 'among organic fossils for any such gradations of form as even to suggest a process of transmutation. Above all, in relation to man, no fossil form adds a single link to fill up the wide interval between him and the most anthropoid of inferior animals.' This, he contended, is true even if one limited oneself to the purely physical characteristics by which the paleontologist is bound. But once one considered mental characteristics, as the ethnologist must, the challenge to Darwin's theory was even stronger, for 'if the difference between man and the inferior animals, not only in mere physical organization, but still more in all the higher attributes of animal life, be not relative but absolute, then no multiplication of intermediate links can lessen the obstacles to transmutation. One true antidote therefore to such a doctrine, and to the consequent denial of primary distinctions of species, seems to offer itself in such broad and unmistakable lines of demarcation [*sic*] as Professor Owen indicates, between the cerebral structure of man and that of the most highly developed of anthropoid or other animals.'[27] Here was the genesis of Wilson's argument a dozen or so years later that Shakespeare's Caliban could be viewed as the 'missing link.' But unlike the 'missing links' so long sought by later anthropologists, Wilson's did not serve the purpose of establishing once and for all time the strength of the chain of evolution. It was, instead, a means of establishing a kind of buffer between animal and man in creation.

Although Wilson rejected Darwin's theory, he treated the views of the British naturalist with the respect due to any who seriously proposed a significant advance in scientific truth. 'His "Origin of Species," is no product of a rash theorist, but the result of the patient observation and laborious experiments of a highly gifted naturalist.' There could be little doubt that Darwin's work would create as many problems as it solved. It would, Wilson noted, 'tend to ... give courage to other assailants of those views of the permanency of species, which have seemed so indispensable alike to all our preconceived ideas in natural science, and to our interpretations of revealed cosmology.' In the end, Wilson said, no serious harm could come of Darwin's work: if it was incorrect, scientists would prove it so; if correct, new areas of knowledge would be opened. In either case the cause of Truth, through the practice of science, would be served: 'our attitude ought clearly to be that of candid and impartial jurors. We must examine for ourselves, not reject, the evidence thus honestly given ... All truth is of God, alike in relation to the natural and the moral laws, and of the former, as truly as of the latter may we say: "if this counsel or this work be of men, it will come to nought; but if it be of God, ye cannot overthrow it; lest haply ye be found even to fight against God." '[28]

Daniel Wilson's science was not, therefore, tied to a dogmatic commitment to the Mosaic cosmogony; yet in its own way it was still tied to the notion of a providential design and harmony in nature. This resulted, at times, in an apparent abandonment of the essence of scientific inquiry. On the one hand, Wilson applauded the work of the comparative anatomist Richard Owen (who embraced evolution but rejected natural selection) for his 'grand generalizations, based not [as with Darwin] on theory, but on laborious and exhaustive induction, [thereby revealing] to us the plan of the Creator.'[29] Yet, on the other, he admitted that science – even that which is based upon the solid Baconian observation of laws operating in nature – becomes inadequate. 'Science has achieved wondrous triumphs,' he observed in his 1861 presidential address to the Canadian Institute, 'but life is a thing it can neither create nor account for, by mere physics. Nor can we assume even that the whole law of life can be embraced within the process of induction, as carried out by an observer so limited as man is ... Darwin, indeed, builds largely upon hypotheses constructed to supply the gaps in the geological records; but whilst welcoming every new truth which enlarges our conception of the cosmic unity, all nature still says as plainly to us ... "Canst thou by searching find out the Almighty to perfection?" '[30] The reasons for Wilson's fascination with the natural world, protected by the veils of Isis, ultimately lay in the satisfaction he derived from the certainty that, behind each raised veil, was fortunately another which yet preserved the mysteries of life.

The appearance of Darwin's long-awaited sequel to the *The Origin of Species* inaugurated a new wave of anti Darwinian sentiment in Canada. By the end of the 1860s little effective accommodation had been reached in Canada between the defenders of Christianity and the scientific findings of the decade. Articles recounting leading scientific infidelities continued to find a welcome place in the Methodist newspaper, the *Christian Guardian*,[31] as they had throughout the decade of the 1860s. Few Canadians writing for the *Guardian* were willing to accept Darwin's theory of evolution, and virtually none gave countenance to the idea of natural selection.

But with the publication of *The Descent of Man*, Canadian critics of modern science were drawn into a renewed struggle with the latest phase of the Darwinian heresy. Just after the publication of Darwin's new book, but before its contents were known in Canada, a long article entitled 'Darwinism and Christianity' appeared in the *Christian Guardian*. It was well-reasoned and moderate in tone, stating all the major objections of the decade to the theory of evolution and concluding that 'all observation and research extending over the period of human and animal life testify to the permanence of species.'[32] It was the last of such articles to speak with moderation of Darwin, for, within months, copies of the The Descent of Man, stowed in the holds of steam packets plying the North Atlantic, reached Canadian shores. Not a few Canadians may later have wished that the ships carrying the offending cargo had met with a watery fate on the shoals of the St Lawrence.

It was a book that focused the full force of evolutionary theory upon the question of the origins of man, a subject not mentioned by Darwin in *The Origin of Species*. Human beings, Darwin now argued, probably descended from some form of primate. He further enraged the Victorian sensibility by stressing the significance of 'sexual selection,' the choice of a reproductive partner, in the process of evolution. Finally, he argued – and here he challenged conventional mental and moral philosophy – that the intellectual and social faculties of man were adaptive and that his survival or extinction rested upon such changes. Darwin's new book involved not only the study of nature but of human nature. *The Descent of Man* raised questions of fundamental importance in the areas of psychology and philosophy, as well as geology and anthropology. *The Origin of Species* had led men into the new world of geological time; *The Descent of Man* took them on a journey into the interior of the mind.

In the dozen years between 1859 and 1871, Daniel Wilson, in Toronto, had followed the debate over Darwinism and had continued his ethnological researches and writing. As professor of English literature as well as history, however, he had also taught the works of Shakespeare. *Caliban: The Missing Link* (1873), Wilson's response to *The Descent of Man*, was thus a mixture of ethnology and literary criticism. It also contained not a little sheer fancy. In 1887 G. Mercer Adam, in an article for *The Week*, described Wilson's book perfectly: '*Caliban*,' he said, 'is an interesting Shakespearean study, combining great imaginative power with a strong critical faculty, and giving the reader much curious information, with not a little fanciful disquisition, on the Evolution theory.'[33]

It was, however else one might judge it, an extraordinary book. All the more remarkable was the fact that, although the book was based upon Wilson's experience teaching Shakespeare's play *The Tempest* to students of University College, his students doubtless came away from their classes knowing at least as much about Darwin, evolution, and the descent of man as they did about Prospero, drama, and the stuff of dreams. 'The leading purpose of the following pages,' Wilson wrote in his preface, was 'to shew that [Shakespeare's] genius had already created for us the ideal of that imaginary intermediate being, between the true brute and man, which, if the new theory of descent from crudest animal organisms be true, was our predecessor and precursor in the inheritance of the world of humanity ... A comparison between this Caliban of Shakespeare's creation, and the so-called "brute-progenitor of man" of our latest school of science, has proved replete with interest and instruction to the writer's own mind; and the results are embodied in the following pages.'[34]

By the 1870s, Daniel Wilson – aided by his poetic imagination – had left the more certain domain of his scientific expertise to consider the philosophical and psychological implications made necessary by *The Descent of Man*. If one assumed that matter existed eternally, then it was difficult to accept the coming into being (and, hence, existence) of a Divine Creator. Was it not 'more scientific,' Wilson suggested, 'to start with the preoccupation of the mighty void with the Eternal Mind?' But if (the Divine) mind existed before matter, how could this be reconciled with the findings of evolutionary science, which implied that mind was created through 'the development of the intellectual, moral, and spiritual elements of man, through the same natural selection by which his physical evolution is traced, step by step, from the very lowest organic forms'?[35]

The scientific imagination had signally failed to resolve this dilemma; nor had scientists found any fossil evidence that could help. Yet what science had failed to do, 'the creative fancy of the true poet, working within its own legitimate sphere, has accomplished to better purpose.' The 'seductive hypotheses' and the 'severer inductions' of science, Wilson believed, inhibited a solution to the problem of the descent of man. Fortunately, where Baconian inductions had proved inadequate, the poet had succeeded. Shakespeare himself had, in *The Tempest*, 'presented ... the vivid conception of "that amphibious piece between corporeal and spiritual essence" [the quotation is from Sir Thomas Browne's *Religio Medici*], by which, according to modern hypothesis, the human mind is conjoined in nature and origin with the very lowest forms of vital organism. The greatest of poets ... has thus left for us materials not without their value in discussing ... the imaginary perfectibility of the irrational brute; the imaginable degradation of rational man.'[36]

Those last dozen words contain the key to Wilson's interpretation of Caliban as the 'missing link' between animal and man, as well as the reason why he felt obliged to rely upon the poetic imagination in order to bolster his own arguments against evolutionary science. It was the mind of both animal and man which was under consideration, and it was poetic insight, rather than scientific thought, that alone could provide the light necessary for the journey into the interior. 'History tells of the acts, literature tells of the mind,' read the literature notes of one of Wilson's students in the class of 1874.[37] Furthermore, lacking what Wilson had earlier called the 'well-regulated fancy' of the poet, the scientist's vision was limited: he could conceive as scientifically 'imaginable' the degradation of the rational man, but could only see as 'imaginary' the possibility that the 'irrational brute' might develop – that is, might evolve within certain specific limits – to the height of his potential and yet not become man.

For Wilson, Shakespeare's 'hag-born whelp' was just such a creature: 'the highest development of "the beast that wants recourse of reason." He has attained to all the maturity his nature admits of, and so is perfect as the study of a living creature distinct from, yet next in order below the level of humanity.'[38] Wilson's book sought in a variety of ways to make the case for the inviolability and sanctity of the gap between Caliban, the poet's imaginative conception of the 'natural brute mind' developed to its fullest capacity, and even the most degraded of rational human beings.

It was necessary first to dispose of the view that since scientific evidence indisputably showed that man was structurally far more similar to the higher apes than apes were to the lesser quadrumana, he was evolved from the ape. The parallel, Wilson argued, was a false one. Man and the apes are both animals; hence, they are physically similar. Yet it does not necessarily follow that the former evolved from the latter. Darwin had made this mistake in logic, and the result was of immense import for Wilson's thought. It made the journey into the interior both possible and necessary. 'To all appearance,' he wrote of *The Descent of Man*, 'the further process in the assumed descent ... of man from the purely animal to the rational and intellectual stage, is but a question of brain development; and this cerebral growth is the assigned source of the manward progress: not the result of any functional harmonising of mind and brain ... It is difficult to dissociate from such an idea the further conclusion, that reason and mind are not more than the action of the enlarged mind; yet this is not necessarily implied ... The brain is certainly the organ of reasoning, the vital instrument through which the mind acts; but it need not therefore be assumed that brain and mind are one.' Caliban, for Wilson, marked the symbolic midpoint between the brain of animals and the mind of man, the narrow gulf between irrational ape and rational man: 'No being of all ... Shakespeare[an] drama more thoroughly suggests the idea of a pure creation of the poetic fancy than Caliban. He has a nature of his own essentially distinct from the human beings with whom he is brought into contact. He seems indeed the half-human link between the brute and man; and realises, as no degraded Bushman or Australian savage can do, a conceivable intermediate stage of the anthropomorphous existence, as far above the most highly organized ape as it falls short of rational humanity.'[39]

Wilson was not content to rest after writing about 'The Monster Caliban.' His next chapter was entitled 'Caliban, the Metaphysician.' Here he attempted to rebut the evolutionist's claim that all the attributes of humanity – man's 'intellect, his conscience, and his religious beliefs' – were simply part of the evolutionary process. As with Dawson, this was Wilson's central source of concern over the question of man's descent. 'The growing difficulty, indeed,' he wrote when considering the possibility of the evolution of these attributes, 'is not so much to find man's place in nature, as to find any place left for mind.' Nor was this the only problem. 'If conscience, religion, the apprehension of truth, the belief in God and immortality, are all no more than developed or transformed animal sensations; and intellect is only the latest elaboration of the perceptions: it need not surprise us that inquiry has already been extended in search of relations between the inorganic and the organic. On this new hypothesis of evolution ''what a piece of work is man!'' and as for God, it is hard to see what is left for Him to do in the universe.'[40]

It is not surprising, therefore, that Wilson rejected the interpretation of Caliban rendered by Robert Browning in his poem 'Caliban upon Setebos.' The thoughts of Browning's Caliban suggested to Wilson that poor Caliban, after all 'only a poor half-witted brute, – [had got] terribly out of his depth.' Shakespeare's Caliban, and Wilson's, had been a poetic rendering of the 'intermediate, half-brute, missing link.' Browning's was that of the Darwinians: 'the human savage, grovelling before the Manitou of his own conception.'[41]

The essential points have now been made. Wilson responded strenuously and at some length to the challenges posed by evolutionary science to his scientific and religious beliefs. He replied to Darwin from the perspective of his own scientific expertise, but in the course of the dozen years between the publication of *The Origin of Species* and *The Descent of Man* two things happened. First, he abandoned the premises of science in important ways in order to defend the religious heritage he saw under attack, and he did so by returning to the poetic fancy with which he had always been enamoured. Many Canadians, whether university students, clergymen, or Victorian families, perplexed by what they read in the *Christian Guardian* or other newspapers on the subject of evolution, may well have found the writings of Wilson to be the proper response for Christians to make to such heresies; but it is questionable whether to the more reflective among them these writings assuaged the nagging uncertainties that were in the air by the decade of the seventies.

The second observation to be made is that whenever Wilson considered the place of man within the framework of the evolutionary hypothesis, he was forced to deal with questions of immense philosophical import. Darwin's new book called fundamentally into question the various dualisms – spiritual and material, revelation and nature, mind and brain – which were basic to the science and the religion of Wilson and others. It marked the bankruptcy of the Baconian scientific method, which actively avoided hypothetical assertions about the existence of natural laws. Furthermore, it called into question the mechanistic faculty psychology on which their conceptions of the human mind were based. 'The nineteenth century ... has ... failed as yet to arrive at a satisfactory conclusion as to man's place in nature,' wrote another Canadian scientist in 1872. 'We think,' he later stated, 'that any naturalist is justified, as a scientific man, in maintaining that all classifications of man by his anatomical characters alone, are *artificial*, and as such are indefensible. Such classifications do not embrace the totality of man's organization, and can not, therefore, be natural ... man's zoological definition must be made to include something more than his mere physical and anatomical structure. *That* something is man's mental and moral constitution; and we repeat our belief that any naturalist is justified, without disparagement to either his knowledge or his ability, in maintaining that man's physical peculiarities are as much an integral factor of his zoological definition as his physical structure, or perhaps more so.'[42]

Such concerns for the legitimacy of the 'mental and moral constitution' and for man's 'physical peculiarities' may well have been within the scientist's area of inquiry, but they were also laden with philosophical implications which transcended the limits of natural science. The high-water mark of the public influence of the earth sciences had been reached by the 1870s. Thereafter, in an ever-increasing degree, the educated public would look to social philosophers attuned to the new physiological sciences for solutions to the problems posed by modern thought. And by the 1870s, discussions of the nature of the human condition could also take place in forums other than the cloistered confines of Canadian educational institutions and the pages of religious newspapers. The ranks of orthodoxy had been breached, not only by new ideas but also by the fact that members of the lay public could now put forward their considered views in new magazines of informed opinion given their start by strange winds that gusted in the new Canadian nation.

In the end, as we reflect upon the place of Daniel Wilson in the Darwinian debate, we are reminded of one of the better-known aphorisms of a nineteenth-century social philosopher whose stock was never to be very high in Canada. 'The ultimate result of shielding men from the effects of folly,' Herbert Spencer once wrote, 'is to fill the world with fools.'[43]

5

Science, Ethics, and 'Modern Thought'

In English Canada, as elsewhere, the decades of the 1870s and 1880s were ones in which the social implications of evolutionary theory were examined and debated. No one in the country was more instrumental in assuring that this major concern of the age was confronted rather than ignored than writer and critic William Dawson LeSueur, arguably Canada's foremost man of letters in the last quarter of the nineteenth century. In LeSueur, too, the imperatives of science and sentiment received their rightful attention as he and others sought to come to grips with shifts of social assumption occurring within English-Canadian society. In LeSueur's mature thought the spirits of August Comte and St Paul sought reconciliation in the form of an implicit union of evolutionary naturalism and philosophical idealism. The manner of this accommodation parallels, and possibly helped facilitate, the empirical yet essentially moralistic character of early social science in English Canada. This essay is derived from the editorial comments in my critical edition, A Critical Spirit: The Thought of William Dawson LeSueur (Toronto 1977), xii–xiv, 71–94.

In April 1871 an article on the French poet and critic Ste-Beuve appeared in the *Westminster Review*. It was for the most part highly appreciative of Ste-Beuve's life-long commitment to 'the critical spirit.' In 1830 Ste-Beuve had written: 'It is the nature of the critical spirit to be quick, suggestive, versatile, and comprehensive. The critical spirit is like a large, clear stream, which winds and spreads out around the works and monuments of poetry.' Quoting this passage in the original French, the author of the *Westminster Review* article added that 'No words could more happily or accurately describe what criticism was, in his hands, throughout the whole of his long career.'[1] Moreover, the writer claimed, Ste-Beuve was important not simply because he was critical but also because he was systematic about it. 'The first thing that strikes us when we look into [Ste-Beuve's] works is, that criticism with him is not a mere thing of rules and precedents, but, so to speak, a living science.' Ste-Beuve had been adverse to all rigid systems of thought, and therefore was suspicious when criticism was subordinated to any preconceived idea or pre-established authority. Nevertheless, his criticism was not without its own controlling idea: it should consist of systematic intellectual inquiry. 'One consequence of the effort which Ste-Beuve made to pursue criticism in a scientific spirit, is that of all critics he is the least dogmatic. 'Indeed, concluded the anonymous reviewer, he is 'less a judge than an enquirer who tells us of his discoveries, and invites us to verify them for ourselves.'[2]

The author of that essay had also been an enquirer more than a judge. Exactly a year earlier he had appeared before the Literary and Scientific Society of Ottawa to deliver a shorter version of the *Westminster Review* piece. Then entitled 'The Greatest Critic of the Age,' this critical appreciation of the French poet-critic (who had died only a few months earlier) was by a young Canadian civil servant named William Dawson LeSueur.[3] By the year 1871, LeSueur, born in 1840, had worked for the Post Office Department of the Canadian civil service for fifteen years. He had by then completed his formal education, which had taken him from the Montreal High School to the Ontario Law School and the University of Toronto. There he graduated as Silver Medallist in classics in 1863. In his career as a civil servant he remained with the Post Office until his retirement in 1902 (from 1888 to 1902 he was chief of the Post Office money order system). After his retirement he became the secretary of the Dominion Board of Civil Service Examiners.[4]

W.D. LeSueur's connection with the Literary and Scientific Society of Ottawa was also a long one. Almost every year from 1871 until the turn of the twentieth century, LeSueur held an executive position with the group, either as librarian, vice-president, or (most frequently) president.[5] This long association with an organization dedicated to the joint study of literature and science indicates that while LeSueur's occupation was that of a civil servant, his preoccupations far transcended the normal concerns of the administrator. Much of his biography must therefore be seen as an inner one, for his significant life was primarily that of the mind.

Ste-Beuve had been twenty-five years of age when he put forward his conception of the nature of the critical spirit; LeSueur was thirty-one when he revealed to his Ottawa audience an acceptance of the necessity for – and dictates of – such a spirit. A long and distinguished career in Canadian letters had begun. For the next forty years and more, LeSueur put before Canadian and international audiences alike a constructive criticism of various aspects of the life and thought of his day. This career was to see him engaged constantly in debate with various orthodoxies which in his view hampered the activity of the critical intellect. Whether attacking an orthodoxy that was religious or scientific, political or historical, LeSueur insisted throughout his life that the essence of civilization lay in an individual's ability to exercise, in a responsible fashion, a critical inquiry that asked nothing more than honesty and sincerity and sought nothing less than truth. His was a moral as well as an intellectual vision. The thought of William Dawson LeSueur, as set forth in scores of essays published over the last quarter of the nineteenth century, provides abundant evidence of a mind that knew few intellectual boundaries. The range of its interests and the sources of its concern were those of its age. LeSueur deserves, then, the attention of anyone interested in the intellectual and cultural history of Canada. The modern student will not only rediscover the most diverse and pre-eminent Canadian intellect of the age of Macdonald and Laurier, but also enter into the transatlantic nature of the controversies in which intellectuals of LeSueur's generation engaged. Of first importance among such disputes was that over the social and ethical implications of what LeSueur's generation chose to call 'modern thought.' We must now turn to the general context in which this most earnest of Victorian controversies raged.

Everybody, wrote Sara Jeannette Duncan in 1887, talks about 'the age.' Moreover, they do so almost as if 'the age' has an existence independent of the actual lives of men. This, she said, indicates an attitude as curious and interesting as anything men in fact said of their age: 'Forgetting, apparently, that we are part and parcel of it, and individually responsible for its having done those things which it ought not to do, and left undone those things which it ought to have done, we elect ourselves a grand jury to indict and try the age.'[6] Miss Duncan was writing for a Canadian periodical, *The Week*, her audience a Canadian one; and while her accusation was by no means applicable only to her own readers, by the time she put her comments to paper she could have provided numerous examples of Canadians' judgments about the age in which they lived.

This was the case partly because by the late 1880s Canadians had been able to publish their views continuously in one national forum or another for almost two decades.[7] It was equally the case, however, because the 'age' in which Canadian periodical literature came into its own was also that of Charles Darwin, Herbert Spencer, and T.H. Huxley. The age that was observed and characterized in the 1870s and 1880s was thus one in which the various claims of science and religion were set forward and debated by the literate middle classes, including those in Canada. 'Whatever sins of omission or commission may be fairly laid to the charge of our age and generation, indifference to the momentous problems of human life and destiny is not one of them,' wrote W.J. Rattray in 1878. 'Men are far too seriously-minded in their search after truth ... to treat the solemn questions which persistently obtrude themselves for solution on every age, with levity, scorn or a flippant superficiality.'[8] The opening sentences of many articles published in Canadian literary periodicals during these decades clearly illustrate the extent to which Rattray's claim was true. 'If any one thing is more characteristic of this age than another,' Kingston's Agnes Maule Machar wrote, 'it is the restless mental activity which questions all things formerly received; a general "shaking" and revising of opinions, which, however much temporary pain and disorganization it may produce, must at least end in the result "that the things which cannot be shaken should remain." '[9]

Agnes Machar was one of the most articulate and intelligent Canadian lay defenders of Christian orthodoxy during one of the most difficult periods in the history of the Christian religion. Well-read and open-minded, yet deeply committed to her Presbyterian heritage, she never doubted the fundamental truths of her religion. Yet not everyone in Canada at the time was able to enjoy such certitude. Goldwin Smith opened one article in the *Canadian Monthly* with the words: 'The intellectual world is at present the scene of a great revolution, one of the most dangerous features of which is that the clergy, an order of men specially set apart as Ministers of Truth, are rendered incapable of performing the intellectual part of their functions properly by the pressure of creeds.' The consequences of this 'intellectual revolution' for Smith were both profound and painful, for while the claims of modern science convinced him of the weakness of many traditional articles of the Christian faith, they provided no adequate substitute for the certainty that was lost. 'Doubt,' he wrote, 'is no longer locked in the bosom or only whispered in the ear.'[10]

The spectre of doubt was abroad. 'The visible encroaches on the invisible,' said the American Anglican divine James DeKoven in 1878: 'Between us and God appear to come laws and forces, and powers, the duration and extent of which we can grasp and measure ... What, then, if these laws begin to take ... the place of God?'[11] By the 1870s and 1880s the progress of science seemed to be making its mark everywhere, especially when science was extended into the area of technology. Few attacks were made upon it on that account by English-speaking North Americans. It was the extension of science into the realm of cosmogony, ethics, and man's spiritual life which turned many who accepted the desirability of the material progress brought about by science into its strongest accusers, and rendered others unable to believe in either a science seemingly validated by 'progress' or a religion that stood only on faith. The claim by one Canadian university student of the 1870s that 'There can be little doubt that of late years the argument for the existence of a God from the proofs of design in Nature, has not met with so general an acceptance as formerly' was understandable in a decade when traditional Christian teleology was in the process of dissolution. This particular student's conclusions illustrate clearly the dilemma in which many of his fellow students probably found themselves. First, he accepted the validity of the findings of modern science: it 'steps in and dispels such fancies' as the evidences in nature of 'a great and invisible Design and Lawgiver.' Indeed, science proclaims physical nature to be solely under the dominion of natural laws. Yet the consequences of that acceptance were immense, for the student found that the tendency of modern science was 'to remove God more and more into the background. 'Even worse,' some of its professors in their wisdom even think that they can dispense with him altogether.' While the student thus accepted the reality of a world governed by physical laws, and while he noted that 'Everywhere around us, if we will but open our eyes, are the signs of a great and terrible struggle for existence,' such 'explanations' nevertheless did not further his own understanding. The Darwinian world provided abundant evidence of the 'agency of evil,' he said, but no *reason* for it. In the end the student was left to fall back upon the rhetoric rather than the substance of an earlier natural theology. Science had invalidated the premises of the argument from design, but the student had been given nothing to take its place. For this student the traditional Christian teleology had been shattered by the findings of modern science, yet the traditional Christian conception of rationality, the correspondence of human reason with the perception of design and purpose in nature, remained very much with him. He could not trust the evidence of a reason guided solely by intellect: 'Starting indeed with the knowledge of its great Architect, we can trace his handiwork in pillar and cornice, ceiling and floor: but with our own unguided reason we could never regard it as in all its parts a fitting monument of Omnipotence and Wisdom divine.' Nor could he even trust the empirical evidence of his own observations of nature, for 'Nature furnishes us with no solution of the enigmas of life: Revelation [alone] reveals the essential truths of existence to every humble enquirer.'[12]

The problem of reconciling Christianity, as a revealed religion, with the findings of modern science was one which preyed upon the minds of many young men and women at Anglo-Canadian universities during the 1870s and 1880s. John Fiske and others, as Carl Berger has claimed, may have affected a reconciliation of evolution and religion during the 1870s, but their efforts perhaps best met their own psychological needs.[13] One sees little evidence of solace derived from such sources in, for example, the pages of Victoria College's newspaper *Acta Victoriana*, Queen's University's *Queen's Journal*, or Dalhousie University's *Dalhousie Gazette* in those years. To be sure, there is a note of optimism in students' opinions that the problems of reconciliation between revelation and science will ultimately be worked out once 'the book of nature' is 'rightly understood' and a '*true* science' developed. But it is a superficial optimism at best. The 'day was fast approaching,' concluded one such student, 'when all mysteries shall be unfolded before our rejoicing intellects.'[14] Another waited for the day when 'the rays shot into the darkness by intellect' would reveal that perhaps the Darwinian theory of descent and the traditional Christian conception of design were consistent with one another.[15] In the meantime, however, their student essays, always utterly serious in tone, bespoke far more of the generally optimistic enthusiasm of youth than of any true reconciliation within their own minds of the twin systems of scientific and religious belief. 'We have but launched our bark on the Ocean of Life,' said one student in a paper with a furrowed-brow title, 'The Age and Its Tendencies,' 'and though we see a current in one direction, and a countercurrent in another, we have yet scarcely found out in what direction the whole mass is drifting; yet we know the course is ever onward.'[16]

While Anglo-Canadian university students wrote articles such as these for their college newspapers, men and women of their parents' generation put into print their own views on the question of science. In a host of articles in the *Canadian Methodist Magazine*, as Berger has pointed out, Canadian clergymen felt compelled to draw upon whatever sources they could in order to plead for the necessary oneness of the author of revelation and the author of nature. Evolution itself, they argued, was part of the on-going design of God.[17] Yet, like those of their sons and daughters, theirs was at best a defensive argument. It could offer no certitude, only the possibility of a new direction in which to follow 'truth' – whatever that now was. A poem entitled 'One Faith in Many Forms,' reprinted in *Rose-Belford's Canadian Monthly* from the London *Spectator* in 1881, expressed the dilemma well:

> Him, –
> What is His Name? What name will all express
>   The mighty whole, of whom we are but part –
> So that all differing tongues may join a worship
>   Echoing in every heart?
> Then answers one – 'God is an endless sequence,
>   Incapable of either break or flaw,
> Which we discern but dimly and in fragments!
>   God is unchanging ... Law.'
> 'Nay,' said another, 'Law is but His method;
>   Look back, behind the sequence to his source!
> Behind all phases and all changes seek Him!
>   God is the primal Force!'

The poet denied in subsequent stanzas that God was either 'unchanging Law' or 'primal Force.' Nor was He solely manifested through a love for an equally vague humanity. God incorporates all – 'Love, beauty, wisdom and force': 'God includes them, as some great cathedral / Includes each separate shrine.'[18] The effect on the poem's readers was probably to further the desire for such an all-embracing God; yet the basic problem remained unresolved – for the shrines remained separate.

It was from separate shrines, each devoted to fundamentally the same end, that W.D. LeSueur and his Canadian critics engaged in polite, yet utterly serious, argumentative battle from the mid-1870s through the 1880s. The opposing battlements were those of modern scientific thought and Christian orthodoxy; the battlegrounds the newspapers, periodical press, and pamphlets. At stake was the nature of the ethical systems by which men govern their lives. As an editorial writer for the Toronto *Mail* wrote, when responding critically to LeSueur's article, 'The Future of Morality': 'one of the questions which our age is debating somewhat anxiously is the connection between the ethics of a nation and its faith.'[19]

Basically, the various charges made by critics of the 'Science' of the day fell into a few general areas. First, they claimed that – extended in the realm of ethics – science led to materialism, agnosticism, and scepticism. Second, as such, it was devoid of any real spiritual substance; hence it could put forward no adequate guide for human conduct. Third, it was guilty of the very sin with which it charged Christianity: dogmatism. These were the charges which LeSueur sought to dispel in his various writings on science and 'modern thought' during the 1870s and 1880s. He did so in a number of articles published over a twenty-year period; yet the essentials of his defence of 'modern thought' can be gleaned in a half dozen pieces.

The articles 'Science and Materialism' (1877) and 'The Scientific Spirit' (1879) extended LeSueur's fundamental commitment to critical inquiry into the scientific endeavour. These articles also attempted to disabuse science of the charge that it was guilty of a negative scepticism and a crass materialism. In 'Morality and Religion' and 'A Vindication of Scientific Ethics,' both published in 1880, he sought to elaborate further his conviction that the scientific spirit *could* exert an ethical influence. He did so through an explication and defence of Herbert Spencer's book, *The Data of Ethics*, published a year earlier and at the time under fierce attack.[20] It was as reasonable to believe that systems of morals could be developed from the study of the history of human conduct in the natural world, Spencer had claimed, as it was to assume that the regulation of conduct could only come about through supernatural agencies.[21] Finally, in 'Materialism and Positivism' (1882) and 'A Defence of Modern Thought' (1884), he attempted to divorce positivist social theory from the charge that it was materialistic and denied that 'modern thought' in general, which sought to rebuild society around scientific principles, was agnostic in its spirit or its tendencies.

That science fostered a materialistic and sceptical outlook on life was the most frequent charge made against it in the 1870s and 1880s. Indeed, some critics claimed that by its very nature it was materialistic and sceptical.[22] Defenders of Christianity could give substance to the truth of these propositions by pointing out the influence of both Epicureanism and sensationalism upon scientists; they could note the way in which the Scottish philosopher, Alexander Bain, took the empiricist tradition into the realm of psychology by tracing both thoughts and 'moral apprehensions' to the bodily system; they could illustrate the agnostic 'materialism' in Herbert Spencer's social evolutionism by quoting him without due regard to the corpus of his thought; similarly, they could support their arguments by drawing evidence from T.H. Huxley's article on protoplasm as the physical basis of life. They could also allow such 'materialists' to ridicule themselves by quoting, equally without adequate regard for context, such snippets as 'The brain secretes thought as the liver secretes bile'; 'The soul is the product of a peculiar combination of matter'; or 'Mental activity is a function of the cerebral substance.'[23]

Charges that modern science was materialistic reached their peak, however, after the delivery and publication of John Tyndall's 'Belfast Address,' given to the British Association for the Advancement of Science in 1874. Tyndall, professor of natural philosophy in the Royal Institution, enjoyed a widespread reputation in the 1860s and 1870s, due mainly to the many lectures he gave for laymen. The opinions expressed in his 1874 Presidential Address to the BAAS were all the more horrifying because they came from one of the most eminent and respected British scientific authorities.

Tyndall infuriated his listeners, and later his readers, because he sought to unite the findings of the science of his day – in biology, physics, chemistry, and psychology – with the philosophical atomism of the ancients, especially Democritus. Tyndall's own religious convictions led him to advocate a vague sort of pantheism and to put forward his belief that religious feelings could not aid man in arriving at an objective understanding of his place in nature. Only science could do this. Science, he concluded, had by 1874 reached an 'impregnable position' which he claimed could be described in a few words: 'We claim, and we shall wrest, from theology the entire domain of cosmological theory. All schemes and systems which thus infringe upon the domain of science must *in so far as they do this*, submit to its control, and relinquish all thought of controlling it.'[24] Here, it seemed, was excellent evidence of the materialistic nature of an agnostic, dogmatic, and arrogant science.

Within hours of the delivery of the Belfast address, its author was under attack in England. The next day, a London merchant suggested to the home secretary that Tyndall be brought to trial under a British statute which dealt with the expression of blasphemous opinions. *Punch* satirized him in poems and cartoons. So did the Scottish physicist James Clerk Maxwell in the following light verse: 'From nothing comes nothing they told us, / naught happens by chance but by fate; / There is nothing but atoms and void, all else / is mere whims out of date.'[25] The debate between Tyndall, his defenders, and his opponents continued into the late 1870s. The very phrase 'Belfast Address' became synonymous with words, such as 'materialism,' which were seen to pose dire threats against orthodox religious belief.

This was no less the case in the new Canadian nation than it was in the more serene atmosphere of the English parsonage. In 1876 the professor of mathematics and natural philosophy at McGill University, Alexander Johnson (who was also vice-dean of the Faculty of Arts), was called upon to convince the university's students in engineering and theoretical physics that in entering their new professions they were not enlisting in the ranks of the materialists. 'My subject is one that has been agitating the minds of many during nearly two years past,' he said:

[A] wave of disturbance originating in the address of the President of the British Association for the advancement of Science in 1874 has rolled over the mother country, and crossing the Atlantic, diffused itself here far and wide. The disturbance then excited, the agitation of men's minds, and the discussions that followed, are still in full vigour, not only in Great Britain, but here in Canada ...

The discussions are carried on or noticed, not only in books, reviews and pamphlets, but in newspapers and in the social circle. When the newspapers teem with quotations from Tyndall, Huxley, Darwin and Herbert Spencer (no later than this morning I saw one from the last mentioned), and the mind of the nation in general is agitated, it is not to be supposed that the student's mind will escape that apprehension which lays hold of many when they are told that Science and Religion are irreconcileably at variance. When after this, the student hears, as he must do, in his lectures, of 'molecules,' 'atoms,' 'vibrations,' and other terms which are bandied about so freely in these discussions, he may have some fears that he is entering on dangerous ground, and a feeling of uneasiness may seize hold of him, though he can see no precise cause of it.[26]

Professor Johnson judged that by the questions asked of him in the classroom during the academic year that had just concluded such an uneasiness was indeed present in the minds of his students. The remainder of his address was therefore an attempt to persuade them that, in his own words, 'there are no good grounds for the impression that what are called the Atheistic or Materialistic conclusions, so loudly proclaimed by certain scientific men and among them, by Dr. Tyndall, have any support in Physical Science.'[27]

The spectre of Tyndall and his 'Belfast Address' was thus part of the intellectual context within which the debate over science and religion was conducted in Canada. Both Graeme Mercer Adam, the energetic editor of the *Canadian Monthly*, and Goldwin Smith, mentor of the Canadian periodical press for the last quarter of the nineteenth century, were well-read in much of the 'heterodox' thought of the day; and not a little of it found its way into the pages of their various journalistic enterprises. John Tyndall's 'Reply to Critics of the Belfast Address' appeared in the *Canadian Monthly* in February 1875. A month later appeared a long exposition and review of George J. Romanes's book, *Christian Prayer and General Laws*.[28] From then until the last issue of the *Canadian Monthly* was published in 1878, its pages were filled with articles which attacked or defended the arguments set forward by Tyndall and Romanes. They were of three basic sorts: first, those the subject of which was 'materialism' proper; second, those which debated the extent to which the physical laws which governed the natural world also exercised a control over the world of the spirit; third, those which debated the possibility of an evolutionary system of morality. The first of these centred on Tyndall, whose 'heresies' were kept in the reader's mind by the republication of articles such as his address, 'Materialism and Its Opponents.' LeSueur's essay, 'Science and Materialism' (1877), was written in the midst of this debate.[29] The second area of controversy, that over the domain of physical laws, took Romanes's book as its launching point. 'The Prayer question,' as Romanes himself called it when opening an article for the *Canadian Monthly*, was among the most fiercely argued of the religious debates in the 1870s in Canada.[30] Without mentioning this controversy specifically, LeSueur's 1880 article, 'Morality and Religion,' was a summation of his general attitude towards Christianity as set forward in the 'Prayer question.'

This article, written shortly after the publication of *The Data of Ethics*, also marked his entrance into the third area of debate, for this was in large measure an enlargement of that over natural laws. The prayer question had begun with the query: 'Given the fact that we live in a world which science shows is governed by natural laws, to what extent can we petition God to have our prayers answered?' (To what extent, that is, can we expect God to 'violate' those natural laws?) The debate over evolutionary ethics began essentially with the question: 'Given the fact that we live in a world which science shows to be governed by natural laws, to what extent can those laws serve as the basis for our systems of belief and conduct?' The debate thus included discussions of the validity of evolutionary theory, the evidences for the truth of the Christian doctrine of the immortality of the soul (as well as the question of the very existence of such an entity), and the possibility of establishing an evolutionary or natural system of morality. This last debate began with considerations of the scientific work of Darwin and the speculations of Goldwin Smith, continued with attacks upon and defences of *The Data of Ethics*, and came to a conclusion (as an on-going debate, not as a question) with the Canadian reactions to Goldwin Smith's pessimistic essay, 'The Prospect of a Moral Interregnum.'[31]

It is not necessary to trace here the arguments set forward by the major participants in these controversies. Our purpose may be served by noting that W.D. LeSueur found himself in the midst of each. It is sufficient to say that, with few exceptions,[32] LeSueur's contributions to the debates were the only ones which derived from the framework of scientific assumptions; and with the exception of certain articles by John Watson, the British Hegelian philosopher at Queen's University, Kingston,[33] LeSueur's were the only pieces which sought to move beyond special pleading to a larger synthesis that could reconcile the two warring camps by setting forward a coherent philosophy of life. It cannot be said that his viewpoint was without significant points of weakness, or even that he managed at all times to measure up to the standards of criticism he set for himself.[34] Yet the articles indicate clearly that LeSueur's writings in defence of science were above all an extension of his plea for a critical spirit in all areas of inquiry. The scientific spirit was, in essence, simply the critical spirit in a special form, and whether LeSueur addressed himself to such American eminences as the cosmic evolutionist John Fiske, the evangelical preacher Lyman Abbott, and the ex-president of Yale University, Noah Porter, or to their Canadian counterparts such as the Presbyterian divine G.M. Grant, or the Anglican archbishop of Ontario, John Travers Lewis, this spirit underlay all his arguments.[35]

It was entirely appropriate that W.D. LeSueur's essays on science, ethics, and modern thought began to appear at about the same time as his essays on the critical spirit, for his conception of the nature of science was derived from the same premises as his theory of criticism. In essence, he claimed, the purpose of science is not to determine inviolable truths. It is a simple matter of inquiry. From the time of Bacon, Science had 'kept to the true path,' because it had been Bacon who first conceived of science as 'a progressive interrogation of nature.' Its prime function is 'to interpret to man the world in which he lives.' Since at the level of the mind it is the intellect which renders the randomness of experience into an intelligible order, thus making such an interpretation possible, the intellect itself – in a very real sense – *is* science. 'Science,' LeSueur wrote, 'is the minister of man's thinking faculty'; it 'is simply the intellect of man, exercising itself in a certain direction.' Once again LeSueur's insistence that 'truth' is not an objective body of data is to be noted. Just as he conceived the critical spirit to be a continual and open process of affirmation and rejection by which judgments are made, so he saw the scientific spirit as simply the critical process extended into the observation of the natural world. 'Science,' he wrote in 1889, 'is nothing else than knowledge of the facts and laws of the universe.' But these 'facts and laws' do not constitute an absolute truth any more than do religious creeds. Science does not advance the interests of an absolute truth. Those engaged in modern science, LeSueur concluded, have a far more humble task: they 'are simply gathering facts and deducing laws, subject to rectification when further facts shall have been gathered.'[36]

This commitment to a scientific spirit conceived largely as the process of continual critical inquiry was most evident in LeSueur's response to the charge that the science of his day was as dogmatic as the institutional Christianity which was then under attack. No article published in Canada set this charge forward more clearly, or with more force, than 'The Marvels of Scientific Logic,' by 'G,' of Toronto. The triumphs of physical science since the time of Bacon, said 'G,' were both magnificent and indisputable. Science had liberated itself from the 'fetters' of theological 'slavery' and the 'tyranny of mind' that such a restriction imposed. Yet it had liberated men from one form of mental slavery only to subject them to another, 'a dogmatism which makes man the foolish sport of undesigning chance.'[37] With its emphasis on the reality of the 'Seen' as opposed to the 'Unseen' and its commitment to sensory experience as the datum of consciousness and belief, it declares triumphantly that Haeckel and Huxley have a better *a priori* claim on 'truth' than St Paul. It insists on positive 'proof' for the verification of all laws, yet though it cannot disprove the existence of an intelligent Creator of the universe or the existence of a universal moral order derived from laws of the world of the Spirit, it nevertheless rejects these as patently false mainly on the basis of their inconsistency with scientific postulates. 'If she cannot fully explain the mystery that lies all around her,' concluded 'G,' 'let her confess that for her at least the *super*natural exists, and let her learn humility.'[38]

LeSueur was scarcely one to take the problems of dogmatism lightly. 'The great intellectual issue of the present day,' he wrote in 1886, 'however some may try to disguise it, is that between dogma on the one hand the free spirit of scientific enquiry on the other.'[39] He made no attempt to conceal the fact, as his article 'Morality and Religion' shows, that to his mind specific religious 'systems' – theologies – constituted 'dogmatism' as he elsewhere defined it: 'a traditional opinion held and defended on account of its assumed practical value, rather than on account of its truth.'[40] The scientific spirit stood in direct opposition to dogmatism; yet LeSueur admitted that science was not always undogmatic. Its very success in enlarging men's understanding of their world had led it to this dangerous trap. 'Dogmatism,' he warned when discussing the scientific spirit, 'is nothing but the temper of command unreasonably exercised. Science in the present day wields command, and it only too easily falls into the snare of dogmatism.' The remedy for this situation was for scientists constantly to remind themselves that all scientific theories are essentially provisional, and any theory framed by them is 'a working hypothesis and no more.' Hence the scientific spirit, like the critical spirit in general, must also be characterized by humility. Again like the critical spirit it must also have as its ultimate end the pursuit of culture, the quest for individual, social, and moral perfection. If the scientist is to assume the momentous task of aiding man 'to interpret [to other men] ... the world in which he lives,' he has assumed a burden which he must not take lightly: '[I]t is, therefore, of vast importance that the leaders in scientific investigation should set clearly before the world where the chief interest and glory of science lies, that they should visibly make it the instructor of humanity to all noble ends, that they should put it forward as the great liberaliser of thought, the enemy of superstition and confusion, the beautifier of life, and that in which man's highest faculties can find unfailing exercise and satisfaction.'

This assertion of the cultural aims of science would have been severely undermined, however, if LeSueur had been unable to counter the charge that science was materialistic. LeSueur's conception of social progress was that of an evolutionary and positivistic naturalist. How, then, could he separate himself and his philosophical outlook from this charge? One writer in *Rose-Belford's Canadian Monthly* had asked, rhetorically, what 'materialism' was and then defined it: 'It is the supposition that all the changes of the universe, all the phenomena of the natural and of what *we* may call the spiritual world, are due to the combination of primordial atoms whose "essential properties are extension and solidarity." '[41] Was this not a more or less accurate description of LeSueur's philosophy, and was his talk of science as the 'beautifier of life' and the minister of 'man's highest faculties' not simply a gratuitous addendum to a materialistic view of life?

The answer to this question lies not in LeSueur's social philosophy but in his psychology. In his thinking about the mind he accepted the 'scheme of scientific ideas' which, as Alfred North Whitehead claimed, has dominated thought since the seventeenth century. This thought, Whitehead stated, 'involves a fundamental duality, with *material* on one hand, and on the other hand *mind*.'[42] This was one of the costs of the scientific revolution of that century, for it resulted, as one historian of psychology has observed, in 'the isolation of mind from nature and the study of purposive behaviour from the advance of the scientific method. The fragmentation of the world into primary and secondary qualities, outer and inner, body and mind, and the exclusion of final causes from science have plagued the study of mind and behavior at least since Descartes.'[43] LeSueur was a dualist within this tradition, an observer whose belief in the inviolable distinctions between 'mind' and 'matter' was entrenched by the authority of science. Yet his dualism, perhaps reinforced by his original training in the tenets of 'Common Sense,' was articulated at a time when scientists such as Karl Vogt and his followers, working in the area of physiology, were uncovering the mysteries of the central nervous system and making the distinction between 'mind' and 'brain' increasingly murky.[44] The fragmentation of the old mind-body dichotomy introduced immense problems for many individuals, especially those who dealt professionally with the mentally ill. In Canada, for example, both Dr Daniel Clark, in charge of the Toronto Asylum for the Insane, and Dr R.M. Bucke, superintendant of the Provincial Asylum in London, Ontario, went through much intellectual agony to reconcile the findings of the new developments in physiology with their own moral and emotional constitutions.[45]

The extent to which LeSueur knew of the work of such psychologists as Franz Joseph Gall, Johannes Muller, and Sir David Ferrier is not known. What is certain is that he did not relinquish his belief in the dualism of mind and body. For him, as for R.M. Bucke, the mind and the body were essentially distinct: the processes of thought and the processes of biology operated at different yet parallel planes. LeSueur therefore rejected flatly the findings of 'the typical physiologist' of his day, 'whose passion was to show that the various modes of social action were nothing more or higher than the processes of secretion, digestion, nutrition, &c., with which his peculiar studies had rendered him familiar.' Even more reprehensible to LeSueur than this materialistic physiologist, who extended the principles of biology into the study of social action, was the materialist who 'loves to dwell on the physical basis of mind, and to ignore the utter impossibility of expressing any of the phenomena of mind in terms of matter.' Here LeSueur agreed with Tyndall: matter cannot be transformed into thought. To accept such an unthinkable notion would undermine the basis of moral judgment and render statements of value – words like 'wise or foolish, just or unjust, brave or cowardly' – meaningless. Furthermore, it would degrade the idea of thought itself. The 'true scientist,' whose aim, like the philosopher, is the pursuit of culture, will not accept such a false view of the scientific spirit: 'no one knows better than a true man of science,' LeSueur wrote, 'that nerve vibrations and molecular movements in the brain are no more the equivalent of thought than the pen with which Tennyson wrote, was the equivalent of 'In Memoriam.' ''

Here is a perfect example of the way certain scientific findings can be drawn upon and others ignored to support an individual's moral and intellectual point of view. LeSueur clearly recognized that an acceptance of the findings of certain of the physiologists and psychologists of his day would have called severely into question the whole superstructure upon which Christian metaphysics rested; yet such an acceptance would thereby have also challenged the reality of a spiritual world independent of both matter and Christianity. He was unwilling to give that world up.

An examination of LeSueur's essay 'Materialist and Positivism' shows a fundamental belief in two inviolable orders of phenomena, one of mind or spirit and another of matter. Comtean positivism appealed to LeSueur not only because it was progressivist, organic, and universalistic, but also because it did not essentially challenge the existence of the spiritual world. It did not doubt the existence of a universal moral order. It was a 'positive philosophy' because it did not seek to invoke spiritual authorities; it was content to deal with facts – that is, with 'whatever produces a complete and definite impression upon the mind.' Yet it was *not* materialistic, for it did not necessarily limit 'facts,' positive knowledge, to the world of material substance. 'Now, the difference between the materialist and the positivist lies in just this,' he wrote, 'that the former is embarrassed at the decided effects which he sees produced by impalpable things, while the latter escapes such embarrassment entirely, simply by not having set up any arbitrary standard of what constitutes reality. The materialist does not want to recognize anything as real that does not more or less resemble his piece of granite, that does not affect the tactual sense; while the positivist is content to recognize all things as real that reveal their existence to the mind by affecting it in a definite manner.' Here LeSueur's dualism came in very handy. Just as there is a faculty of mind which operates at a separate plane from the bodily functions, so there is also a distinct emotional and moral nature which functions in relationship to a 'reality' different from that involved in man's physical relationship with nature. The hold upon the Victorian mind of the school of Reid and Stewart was a tenacious one indeed.

It is important to recall the extent to which such a view was as fundamental an intellectual assumption in LeSueur's day as the 'reality' of the 'stimulus-response' construct is to ours. In 1879 LeSueur reviewed R.M. Bucke's book *Man's Moral Nature* (1879) and confessed that he was 'struck' by it. By 1879 Bucke had begun to acquire a reputation on the North American continent as one of the most innovative medics engaged in psychological research. One passage in particular from the book of this authority on human psychology engaged LeSueur's interest: 'The activity and efficiency of the intellectual nature is largely dependent upon the degree of development of the moral nature, which last is undoubtedly the driving-power of our mental mechanism, as the great sympathetic is the driving-power of our bodily organization. What I mean is, and I think everyone will agree with me here, that, with the same intellectual power, the outcome of that power will be vastly greater with a high moral nature behind it than it will be with a low moral nature behind it. In other words, that, with a given brain, a man who has strong and high desires will arrive at more and truer results of reflection than if, with the same brain, his desires are comparatively mean and low.'[46] Bucke, like LeSueur, assumed that the moral nature had a distinct and autonomous existence within the human constitution. Like LeSueur (and like Comte), he also believed that this moral nature existed in different men at different levels.

LeSueur was convinced that Bucke was right: the lessons of everyday experience told him so. Some men, even though intelligent, fail to make a mark on society because they have a poorly developed moral nature. They have no distinct 'moral aims,' do not 'aspire to moral influence,' are not 'compelled to any enterprises of moral conquest,' and 'do not appeal to the emotional side of any one's nature.'[47] At the same time, men of 'culture and humanity' do not lead such narrow lives. 'Theirs is an intellectual power energized and given direction by a highly developed moral nature. They see what others fail to see: *They see into themselves*, and seeing into themselves, they see into others. They are at home, so to speak, in the region of the soul.' The ultimate lesson of Bucke's book was thus also the lesson of Arnold's *Culture and Anarchy*: Bucke showed 'in a very striking manner how natural is the connection between "Sweetness" and "light."'[48]

The operation of these assumptions within LeSueur's mind made Herbert Spencer a likely authority upon whom to draw for ideas. In the 1870s and 1880s Spencer's reputation as the greatest man of his age reached its peak in the Anglo-American community. His 'synthetic philosophy' was both comprehensive and scientific and made the British social philosopher, in the words of Richard Hofstadter, 'the metaphysician of the homemade intellectual, and the prophet of the crackerbarrel agnostic.'[49] His was a philosophy that – because of its comprehensiveness – was all things to all men, and scarcely an intellectual in the transatlantic community remained unaware of 'Spencerism.'[50]

The dominant view of Spencer's social philosophy that emerges from Richard Hofstadter's book *Social Darwinism in American Thought* (1944) is of a grand 'scientific' justification for an economic enterprise unimpeded by government regulation or control, a philosophy which, in the hands of Spencerian disciples such as the American social theorist William Graham Sumner, could give sanction to such claims as that which said: 'The millionaires are a product of natural selection, acting on the whole body of men to pick out those who can meet the requirement of certain work to be done.'[51] W.D. LeSueur drew no such conclusions from his own reading of either Spencer or Darwin. He objected strenuously in 1885 to John Fiske's claim that 'in the desperate struggle for existence no peculiarity has been too insignificant for natural selection to seize and enhance,' for such a view seemed to suggest that natural selection was 'some vigilant intelligence watching for opportunities to advance its designs.'[52] Natural selection, he insisted, carried with it no differentiation into 'good' or 'bad.' 'Darwin has discovered no law in nature by which good qualities (as such) are produced; he has simply discovered a law by which all kinds of qualities (differentiations), good, bad, and indifferent, are produced, and by which the bad ones (bad, i.e., in relation to the environment) are knocked off, like so many projection angles, by the destruction of the individuals manifesting them ... If, therefore, we believe in natural selection, let us believe in it as it is, and be content to speak of it as it is. *Let us not make a god what is, in its essence, the very negation of intelligent action.*'[53]

LeSueur's insistence upon a radical separation of ethics from the mechanism by which evolution took place did not presume, however, a divorce of ethics from the evolutionary process itself. It was precisely because Spencer's 'synthetic philosophy' was also fundamentally an ethical one (see note 21) that he was attracted to it. Furthermore, while Spencer's comprehensive system treated all things as subject to natural laws it did not deny the possibility of a divinity and the existence of universal moral laws, or obliterate the spiritual-material dualism which was so basic to LeSueur's discussions of the 'moral nature' of man. Against the charge that a 'natural' system of morality is impossible since morality is derived from theology, LeSueur replied: 'The broad fact that everywhere we see traces, however rude, of moral feeling is precisely the foundation upon which my whole argument is built; men cannot live together unless they are partially moral; unless in other words, some general good results from their association.' He also denied emphatically that the evolutionism of Darwin and Spencer 'materialized' the human spirit and involved 'caprice in morality, tyranny in government, uncertainty in science' along with 'a denial of immortality and a disbelief in the personality of man and of God,' and did so on the grounds that Spencer in no way challenged the existence of the world of spirit or mind: 'Evolution, as taught by Herbert Spencer, does nothing to weaken the fundamental distinction between subject and object, between mind and matter. If Spencer teaches that both these aspects of existence may, or rather must, find their union and identification in the Unknowable Cause, he does no more than the Christian, who believes that God is the author both of the visible world and of the human spirit. Evolution gives material laws for human thought, only in so far as it shows the dependence of each higher plan of life on those below it.'[54] Nor, he added, did evolutionism *ipso facto* seek to subvert belief in immortality or in a personal God: 'The doctrine of evolution is simply a mode of conceiving and accounting for the succession of events on the earth. It is in no sense a metaphysical or ontological doctrine, and lays no claim to the absoluteness with which metaphysical and ontological doctrines are invested. It does not pretend to penetrate to essences or to unveil final causes. If it is regarded by some as solving all mysteries, that is simply because they do not adequately understand it. Mr. Spencer certainly has never given countenance to such an idea. It does, however, as Darwin said of his philosophy, call constant attention to the need for providing all things. It strikes at the idea of authority, always excepting the constitutional authority, as we may term it, of demonstrated truth.'[55] The doctrines of immortality and the idea of God, LeSueur concluded, were undermined only in the sense that modern science had discredited the theological system which served as the authority upon which such doctrines had been taught. Science, he added, does not doubt that such notions may be true; it simply asks that they be given 'more conclusive demonstration' by defending them 'in the open field of philosophy.'[56]

This chapter of W.D. LeSueur's inner biography was in general an optimistic one. It saw him reject theological systems of morals in favour of the edifice of positivism and, in particular, of Herbert Spencer's attempt to show 'the evolution of morality as an objective process.' History, for Spencer and for LeSueur, was primarily the study of human conduct, and morality was one aspect of that conduct – 'developed conduct.' History seemed to show that human conduct, if looked at objectively (that is, from a social point of view rather than from the perspective of one's own consciousness), was in a state of constant ascendance from lower to higher, simplicity to complexity. In the long course of human evolution a point beyond the struggle for subsistence had been reached in certain societies, a stage at which the power of ethical choice in human action had become possible. Spencer's view was that the best interest of the individual is generally with obeying the dictates of his 'higher' (later-developed) faculties through the voluntary subordination of the 'lower.' This requires self-control, but subordination of self in this way not only places man in a greater harmony with society but also with himself.

LeSueur drew upon evolutionary science in a way decidedly different from American Social Darwinists such as William Graham Sumner. He used Spencer's naturalism, his organicism, and his universalism as a means of consolidating the social bond, not as a rationalization for the existence or hegemony of an individualistic ethic. In part, this response was due to the dictates of LeSueur's own intellectual and moral premises. But if his life can be seen as one manifestation of the Anglo-Canadian moral imagination – if, that is, it represents part of a continuing tradition in Canadian social thought – then perhaps LeSueur's particular use of Spencer's ideas is a small but not insignificant commentary on the nature of the Canadian cultural experience itself. Late nineteenth-century America can perhaps generally be characterized as a country overwhelmingly dominated by Frye's myth of freedom; and Sumnerian Social Darwinism gave reign to such freedom in the sphere of economic action. The myth of freedom in Victorian Canada was compromised significantly by a stronger presence of the myth of concern. Physically in the New World but culturally of the Old, those such as LeSueur drew naturally upon the historical ties and organic evolution of Canadian society.

Herbert Spencer, as LeSueur understood him, had much to contribute to an understanding of such a culture and society. The organic analogy which was the basis of Spencer's thought could be used to criticize a *laissez-faire* society, for it stressed interrelationships and mutual dependence. While Spencer's methodological individualism allowed him to elevate the role of the individual within society ('society existed for the benefit of its members,' not the other way around), his rejection of a mechanistic model of society in favour of the idea of 'The Social Organism' (as he often called his basic metaphor) equally insisted upon the symbiotic relationship of individual and society:

The individual citizen [is] embedded in the social organism as one of its units, moulded by its influence and aiding reciprocally to remould it.

The cardinal truth, difficult to appreciate, is that while the forms and laws of each society are the consolidated products of the emotions and ideas of those who lived through the past, they are made operative by the subordination of existing emotions and ideas to them.[57]

Such ideas could have much meaning for English Canada, which drew seriously from both the liberal and conservative philosophical traditions and the culture of which was something of a fusion of the two.

While not ignoring the individualistic strand in Spencer's philosophy, LeSueur drew upon the organic aspect of his thought to show the way in which Spencer could provide a naturalistic social ethic for the modern age. 'Let me not hesitate to say,' he wrote, 'that many in this generation are willing to take their stand, and live their lives, upon such basis of truth as they can discover in nature and in human relations ... Human ties are not less tender or precious for the knowledge that we hold our treasures in earthen vessels.' Here were signs that William Dawson LeSueur, Canada's philosophical radical of the nineteenth century, was 'radical' for a fundamentally 'conservative' purpose. As in his writings on criticism, so too in his writings on the scientific spirit was the tension between the modern myths of freedom and concern and the corresponding polarity of liberty and order present. In the second chapter of his internal biography, LeSueur sought to reconcile the spirit of science with the spirit of Christianity, the concern for inquiry into all things with the concern for the preservation of human community. 'What we want,' said the exponent of the critical path, the opponent of Christian doctrine, 'is a "natural piety" that shall link us in thought and sympathy with both the past and the future of mankind.'

6

The Research Ideal and the University of Toronto

Intellectual reorientation does not occur in an institutional vacuum, and it should not be surprising to find that the internal histories of universities, for example, both reflect and help direct the nature of that reorientation. This essay explores the conflict of two generations of scientists at the University of Toronto, one informed by a traditional Christian metaphysic and reflected by Daniel Wilson, the other dedicated to a scientific research shorn of metaphysical concerns and aimed largely at social needs as defined by the secular state. Here can be seen one point at which intellectual and social history clearly intersect. The paper was originally given as 'The Research Ideal and the University of Toronto, 1870–1906,' at the Centenary meetings of the Royal Society of Canada in 1982. It was published in Transactions of the Royal Society of Canada, *4th series, Centenary Volume (1982): 253–74.*

The colleges and universities of Ontario were not founded in order to advance the state of knowledge; they came into being to promote the causes of denominational religion and to cultivate a disposition both pious and deferential in the minds of what were hoped would be the future leaders of English-Canadian society. Piety meant in fact the suspension of critical judgment and investigation in the face of the will of God as revealed in scripture. Its secular equivalent, the habit of deference, meant acceptance – equally involving the suspension of critical judgment – of existing forms of social and political authority.[1] For much of the nineteenth century the two were in fact inseparable, both having as their object the formation of an educated but 'responsible' citizenry. Both were aimed at the cultivation of 'character,' usually by means of instilling a profound sense of duty in students' minds, and at the creation of appropriate forms of social conduct. Success at the former invariably was seen to lead to success at the latter. The native intelligence of the nineteenth-century English-Canadian undergraduate was to be cultivated and sharpened, but not so much by encouraging original investigation or critical inquiry – indeed, these were regarded with real suspicion – as by inculcating intellectual and social discipline. Virtually no Canadian college president prior to the 1890s encouraged critical inquiry at the risk of undermining appropriate forms of social conduct. In 1890 Sir Daniel Wilson, president of the University of Toronto and one who in his own right had made significant contributions to ethnological knowledge (he is credited with having introduced and given meaning to the word 'prehistoric'), could state at Convocation: 'Our aim in the Faculty of Arts is high culture in its truest sense; the pursuit of knowledge for its own sake and wholly independent of mere professional requirements.'[2]

Wilson, like most of his contemporaries, chose to subordinate both 'pure' and 'practical' forms of research to the pursuit of 'culture' – indeed to 'high culture' – and this, for proponents of the research ideal in the nineteenth century, was their own equivalent to Bacon's exasperation with the unproductive and circular metaphysical speculations of sixteenth-century academicians. To such impatient minds this sort of quest after an undefined and perhaps undefinable 'culture' merely served to repeat endlessly the traditional and irresolvable search for metaphysical 'truth.' Daniel Wilson's convocation addresses as president were models of the Victorian impulsion to forge a compromise between empirical investigation and metaphysical necessity, between the imperatives of nature and culture. While his views probably reflected the assumptions and priorities of most members of the Ontario academic intelligentsia, there were others who by the 1870s viewed such statements as unprogressive obfuscation hindering the real needs of the age: those of science.

Unlike some of his contemporaries,[3] Daniel Wilson was by no means a scientist convinced that new developments in science undermined religious certainty. For this reason he consistently urged the pursuit of scientific research. 'We claim,' he concluded in his 1861 presidential address to the Canadian Institute, 'as associates of this Institute to rank as lovers of science, united for the investigation of the laws of nature, and the discovery of new truths in every department of human knowledge.'[4] With this sort of statement scarcely any Canadian scientist of the nineteenth century disagreed. But to what end was this pursuit of scientific truth to be put? Wilson revealed his own view when he described the scientific community in the same address as 'a phalanx of labourers ... sharers in that glorious advancement of knowledge by which God, who has revealed himself in his word, is making ever new revelations of himself in his works ... May we, while seeking here the pure and elevating enjoyments which spring from the discovery of nature's truths, find knowledge of the humblest works of God an incitement to the adoration and love of him, whom to know is life eternal.'[5] Here Wilson and others like him parted company with a generation of younger advocates of the research ideal. For them, any science that continued to subordinate the pursuit of knowledge to traditional religious metaphysics was simply a science manqué.

This divorce of the cause of science from that of metaphysics in fact predated the Darwinian epoch in Canada. It would be misleading to view it as a result of the intellectual revolution wrought by Darwin's *Origins* in 1859 and thereafter. In the very first issue of the *Canadian Journal*, the magazine of the Toronto scientific community, such a view was in fact set forward. The occasion was an address that had been given in England by the British scientist Lyon Playfair, called 'The National Importance of Studying Abstract Science with a View to the Healthy Progress of Industry.' After noting recent improvements in the production of such items as candles and coal gas, the anonymous author of the *Canadian Journal* report paraphrased with obvious approval the gist of Playfair's message: 'the progress of abstract science is of extreme importance to a nation depending on its manufactures. It is only the overflowing of Science, arising from the very fulness of its measure, that benefit industry. Yet in our Mammonworship we adore the golden calf, and do not see its real creator. It is abstract and not practical science that is the life and soul of industry.'[6] Here, as with the views of Wilson, we note an overt tension between 'abstract' and 'practical' science. And it is one, moreover, given expression from *within* the scientific community itself, not from the camp of those who regarded science as a suspect, heterodox form of inquiry that resulted in materialism. Such debates, whether between proponents of nature or of metaphysics, or, within the community of scientists, between advocates of 'pure' as distinguished from 'practical' science, remained relatively academic arguments from the 1850s through the 1870s. The debate over the future and the tendencies of science (as, for example, that regarding the implications of evolutionary theory) was confined to a relative few and was not a central concern to those who sought to forge a nation out of several disparate colonies. Nor was there the institutional infrastructure that could have made possible any systematic programs of either theoretical *or* practical science.

This state of affairs slowly began to change in the last two decades of the nineteenth century. Scholars have long debated the strengths and weaknesses of Sir John A. Macdonald's National Policy of 1878. It is not necessary to add to it here. The fact remains that – whatever its merits – a national economic policy did exist by the decade of the eighties. That decade saw, as a result, a significant if uneven expansion of the industrial and commercial sectors of the central Canadian economy.[7]

The result, however ambiguous, was significant enough by 1889 to allow Canadian social critics to boast that the country had industrial problems that could match those of other 'developed' countries. *The Royal Commission Report on the Relations of Labor and Capital*, published in that year, provided ample evidence for this claim.[8] The politicians of Ontario had recognized the need for harnessing the potentials of science to the requirements of the provincial economy by the early 1870s, when they began to fund a school of practical science at the provincial university.[9] But the venture was relatively unsuccessful until the economic advances of the eighties gave the matter a degree of urgency that was picked up quickly by both politicians and professors. Then, as now, numerous eyes were cast on the possibilities of the main chance.

In a province witnessing the uneven beginnings of an industrial transformation of major proportions it was understandable that the first major commitments of public funds to scientific research should have been ones made in the direction of engineering, with direct potential for application to industrial purposes and needs. Scientific men of affairs, such as T.C. Keefer and Sandford Fleming, had been urging private investors and governments to support what a later age would call 'strategic research' for years, often with indifferent success.[10] But by the eighties several of the provinces' most distinguished academicians were pursuing the same cause. As president of the provincial university, Daniel Wilson spoke often on public occasions, and as often as not his lectures touched upon the question of science and material progress. But Wilson was as much a poet as he was a scientist,[11] and as a result he would urge support for university research in biology, electricity, optics, acoustics, and other scientific areas yet balance his demands with public assurances that increased scientific inquiry would not distort the fundamental aims of a university education. '[W]hile we view with unalloyed satisfaction the due prominence given to physical sciences,' he stated in 1884, 'there is no disposition to relegate to an inferior place the study of the classics, or of comparative philology and all the invaluable training which philosophy and literature supply.'[12]

Such a statement was on the surface harmless enough, for it sought to encourage scientific research while assuaging the fears of humanistic scholars. Yet it was also of significant import within the University of Toronto. By the early 1870s Toronto had become an academic community highly politicized along several lines which bore upon the place of original research. The University Reform Act of 1873, passed under the direction of provincial attorney general Adam Crooks, had required the election to Senate of fifteen graduates of the university, these to be voted upon by the graduates themselves.[13] The fact that this initiative took place during what Frank Underhill later called 'the first, fine careless rapture' of

Confederation,[14] and in the heyday of the Toronto-based 'Canada First' move-ment,[15] simply exacerbated a tension that already existed between the proponents of more Canadian representation on the university faculty and a number of the current professors who were British in both training and outlook. Among the 'old guard,' for example, had been William Hincks, an anti-Darwinian professor of natural history, appointed to the faculty in the 1850s when his brother, Francis, was premier of Canada West. An unsuccessful candidate for the position had been the young T.H. Huxley.[16] By the 1880s the leader of this generational faction was Daniel Wilson, convinced of the superiority of British forms of higher education and sceptical of the readiness of Canadians to enter university life at the professo-rial level. Typical of Wilson's estimation of the quality of Canadian scholarship was his stance regarding the possibility of creating a Royal Society of Canada pat-terned along British lines. 'The Marquis of Lorne wants me to meet him at Ottawa ...' he wrote in his 'Journal' in October 1881, 'to consult on important matters. The Marquis, with the very best intentions, wants to call into being an academy of Sci-ence and Letters for Canada. The material out of which such an untimely birth must be concocted, or generated rather, is of the most incongruous sort.'[17]

Increasingly at odds with such men and such views was a generation of University of Toronto graduates led by Edward Blake, Thomas Moss, William Mulock, and James Loudon – all of whom took their degrees between 1854 and 1863. It was they who urged the election of graduates to the university's Senate. They achieved their first significant political victory in 1874 when, against the strenuous opposition of Daniel Wilson, then head of University College, Moss was elected to the vice-chancellorship. A full fifty-eight years later, James Loudon's nephew still savoured the sweetness of the triumph when, in a biography of Sir William Mulock, he wrote: 'From that date Progress began to stretch out her hand, and although some of the members of the Senate who had lived in medieval bliss for many years fought valiantly against the new order, yet they were gradually being overwhelmed by the representatives of public opinion. A new star of education was appearing on the horizon; henceforth there was to be no back-sliding. The University might stand still but there would surely be no step back toward the Past.'[18] The old order versus the new, past against future – thus were the battle lines formed for a series of protracted squabbles that would continue to hinder the provincial university for the next thirty years. For much of that time the internal factional squabbles often attracted public attention since professorial appoint-ments, by virtue of the University Act, were made by the minister of education, not by university officials such as the president. As a result, politicians, profes-sors, and public often sought the ear of the minister of education in order to pro-mote their own causes or prevent those of their rivals. 'The reason I write,' said

MPP J.M. Gibson to George Ross in 1887, 'is my desire to get Woods in the staff if it can be brought about ... Have you consulted Mulock at all? I understand both he and Dr Wilson favor Woods' appointment. Isn't the political economy chair more urgent than Physiology?'[19]

This example, dealing with an anticipated appointment to the chair of Latin but touching also upon the question of what priority the provincial government ought to give to other elements of the university curriculum, was typical of hundreds received by the minister of education in the 1880s and 1890s. Politicians wrote when the politics of prospective appointments were 'right' or when they were 'wrong.'[20] Professors wrote when their own salaries were too low or when those of their colleagues were too high. Both wrote when they sought more – or fewer – Canadians on staff. For the whole period under examination, but especially during the uncertain years surrounding university federation in the late eighties when the promotion of self-interest reached frenzied heights under the guise of sacrifice, the position of the university president was consistently undermined. Why talk to President Wilson if one had a problem or a promotion? A five-minute walk to Queen's Park would give the petitioner the ear of the minister himself. This, at least, seems to have been the attitude assumed by many members of the University of Toronto faculty if their letters and the internal memoranda of the Ministry of Education accurately reflect the state of affairs. The ministry itself, we should note, was not entirely the originator of active interference in university affairs, although it was often accused of being so. The blame rested equally on the weakness of the University of Toronto Act, which positively encouraged the petty and often self-serving intrigues of the university faculty. Their acrid letters often reached the minister's desk, and they all but forced him to interfere in the internal affairs of an apparently ungovernable university. Whatever else might be said about the history of academic freedom in Ontario in the nineteenth century, it can unequivocally be stated that the rank and file of the provincial university's professoriate had little notion of it. They seem much more to have preferred to deal with a relatively disinterested political arbiter than with their own president.

It is unfortunate, to think of it, that Messrs Gilbert and Sullivan remained productively occupied in England during the late nineteenth century. A tour to Toronto might well have produced a major comic opera – a silly-little-satire-of-an-academic-sort – of substantial proportions. For no Canadian institution was more ripe for their biting attention than was the University of Toronto between 1875 and 1895. Its history provides as sustained a performance of academic *opéra bouffe* as one can imagine. James Reaney caught some of the comic potential in the high seriousness of the day with his play *The Dismissal*, written to commemorate the 10th anniversary of the university in 1977. Using as his subject the 1895 students' strike – itself the culmination of the 'nativist' controversy that began in the 1870s – Reaney gave as his subtitle the words 'Twisted Beards & Tangled Whiskers.'[21]

Satire, however, is a bastard child of hindsight. Looking back upon those years with less dramatic intent we must conclude that the major historical players on that stage saw nothing of amusement in the state of affairs, however twisted and tangled their beards and whiskers may have been as a result of their frustrations. The man dismissed from the university faculty for criticizing university authorities in a public forum was William Dale, associate professor of Latin and a long-time advocate of Canadian interests within the faculty. There had been no hint of the humorous in a letter he wrote to minister of education George Ross in December 1890:

With respect to appointments I would like to say this. It was your policy in that respect that first made Canadian graduates feel that they had some part in their own University, that to some extent broke down the exotic character of the Institution, & I have no hesitation in saying that I regret that that policy was not carried out to a still greater extent. In the past higher education has been repressed, almost destroyed in the Province from the apparent impossibility of any Canadian ever reaching the higher appointments. The Canadian appointments have I believe been uniformly good, while it is doubtful if the same assertion can be made respecting the foreign appointments. It must have occurred to yourself that there must be something wrong when after a generation of foreign teachers it is said to be impossible to find Canadians to fill any chair in the University, as it has been said. Doubtless we shall have to fight in the future as we have done in the past for every point.[22]

It has been necessary to dwell on these aspects of the internal politics of the University of Toronto because the tangible prerequisites for the development of research at the provincial university – the acquisition of staff, equipment, and laboratory facilities, as well as the possibility of awarding a research degree (PHD) – were debated, promoted, and resisted within this general context of institutional confusion, generational differences, and personality conflict. No person played a more important role in each than did James Loudon.

Born in Toronto, educated at Upper Canada College and at the University of Toronto (where he took his BA and MA degrees in 1862 and 1864), Loudon was ambitious, aggressive, and therefore the most visible example of the local boy made good in the Ontario academic world. For a number of years he taught Latin, Greek, mathematics, and natural philosophy, until in 1875 he became the first Canadian-born scholar to occupy a chair at Toronto with the offer of the professorship of mathematics and physics. Already an acknowledged leader of the nativist faction in the university, Loudon soon established himself as an unwavering champion of the cause of disinterested scientific research. For the next fifteen and more years, as an appropriate place was sought for science within the university, the relationship between its two major exponents – Wilson and Loudon – remained very tense. Loudon had little patience and less respect for most of his former professors, at least in private; even those with whom he had associated in his early years on staff. Of John Cherriman, who had taught him mathematics and whom he replaced, he wrote in his memoirs: 'Cherriman favoured the Cambridge text-books exclusively, and looked for guidance to the Examination papers of the Mathematical Tripos there, until they began to change their character, when he protested. He did not believe in the possibility of any great advances in Mathematics.'[23]

Cherriman's was not a view that Daniel Wilson would have accepted: he was always speaking of the virtually limitless advancements of truth made possible through science. But even Wilson's more enlightened views were clearly inadequate from Loudon's perspective. He scarcely encouraged Wilson's intellectual support when he gave his first major public lecture after assuming the chair of mathematics and physics. As reported in the Toronto *Mail* on 16 October 1875, Loudon had stated: 'It is not the proper function of a scientific teacher to reconcile scientific theory with metaphysical or religious opinion – his duty being, as it appears to me, to investigate facts, to draw legitimate inferences, and declare them to the world to be accepted or refused, upon their merits.' This was a declaration of Loudon's own commitment to a total separation of science from metaphysics; but it was also, as members of the university community would immediately have perceived, a blunt rejection of Daniel Wilson's entire approach to both science and life. The lecture was characteristic of Loudon equally in its straightforward declaration of honest conviction and in its utter lack of diplomatic tact.

If Wilson took offence at Loudon's insistence that the scientist should not take upon himself the task of reconciling science with metaphysics, and if he was annoyed with Loudon's championing of the nativist cause, he was also irritated because Loudon was by implication also accusing the British universities, so valued by Wilson, of having failed to harness science to the needs of the age. Indeed, two years later Loudon was much more direct on this subject in his presidential address to the Canadian Institute. This 1877 address is of major importance for the history of scientific research in Canada, for it was a manifesto declaring Loudon's compete commitment to the German research ideal as found in its universities. And on this matter Loudon would not waver for the rest of his long and distinguished, if stormy, career. Perhaps inspired by the opening of Johns Hopkins University two years earlier, one based on the German model and therefore committed to research as much as to instruction, Loudon declared his approval. The state, as well as scientific societies, must develop ways of rewarding those engaged in independent research; it must increase the number of teachers, thereby enabling the division of labour that would make specialized research possible and productive. Neither British nor American universities, he stated, had yet done so; but it was 'the distinguishing feature of the German universities. In them [Loudon said] the teacher is not relieved from the duties of the lectureroom or the work of the laboratory, but his subject lies within narrow limits, and he is thus not only enabled to teach but to devote a lifetime to his special subject ... Before the German plan, however, can be generally pursued anywhere an enormous revenue must be available; there must be a small standing army of professors, and a highly trained body of recruits.'[24] With Loudon's 1877 address, the mantle of scientific leadership at the University of Toronto passed from Wilson to Loudon, a man twenty-five years Wilson's junior. The future of scientific education thereby resided in the hands of a distinctly different generation.

The redirection and expansion of the university called for by Loudon was not, however, to be easily or quickly won – and for a number of reasons distinct from the numbing factionalism and intrigues of the late nineteenth century. To begin with, the very Britishness of the university and its surrounding community had traditionally made almost any German influence suspect. 'I cannot ... even patiently sit down under the rebukes of any one who has himself drank from German fountains, and believes all wisdom to be with his masters,' William Hincks had written in 1859.[25] A certain amount of this hostility would dissipate in subsequent years, especially after a German-derived philosophical idealism was made both acceptable and popular at Toronto under the influence of the much-revered professor George Paxton Young. But a residuum of British imperial distrust of German ideas and ways remained at the university and in the community, and it would re-emerge during the years of the Great War.[26] Second, the college idea of a broad, humanistic, and liberal education preoccupied with the instillation of 'inherited wisdom' and human values remained strong. The consolidation of the college structure and affiliation with university confederation in 1887 served to buttress this commitment. 'Specialization' became a synonym for challenges to humanistic values, and schemes for specialized scientific research were often regarded as evidence of the imperial and centralizing ambitions of 'the godless institution' at the expense of affiliated colleges and regional institutions such as Queen's or Western.

Finally, even if such forms of resistance had not existed, the fact remained that financial assistance by the state was seldom forthcoming. The funds provided by the provincial legislature necessitated by the disastrous University College fire of 1890 constituted its first significant grant in excess of the annual revenues of the university's endowment funds. The government disbursed this capital grant of $135,151 on the clear understanding that it was not to be construed by the universities as a precedent for future grants. Nevertheless, as Henri Bourassa was to say of Laurier's decision to send a contingent of volunteers to the Boer War in 1899, the precedent lay in the established fact. Each year after 1890 the Ontario government committed public funds, both for operating and capital expenses, to the University of Toronto, although, as E.E. Stewart has noted, 'the general pattern of government expenditures ... were [sic] slightly less in 1900 than they had been in 1891 and ... fell every year between 1890 and 1896 before beginning their slow rise again.'[27]

The Ministry of Education under George Ross continued to play an active role in what were matters of pure academic jurisdiction. Ross dismissed Professor William Dale in 1895 without consulting James Loudon, Wilson's successor as president of the university. Loudon learned of the dismissal through his newspaper. But the financial concerns of the ministry for the university were almost entirely in areas of academic activity that were of direct practical and social utility, and therefore of political benefit. The School of Practical Science in Toronto and the College of Agriculture in Guelph, both under direct government control, were well-financed in comparison with the universities proper; and Principal G.M. Grant's scheme to create a Kingston School of Mining and Agriculture in the early 1890s was given the government's approval and support in spite of substantial Toronto opposition. In this way, a science harnessed directly to the needs of the state was encouraged while general university requirements were neglected.

Acrimony continued to dominate University College in the 1890s, and the colleges federated with the University of Toronto suffered, in the words of E.E. Stewart, from 'progressive deterioration.'[28] By 1895, with a substantially increasing student body but deteriorating and inadequate equipment and facilities, the university Senate issued a 'Report of a Special Committee ... on claims respecting the assets and Endowments of the University,' 'Your committee,' it concluded,

would earnestly impress upon every member of the Senate, and upon every graduate of the University, that they should agree to make it their steadfast policy, and their pledged duty, to obtain for our Provincial University ... a recognition of its right – equally with the subordinate Educational Institutions of the Province, – to a proportionate share in the increased Land Grants which the marvellously rapid progress of the Physical and Social Sciences, and Mechanical Arts has made necessary ... Only to its University, which has long felt the pressing necessity for better educational equipment to meet the scientific and intellectual demands made upon it, has the Province failed in the liberal policy which has made its Educational System famous among other enlightened communities. The result is that, from poverty of means, the available resources of the University are altogether inadequate to meet the modern Educational and Scientific demands of the age.[29]

The Senate report was duly submitted to the legislature, and the result was an 1897 act giving the university lands in northern Ontario sufficient to increase the value of its endowment. Annual revenues generated from them were nevertheless pitifully inadequate, ranging from a low of $895 in 1898 to $8191.81 in 1899. For these princely sums the provincial university paid a high price, for George Ross publicly justified the government's largesse on the grounds that the university was a 'child of the state,' owing its origins to 'the parliament of Ontario' and acknowledging 'no master but that parliament.'[30] In this way, the provincial state consolidated its ability to exercise political control and direction when necessary and financial neglect when possible.

Such a political climate was scarcely conducive to the successful promotion of disinterested research, whether in the sciences or in the humanities. Nor did it facilitate the means by which that research could best be encouraged: the creation of a sustained program of graduate studies, including the PHD. Nevertheless, progress was made – if slowly. As might be expected, leadership of this movement was provided principally by James Loudon. Increasingly in the 1870s and 1880s, Loudon could point to the lead taken in American graduate studies by Johns Hopkins; moreover, he could also consistently draw upon the success and the testimonials of Toronto graduates who had gone to study there.[31] By 1883, with the aid of Edward Blake, who had become chancellor of the University of Toronto, he was able to cajole a reluctant Senate to adopt in principle the desirability of offering the PHD degree. No concrete action was taken, however, by the committee appointed to pursue the matter.

A year earlier the Ontario government had instituted a fellowship system, but these awards (nine in all) were intended as much to provide teaching assistance to an overworked staff as to facilitate the students' research activities. The result, ironically, was that just enough graduate training was made available to encourage fellowship holders to go elsewhere (usually to the United States) for the doctoral degree. But along with their mentor, Loudon, these Toronto alumni were an effective lobby for the establishment of a PHD program at Toronto. They continuously extolled the virtues of American universities in academic research and directly or by implication criticized their alma mater for its shortsightedness. Some of them – such as W.J. Alexander in English and A.B. McCallum in physiology – returned to Toronto after taking doctorates at Johns Hopkins and aided Loudon in his continuing quest for the acceptance of the research ideal as a fundamental element in university life.

Other imperatives – both intellectual and social – came to their aid by the late 1880s and 1890s. In spite of resistance from the undergraduates, the opposition of

Daniel Wilson, the absence of financial support due to the smug indifference of George Ross, the continuing antagonisms left in the wake of the 'University Question' in general, and the conflict between exponents of the 'college' and the 'university' ideals concerning the purpose of higher education as transmitter of inherited wisdom or catalyst for advancing knowledge, the tendencies of the age ultimately favoured the cause of specialized research. The very fragmentation of the pre-Darwinian monistic cosmology in the decades after 1859, in spite of the heroic attempts by idealist philosophers to maintain moral and intellectual unity, paved the way for individualized academic routes to objective 'truth.' The explosion of knowledge made possible by improvements in the technology of communications required the creation of well-defined academic 'disciplines,' for by no other means could any scholar of the late nineteenth century gain command of what he was coming to call his 'field.' In spite of the financial constraints of the eighties and nineties, such specialization necessarily took place.

Earlier, Daniel Wilson could occupy a chair that encompassed all of history and literature; Loudon could hold one in both mathematics and physics; and George Paxton Young's chair in philosophy could embrace not only today's subfields of logic, ethics, metaphysics, and the history of philosophy, but also psychology and political economy – which were then part of the philosopher's domain as 'mental philosophy' and 'civil polity.' Such had been the majestic, unifying sweep of nineteenth-century mental and moral philosophy. But by the 1890s these chairs had each been divided – some said pillaged. In 1887 mathematics and physics had been separated. The following year, English and history were effectively split with the creation of controversial chairs in English and in political economy and constitutional history, occupied, respectively, by W.J. Alexander and W.J. Ashley. By 1894, history was given a status independent of political economy with the appointment of the Rev. George Wrong as professor of history. In each of these new chairs in the humanities and social sciences, the lobby of Toronto nativists played a major role. In most, the successful applicant was a strong advocate of the new research ideal. W.J. Alexander had graduated from Toronto had and later taken a PHD at Johns Hopkins; W.J. Ashley was a graduate of Oxford but had already distinguished himself in social and economic research; George Wrong was a Toronto graduate, had no obvious credentials as an historian, but had married the daughter of Edward Blake, the university's chancellor.

Near the mid-point in this expansion of disciplines the venerated George Paxton Young died. Another major appointment was therefore necessary, and a controversy of major proportions was the result. Ultimately, the dispute touched upon virtually every one of the factors that had divided members of the university community in the eighties: the importance of metaphysical doctrine and of empirical research, which led in turn to a public debate over what constituted an 'acceptable' metaphysics and what was the value of laboratory work; the relationship of philosophy itself to the emergent discipline of psychology (should the latter be taught by professors of mental philosophy or by experts in experimental science?); the question of who should have the responsibility for determining appointments to the provincial university – politicians or professors; the problem of whether qualified Canadians should be given preference over non-Canadians when such appointments were made. The controversy is important enough for these reasons; but for our purpose it is especially so because the appointment that was ultimately made resulted in the first laboratory for empirical psychological research in Canada. Moreover, the story serves to remind us that real advances in the institutional and intellectual conditions necessary for scientific research are at times the result of matters that, strictly speaking, have no bearing upon either science or research.[32]

As might be expected, the Toronto academic community split largely along nationalist lines. Sir Daniel Wilson and the heads of two Toronto-affiliated theological colleges (William Caven of Knox and James Sheraton of Wycliffe) supported the candidacy of James Mark Baldwin, a young American who had studied at Princeton under James McCosh, North America's last major exponent of Scottish Realism or 'Common Sense.' Baldwin had also studied briefly in Germany with the renowned physiological psychologist Wilhelm Wündt. James Loudon, Vice-Chancellor William Mulock, the editors of the *Varsity*, and a number of vociferous University of Toronto graduates favoured the Ontarian James Gibson Hume, a recent Toronto graduate who was a self-proclaimed disciple of George Paxton Young and who had gone for further studies to Johns Hopkins and Harvard. There he had studied variously with G. Stanley Hall, Richard Ely, Josiah Royce, and William James – and had made an excellent impression on each.

The reasons for these allegiances are relatively clear. Loudon, faced with candidates with roughly equal credentials, chose the native son, as did the other supporters of the nativist cause. Wilson, typically, chose the candidate with an international background and therefore (in his view) cosmopolitan outlook. But he probably also favoured Baldwin as much out of reaction to Loudon's choice as out of commitment. Indeed, earlier, when Wilson found out that Loudon had approached the Nova Scotia-born president of Cornell, Jacob Gould Schurman – a candidate Wilson himself supported – he confided to his 'Journal': 'Probably Schurman was communicative with him, and he belongs very specially to the little 'native' clique with Professor 'Mole' as secret wire-puller.'[33] Wilson often referred to Loudon as 'Mole,' just as William Mulock was 'Mule.' Finally, the view of the principals of Presbyterian Knox and Anglican Wycliffe colleges was probably that it was theologically more safe to appoint a graduate of McCosh's Princeton than it would be to award the position to one they viewed as a pale imitation of Young – whom they regarded as irreplaceable. Besides, Baldwin had married the daughter of the president of Princeton Theological Seminary.

Since the appointment of the new professor of philosophy was ultimately, by virtue of the University Act, a political one to be made by Oliver Mowat's cabinet, the debate rapidly became a public one by means of academic deputations to the legislature, letters to Toronto dailies, and front-page newspaper articles with titles such as 'Metafeesicks' and 'M'Cosh, Be Gosh.'[34] There and elsewhere the thundering ironies of the various allegiances soon paraded themselves in full public view. Loudon, the champion of experimental research, had rejected the candidate with laboratory experience under a German psychologist of world rank in favour of a Toronto graduate with none; the clergymen-academics had rejected an exponent of philosophical and religious idealism in favour of a scholar who had spent much of his time in Germany reading the writings of the materialist Lotze in the darkness of the Black Forest.

The Mowat cabinet was also split, with Mowat favouring the appointment of Baldwin but his colleagues, including George Ross, strongly on the side of Hume. Mowat was further caught between the strong support of President Wilson for Baldwin and the weight of a British-Canadian, imperialist, and anti-American public sentiment. In the end, Mowat's decision was truly political: he compromised by splitting Young's all-embracing chair. Baldwin, the American, would be appointed immediately as professor of philosophy, with the understanding that he would specialize in psychological laboratory research. Hume, the Canadian, was ordered to spend two more years of preparation abroad, after which he would return as professor of ethics and the history of philosophy. The hegemony of metaphysics – now gone from the title of the new chairs in philosophy – seemed over at the University of Toronto. By a bizarre series of events the research ideal was finally to be given a tangible presence and government support.

The days of Daniel Wilson were also nearing their end. He was losing both influence and strength. He had neither won nor lost the appointment battle – he merely felt embarrassed and embittered, especially when called upon by Premier Mowat to write anonymous pieces for the *Globe* and the *Mail* praising the wisdom of the government's decision. 'And now I hope my colleagues will be considerate enough,' he wrote in his 'Journal,' to [let] live forever, or at least til I have shuffled off the mortal coil of Presidency or of life ... The aspect in which I find myself viewed by this pack of self seekers as a foreign intruder is comical. I am the last of the hated Hykos kings. If they only had me safe in my sarcophagus the reign of the true native pharoahs would begin.'[35] By 1892 he received both his wish and his prophecy. He died in that year, his beloved University College literally in ashes. James Loudon was appointed president of the university in his place. In a sense, too, James Mark Baldwin was also a victim of the controversy. The disastrous fire that destroyed part of University College, including its library, in 1890 also consumed the future location of Baldwin's anticipated psychological laboratory. His optimistic inaugural address declared him to be an 'apostle' of the new experimental psychology,[36] but the inferno left him with little but his own energetic enthusiasm. Nevertheless, by literally begging and borrowing he was able to announce the existence of a laboratory for the opening of the 1891–2 academic year. Not in fact ready until the spring of 1892, the facilities – the first that were solely committed to putting the research ideal into practice at Toronto – cost a total of $919.21. Baldwin received no aid from either government or university in meeting his request for a laboratory demonstrator, and this was essential for serious and sustained experimental work. As a result he began seriously to consider accepting one of several offers from other universities, including one from his alma mater, Princeton. Knowledge of the likelihood of losing Baldwin (as well as W.J. Ashley to Harvard) was enough, together with the legacy of the fire, to send Wilson into the coma from which he did not recover.

Baldwin (and Ashley) did choose to leave Toronto, and both forged exceptionally distinguished careers.[37] In the ensuing political struggle over the leadership and direction of the philosophy department the metaphysicians and the nativists took their revenge. Baldwin's departure left Hume as head of the department, free to promote his own brand of Youngian idealism at Toronto. Baldwin's eventual successor in the psychological laboratory, August Kirschmann – a solid scholar specializing in experimental psychophysics – was appointed (after a virtual replication of the original squabble) only at the lecturer level. He did not receive professorial rank until 1898. In spite of the fact that Kirschmann managed to give psychophysical experimentation at Toronto an international reputation within a decade, he left in 1909. Meanwhile, James Gibson Hume, with the aid of Francis Tracy, a Toronto graduate moulded in the image of Hume as much as Hume was of Young, shaped the Department of Philosophy along broadly idealist lines – lines that were to continue well into the twentieth century in its preoccupation with ethics and 'social philosophy.' It is not too much to say that at Toronto there was established a clear and continuous intellectual and moral line from Paxton Young and James Hume to Marcus Long and John Irving, and that takes us from the latter days of the Victorian era to the early 1960s. The research ideal did not have an easy course at the University of Toronto, in philosophy as elsewhere, for the concern for values continued to be a major preoccupation of many at the provincial university long after universities elsewhere in the industrial world had shifted much of their attention to more tangible concerns.

The research ideal scarcely achieved an unambiguous triumph within the confines of the university's philosophy department. Yet the episode is important historically in a different way. It involved the question – central to many minds at the time, politics aside – of whether empirical research deserved more in the way of tangible reward than did the wide-ranging reflections or speculations of the 'unscientific' academic mind. The University of Toronto is not today primarily known for its pioneering efforts in psychological research; it is, however, known for the broad-ranging speculative work of scholars such as Harold Innis, Charles Norris Cochrane, Marshall McLuhan, and Northrop Frye. None of these scholars owes his reputation directly to the 'research ideal' as set forward by men such as James Loudon (although Innis built upon it). But each owes his place within the provincial university, however indirectly, to the acrimonious yet intense debate within the university community that occurred in the late nineteenth century. The fundamental academic directions, one might say the 'balance,' of the university were set in the 1890s.

The legacy of the nineteenth century ultimately allowed for a strong presence of the humanities at the University of Toronto in spite of the utilitarian concerns of the provincial government. It provided too, however inadvertently, for the continuation of the introspective, acrimonious, yet probably productive debate between exponents of the arts and the sciences. The institutional structure of federated denominational colleges, cumbersome as it may have been, protected the moralistic character of humanistic research.

Yet social and economic imperatives gave the cause of pure research increasing momentum. Throughout the nineties university enrolment increased significantly, partly because of the success of the provincial high school system and partly because the maturing provincial economy now required university graduates with specialized skills. By the first years of the twentieth century, *Industrial Canada*, the journal of the Canadian Manufacturers' Association, was active in promoting the cause of industrial research at the universities.[38] In 1878, when the university had first constructed laboratories in chemistry, geology and mineralogy, biology, and physics for the students of the School of Practical Science, a professor of English could ask Loudon: 'Why go to the expense of purchasing this elaborate equipment until the physicists have made an end of making discoveries?'[39] Twenty years later that battle had partially been won. In 1897 Loudon, with the aid of Toronto alumni such as A.B. Macallum and W.J. Alexander (now on staff), was finally successful in getting the university Senate to pass his 1883 motion – never rescinded but never acted on – to introduce the PHD degree 'for the purpose of encouraging research.' Departments now offering the degree were biology, chemistry, physics, geology, philosophy, orientals, and political science. But it should be noted that history, Latin and Greek, mathematics, and modern languages refused to participate.[40] A turning-point had been reached. From 1897 on, the university , in its attempt to meet the increasing demands of the resource-rich and industrial 'New Ontario,' was forced to declare major deficits, and the reluctant and fatigued Liberal government of the province had no choice but to respond with grants of increasing size,[41] usually earmarked for scientific facilities, training, and research of direct applicability to industry.

The year 1897 had also seen the celebration of Queen Victoria's Diamond Jubilee. Partly to mark the occasion, the British Association for the Advancement of Science met in Toronto. Imperial fervour was near its height in Ontario and the call by the assembled scientists for a co-ordinated system of research, to be led by the universities of the British empire in order to maintain Great Britain's traditional industrial supremacy over Germany, met with general public approval. James Loudon, still the provincial leader of the cause of pure research, was therefore able to wed the needs of science to the growth of imperial-nationalist sentiment. He could support the call for more technical education, as he did in his convocation address of 1900 to the University of Toronto,[42] but he was able to insist equally, with increasing support, that 'no diffusion of technical training will in itself be effective if we do not take care to maintain the higher and highest kind of scientific instruction.'[43] And by the turn of the century the task was also made easier by the fact that he could now point to the newly created University of Birmingham – with Joseph Chamberlain as chancellor – as an example of a *British* university committed to the German research ideal.[44]

Loudon made significant progress in popularizing the need for (and desirability of) pure research. In 1902 he began his presidential address to the Royal Society of Canada by saying: 'It is now many years since I came to the conclusion that the provision of adequate facilities for research is one of the prime necessities of university education in Canada.'[45] He could, by then, justly claim major credit for helping convince politicians, professors, and public that his convictions regarding research needs were justified. But at his own university he continued to meet with frustration and be thwarted by internal unrest due ultimately to the near-impossibility of governing under the existing University Act. Sir Daniel Wilson, secure, presumably, in his sarcophagus, may well have been seen to smile between 1892 and 1906, for the 'Loudon Years' were – if possible – even more tumultuous than those of Wilson. They opened with the 1895 Students' Strike and closed with the university in such general disarray that a wide-ranging royal commission, appointed by the new Conservative government of James P. Whitney, was required to establish it along more secure lines. To an extent these problems were of Loudon's own making, for he seemed 'to have been a man who carried his own black cloud with him.'[46] But in fairness to Loudon, probably no one could have governed the provincial university adequately under the existing University Act. Its inadequacies played into the hands of the Liberal administrations of Mowat and Ross, both of which were quite willing to interfere in academic affairs in order to maintain political control. To them must also be apportioned much of the blame for the university's pathetic state by the end of their regime.

The 1906 University of Toronto Act, drawn up by the members of the royal commission appointed to examine the state of the provincial university, signalled the end of Loudon's tenure as president. But it was also, arguably, the most important piece of legislation in the history of higher education in Ontario – and certainly in the history of the University of Toronto. It provided the basis for effective management; ended, as Whitney had long claimed he would, the constitutional basis for political control over internal university affairs; and recognized the necessity of adequate financial support by the state. It provided, in short, the basis for ending in a remarkably abrupt fashion the *opéra bouffe* performances of the previous quarter century. Moreover, it provided a secure means of engaging more fruitfully in the central questions of university life. 'We have arrived at a critical juncture in the progress of University education,' wrote the commissioners. 'The question presents itself, whether the main object shall be, as it has hitherto been, intellectual culture, or the knowledge which qualifies directly for gainful pursuits ... Science, properly so-called, is culture of its kind and those who pursue it may in turn imbibe the spirit of culture by association. We could not pretend, in confronting this great question, to forecast or regulate the future. We could do no more than provide a home for culture and science under the same academical roof.'[47]

By 1906 a rough equilibrium had been established in the provincial university for culture and for science, for metaphysics and for research. Until then, Queen's, secure in its genteel poverty and in its relative isolation from political intrigue, had accomplished far more in the humanities and the arts; the Royal Society of Canada had provided a much greater forum for research in all fields; and the Canadian Institute and federal and provincial agencies such as the Geological Survey, the astronomical and magnetic surveys, and agricultural experimental farms had done more in the way of original scientific research. To an extent this pattern would continue, especially with government research establishments. But the future of the University of Toronto would prove to be much different from its troubled past. The basis had been laid by 1906 for the creation, within a single generation, of what President Bissell has called 'The Great Good Place.'[48] Reflection and research could now co-exist in a propinquity of continuing unease but relative security, as well they should.

7

The Idealist Legacy

Philosophical idealism, especially that given expression by professors in English-Canadian universities, became a major way of accommodating science and religion in late Victorian Canada. No philosopher, then or since, was as influential as John Watson of Queen's University, who, with Edward Caird of Great Britain and Josiah Royce of the United States, completed a triumvirate of Hegelian idealists at the apex of Anglo-American academic life in the late nineteenth century. But in thought, as in other aspects of life, intentions often have consequences profoundly different from those desired by their authors. The legacy of idealist thought, given its most profound expression by Watson, was ironic in just such a way. At the conclusion of Watson's career it was debatable whether his desire to preserve the essentials of the Christian religion had resulted in preservation or destruction. In any event, the legacy was profound, extending beyond the boundaries of philosophy and religion into public education. B. Anne Wood, for example, extends my interpretation into this area in Idealism Transformed: The Making of a Progressive Educator *(Kingston and Montreal 1985). This paper was published as* 'John Watson and the Idealist Legacy' *in the Intellectual History issue of* Canadian Literature *83 (winter 1979): 72–89.*

The historian of ideas in Canada quickly discovers how central the philosophy studied at Canadian universities was in helping to bring about the intellectual and spiritual accommodations made necessary in the Victorian era. Much of that accommodation involved the interplay among certain strands of religion, science, and philosophy that found their way, as a kind of intellectual patchwork quilt, into the homes, universities, and churches of British North Americans in the nineteenth century.[1]

Readers of the *Literary History of Canada* will recognize immediately that central to this process of accommodation, and dominating philosophical inquiry generally in Canada between 1872 (when he arrived from Scotland on the campus of Queen's University at the ripe old age of twenty-five) and 1922 (when he retired from teaching), was John Watson. John Irving's lengthy account in the *Literary History* of Watson's signal achievements in the field of international philosophical scholarship need not be repeated here. It might simply be noted that the Garland publishing company in New York reminded Canadians in 1976 that his scholarship has been of enduring value: in a republication of the eleven most important studies of Kant since that philosopher's death, two of the volumes selected were by John Watson of Queen's.[2]

Yet Watson was not significant for his contributions to scholarship alone. More important to consider is the crucial role he and his philosophy played in the transition of the overtly Christian mental and moral philosophy of the nineteenth century in Canada into a broadly secular moral outlook which has dominated much of English-Canadian thought in the twentieth. When fully examined as part of the general intellectual and cultural history of English-speaking Canada, the legacy of nineteenth-century mental and moral philosophy will perhaps be seen to have been a profound one, part of what, in *A Disciplined Intelligence*, I have called a 'moral imperative' that links the thought of Thomas McCulloch to that of Northrop Frye, and that will allow an historical connection to be made between moralists such as George Grant, W.L. Morton, Hugh MacLennan, Harold Innis, and Robertson Davies and the Victorian philosophic temperament.

This essay provides part of that background. To be explored here is the influence of the critical intellect of the speculative idealists, led by John Watson, upon the major religious phenomenon of early twentieth-century Canada: the liberalizing movement within Protestantism known as the Social Gospel. In the process, some light will be shed on the interrelationship between philosophical and theological suppositions at a crucial stage in Canada's history, and some of the shifts and continuities in Canadian intellectual history which continue to affect Canadian cultural development will be suggested.

At the end of the nineteenth century, Anglo-Canadian thought had reached a watershed. For a half century, those who dominated religious, scientific, and philosophical thinking in Canada had been intensely suspicious of the critical intellect that emerged in the popular realm during Victoria's reign. Anglo-Canadian educators had, in effect, established an orthodoxy of ideas and assumptions in the formative years of the university *curricula* in the country. Yet by the end of the century that orthodoxy was everywhere under assault. In the first place, the Baconian scientific ideal (which stressed observation while eschewing speculation), reflected in the work of Toronto's Daniel Wilson and McGill's William Dawson, had proven inadequate under the onslaught of Darwinian science. Second, the Scottish Common Sense philosophy, which pervaded the teachings of

James George at Queen's and William Lyall at Dalhousie in the third quarter of the century, had gradually been dismissed by younger minds as inadequate in its psychology to meet the needs and the challenges of an age of inquiry and analysis. Finally, the third and to an extent the most central element in this triumvirate of early Victorian orthodoxy, the Paleyite natural theology given expression by James Beaven and James Bovell at Toronto in the 1850s and 1860s, had, by the 1890s, largely been replaced. Originally of value as a means of preserving the argument from design while utilizing the frameworks of both faculty psychology and Baconian observation, it had, by then, been supplanted by an equally teleological, but dynamic, Hegelian conception of social evolution. In short, by the end of the century the old orthodoxy of ideas, anti-speculative by nature, founded on social constraint, and aimed at instilling students with a traditional Christian piety, had been shattered. In its place had emerged a Canadian variation of British speculative idealism.

In the twenty years after the arrival of Watson and Idealism in Canada in 1872, that philosophical creed seemed to have resolved certain problems critically important for the generation who had been trained under the assumptions of the old intellectual orthodoxy but who lived through the Darwinian revolution. Watson's confident philosophy seemed to resolve the problems faced by the Common Sense school in the decades which explored the intricacies of the central nervous system (or, as Richard Maurice Bucke chose to call it, 'the Great Sympathetic'), for it could maintain the existence of the 'moral nature' of man while asserting the active powers of mind. It constituted a new conception of design and purpose operating in the universe, one that could encompass rather than capitulate to evolutionary science. It offered a critique of empiricism and put empiricists on the defensive by revealing the limitations of scientific enterprise without attacking science *ad hominem*. It cultivated a pious disposition, yet did not belittle intellectual inquiry. It showed the essential 'rationality' of the universe and placed everything within the perspective of a new and modern interpretation of the Christian experience, even while defending the essentials of the faith as it conceived them.

For these basic reasons, the speculative Hegelian idealism whose British mentor was Watson's teacher Edward Caird and whose major Canadian voice was Watson himself found increasing acceptance among Canadian professors, clergymen, and students in the late nineteenth century. Yet even though Watson was, by 1890, a scholar of international stature, idealism was still a fresh intellectual force, a force for intellectual change that was coming to dominance in a decade when change in the country was everywhere.

The hegemony of idealism had begun, but only the first signs of its ultimate influence could then have been discerned. Every epoch is, in its own way, a time of transformation; but the 1890s marked a clear departure from the past in the nature and quality of Canadian life. John Watson's *Outline of Philosophy* (1895) was put before a Canadian reading public that witnessed in the decades to come a social and industrial upheaval for which there was no precedent in the history of the nation. His *Christianity and Idealism* (1897), a series of lectures given before the Philosophical Union of the University of California at Berkeley, appeared in the first flush of the Laurier boom; his Gifford Lectures, published in 1912 as *The Interpretation of Religious Experience*, were given when the rate of social and industrial change had reached its height.

This was, above all, a social transformation, and the idealist preached what was fundamentally a social ethic. Even at the level of intellectual speculation the social good was necessarily to prevail. And as with thought, so lives and careers were also seen to be meaningful only when regarded from a universal perspective. Society, it was argued, must be conceived as an organism. The individual must subordinate private interests to serve the greater whole. Watson had spoken from the first of 'the various spheres of the universe,' each forming 'an ascending series, in which each higher realm includes while it transcends the lower ...'[3] Each 'sphere' could become a focus of attention for Canadians whose thought was informed by this new moral imperative, articulated in a different form for a new age. One could perform one's social duties in ascending higher forms of service to an ever greater good, whether at the level of the church, the civil service, or the empire. During the thirty years that followed 1890, Canadian intellectual life was thus suffused with the idealist variant of the Anglo-Canadian moral imperative.[4]

Idealism exerted its greatest influence, however, on Canadian Protestant thought and practice. The full nature and extent of this influence will be determined only with more substantial historical investigation, yet a brief examination of the thought of certain key figures in early twentieth-century Protestant circles may serve for the present purpose to suggest the general nature of the intrusion of idealist assumptions upon Protestant thought in Canada.

The late nineteenth-century idealist delighted in using his creed to resolve seemingly irresolvable problems, and in Canada he took great pleasure in being simultaneously a force upholding the essentials of the Christian experience while inaugurating a profound transformation in religious life. The result, however, was a reorientation of Canadian Protestantism that by the 1920s scarcely resembled that desired by the nineteenth-century clerical advocates of a reconciliation of science and religion through idealism.

Idealists inspired by Watson taught that reality consisted of the secular process of history infused with a spiritual principle that was at once the heart of knowledge and synonymous with the Mind of God. 'In God we "live and move and have our being,''' Watson told a Kingston meeting of the YMCA in 1901; 'we are spirits capable of communion with the Spirit of all things; the meanest as well as the highest object within our reach witnesses of this universal spirit; and, living in it, we may become worthy members of the family, the community, the state, the race. To realize this spirit in all its forms is our true life work.'[5] So it was, but it was also a quest with a profoundly ambiguous legacy.

Watson's address had been entitled 'The Sadness and Joy of Knowledge,' its text taken from Ecclesiastes I: 18, which said: 'In much wisdom is much grief: and He that Increaseth knowledge Increaseth sorrow.' This was a paradox such as Watson delighted in resolving, for the idealist's universal vision and dialectical mode of argument could show how the 'perils and storms of the intellectual life' – the sorrow – would be quelled by the simple recognition that in this very sadness lay the source of joy. Strenuous effort in the search for universal truth by means of intellectual inquiry would gradually result in a deeper consciousness of reality, one in which 'at each step we feel we are penetrating a little deeper into the nature of things, and learning to re-think the embodied thoughts of God.' A generation earlier, such a statement would have been roundly condemned in Canadian Protestant circles, for it would have been seen as the height of intellectual arrogance. Watson's large claim was an expression of a piety shorn of the Christian's awareness that because of the sinfulness of man he could never fully achieve identity with the Mind of God, however much he might strive for it. But by the twentieth century this was a notion that found increasing acceptance in Canadian churches and Protestant denominational colleges.

The pervasiveness of idealist assumptions in Canadian university circles is suggested by even the most cursory of examinations of student newspapers such as *Queen's Journal* or Victoria College's *Acta Victoriana*. This is likewise the case with the fledgling academic journals *University of Toronto Quarterly*, which began in 1895, and *Queen's Quarterly*, first published two years earlier. The editors of the latter proclaimed solemnly in an opening statement that their quarterly sought to keep its readers aware 'of what Queen's is doing and thinking,' and 'to try to throw some rays of light on the questions that men's minds must always be most concerned about.'[6]

Not surprisingly, the honour of making the first statement about such weighty questions fell to John Watson, who provided a piece called 'The Middle Ages and the Reformation.' Luther's reformation, Watson stated, was based upon the simple principle that reconciliation with God was possible only through 'a spiritual act, an act of faith.' Yet he had not gone far enough in assessing the application of his own principle. Watson insisted that Luther had failed to take into account the fact that 'the individual's consciousness of God' transcends individuality and 'is conditioned by the past history of the consciousness of the race.'

Luther, that is to say, had not, for Watson, taken into account the principle of development, since he had not recognized that religious consciousness evolved 'with the growing intelligence and will of humanity.' Once wedded to the idea of the progressive development of consciousness, however, Protestantism would, in Watson's view, 'purify the state by making it an embodiment of reason.' This was the 'logical consequence of the Protestant idea,' one in which 'the ideal is the real, and what contradicts the ideal must ultimately be annulled.'[7]

Watson's *Queen's Quarterly* essay appeared in July 1893. In February of that year a very important event in the history of university extension in Canada had occurred. Initiated by Principal G.M. Grant, the First Theological Alumni Conference took place on the campus of Queen's University. Lasting for ten days, it was attended by Presbyterian ministers across the dominion. Others, not graduates of Queen's but attracted by the intellectual vitality of the place, also attended. There they heard the principal speak on a variety of doctrinal and practical subjects, and they were also exposed – as the alumni had been as undergraduates – to John Watson's hermetic philosophy. A sign of their appreciation of his views came in their closing resolutions, for they recommended the inauguration of a permanent lectureship and stipulated that it first be held by a professor from Queen's and that he 'should treat some subject bearing on the relations of Philosophy and Theology.' Any doubt as to who they wished to hold the first lectureship was dispelled when Chancellor Fleming announced later in the year his intention to sponsor the desired lecture series, stipulating that 'no one could better fill the position than Dr. Watson, who did so much to make the first conference a success.'[8]

Watson and his followers were not without their critics, but there can be no doubt that by the early twentieth century their distinctive Protestant vision was beginning to have its effect. In February 1906, for example, a correspondent in Montreal reported to Albert Carman, general superintendent of the Methodist Church in Canada, that 'many in this Conference [are] saturated with what they call "The new ideas," and it has become a sort of fad – a pretence of scholarship – to parade radical ideas. I have raised a few conflicts thus far, and expect to have more as I come in contact with these men. When the strife comes I find it is not so much the Higher Criticism ... that I am forced to combat, but the Hegelian philosophy ... I find that nearly every man who has passed through "Queen's University," and a coterie who follow this set, are preaching Hegelianism. It is a sad plight.'[9] So it was, indeed, for Methodists or Presbyterians who wished in the early twentieth century to retain the fundamentals of their faith as they had been handed down from earlier generations.

This was no easier at Victoria College, Toronto, than it was at Queen's. There, idealism was given sustained expression early in the century by a philosopher only at the outset of his career: George John Blewett. In 1897 Blewett had won the

Governor General's Gold Medal at 'Vic,' placing first in his philosophy class, and, aided by the George Paxton Young Memorial Fellowship, he then did graduate work at Harvard, in Germany, and finally at Oxford under Edward Caird (by then master of Balliol). After a stint at Wesley College, Winnipeg, he returned to Victoria College where he taught and wrote until his untimely death in 1912. By then, like Young before him he had gained disciples – both through his brilliant and inspiring lectures and through his two books, *The Study of Nature and the Vision of God* (1907) and *The Christian View of the World* (1910). In a preface to the former, Blewett noted that he had first been introduced to philosophy through T.H. Green's *Prolegomena to Ethics*. Yet the book was stamped with the mark of Caird. He had not been exaggerating when, also in his preface, he had written of his 'reverence and gratitude' to Caird, 'whose venerable primacy in philosophy among English-speaking men makes him "our father Parmenides." ' [10]

The combination of the views of Blewett (who could write that 'the nature of God ... may be expressed by putting together the three words, reason, righteousness, love') with the more abrasive and less spiritualistic rationalism of the Higher Criticism was a powerful force for change in Canadian religious thought. However much idealists such as Blewett and Watson attempted to infuse reason with a Christian spirituality, the fact was that in stressing the way early Christianity 'had inherited the intellectual spirit of the Greeks' they helped clear the path toward the application of an essentially secular version of the Christian revelation.

To the philosophically astute, Blewett's conception of a reason that transcended but did not challenge faith was distinctly different from one that simply equated faith with irrationality and therefore dismissed it. But to someone less initiated into the subtleties and the rhetoric of idealist philosophy, someone who found the argument persuasive but the logic and the jargon difficult at times to follow, such distinctions were perhaps never fully clear. For such a person it may have been sufficient simply to remember that Caird, Watson, and Blewett had said that Christianity was evolving through the secular process of history; that this religious progress was essentially a spiritual one which nevertheless was everywhere manifested in concrete terms; that in this (admittedly vague) unfolding of the consciousness of the race, religious faith could be better comprehended through rational – even intellectual – understanding; that piety and intellectual activity were not at odds since faith could not be faith if it defied intellectual inquiry; and that, finally, somehow in this ongoing cosmic process the old divisions between the spiritual and the material, the sacred and the secular, God and man, were obliterated.

Perhaps the potential legacy of the idealist's view of Christianity is best illustrated in the culmination of the correspondence between Watson and one of his lay admirers, a Mr J.M. Grant of Toronto. The troubled Mr Grant could not quite reconcile Watson's notion of the absolute with the doctrine of the Trinity, failed to see how objective idealism was not a form of pantheism, and, between 1911 and 1918, expressed to Watson, often in lengthy and tortuous letters, numerous other difficulties. Always Watson replied, and at length, in his reassuring and controlled hand. Always, Grant found, for a time, solace in a re-reading of Watson's *Philosophical Basis of Religion*; but only for a time. Finally, Grant announced that he felt compelled to resign his position as a Presbyterian Sunday school superintendent because of his doctrinal uncertainties. He had no choice, he said, but to join the Unitarian church. 'Do you think it really matters,' Watson replied in a letter marked 'confidential,' 'from the point of view of the essence of religion, whether one accepts what is called the divinity of Christ? ... You will understand,' he went on, 'that I cannot accept any of the doctrines of any Church literally.'[11] He then went on to dismiss, in their traditional forms, each of the doctrines which Grant found impossible to reconcile with speculative idealism.

Like his mentor, Edward Caird, Watson desired above all to reassert the moral and religious dimension of life undermined by modern scepticism. Yet his method of doing so resulted, ironically, in a form of belief that bore a distinct resemblance to the declared enemy, evolutionary naturalism. Both accepted the principle of evolutionary change; both asserted the fundamental unity of nature. This convergence between Hegelian idealism and the new naturalism, John Passmore has argued, was one of the most important and distinctive results of Darwin's impact on British metaphysics. 'It has been said,' Passmore wrote, 'that pantheism is a polite form of atheism: to assert that everything is God is certainly to deny that there is a God, as that word is ordinarily understood. And similarly one cannot but be struck by the resemblances between naturalism and the Absolute Idealism of philosophers like Caird and Bosanquet: so concerned are they to insist that there is nowhere a gap between the spiritual and the material, between the human and the natural, that one is often inclined to say – Absolute Idealism is the polite form of naturalism.'[12] The spiritual agony of J.M. Grant, struggling with the competing messages of the Westminster Confession and Watson's *Interpretation of Religious Experience*, is an illustration of what could result when one honestly attempted to follow speculative idealism to its apparent conclusions. Grant found Watson's reply to his own urgent letter 'so radical that it demands my most careful thought.' Accordingly, he began the repeated study of Watson's *Interpretation*. A couple of years later he became a Christian Scientist.

One can only wonder about the extent to which other earnest Presbyterians and Methodists were similarly affected by the idealists' perception of the essence of Christianity; their willingness, in effect, to scrap much in order to 'preserve the essence of the Christian consciousness – the unity of man & God.' The Trinity, the divinity of Christ, original sin, the atonement, eternal life, the resurrection – each in its generally accepted meaning was an impediment to an understanding of the union of God, man, and reason. 'No creed of any church can be accepted,' Watson had written to Grant at the height of the latter's crisis, 'and I don't think the Church be based upon any belief except that it is an organization for making men better.'[13] How many of the divinity students trained under Watson in the fifty years from 1872 to 1922 came to accept Watson's simple definition of the church, and to view traditional doctrines as impedimenta hindering the growth of consciousness?

For some, it is clear, the idealist philosophy was a revelation equal to that imparted to Watson by the Caird brothers in the 1860s. The Social Gospel movement in Canada was diverse both in its membership and in its origins; men and women drew their ideas on the social teachings of the gospels from sources as different as Ralph Waldo Emerson and Albrecht Ritschl. But they also drew, and perhaps in a more sustained and direct fashion, from the messages of men such as John Watson, George Monro Grant, George Blewett, and S.D. Chown (who became general superintendent of the Methodist church in 1910 and who continued in the position until Church Union in 1925). These intellectual and institutional leaders of Canadian Methodism and Presbyterianism helped provide the intellectual foundations upon which the Social Gospel movement in Canada was constructed between 1890 and 1914.

The 'Queen's spirit' of the 1890s, led by the contemplative Watson and the active Grant, inspired numerous individuals to engage in different forms of social service and to strive in their secular pursuits to bring about the Kingdom of God on Earth. Some, such as Adam Shortt (a gold medallist in philosophy under Watson) and O.D. Skelton, became prominent federal civil servants; others, a far greater proportion than the population of Queen's warranted, became teachers throughout the country and sought to live up to the moral example set them by Grant and Watson. Still others sought to be instrumental in the reorientation of the Canadian religious order. No one more exemplified this ambitious spirit than the Methodist preacher Salem Bland, who was to become the most radical of the social gospellers in Canada.[14]

Born in 1859, Bland, the son of a Methodist preacher, had been present in Kingston from 1884 through the 1890s, and in every respect he was a 'Queen's man,' proud to call himself a student of Watson and a disciple of Grant. Though never formally enrolled as a student at Queen's, he nevertheless read Kant with Watson, attended political meetings and Sunday afternoon addresses with Grant, and thoroughly imbibed the new social and critical spirit of the nineties. The novelist Robert E. Knowles, himself a graduate of Queen's in the 1890s, noted when Bland retired from public life that he had 'enlisted and enmeshed and engaged in all her life and ferment. Few faces were more familiar about her halls.'[15] There, instructed by Watson (and through him Hegel and Caird) and Grant, Bland's life and mind took a new direction. Signs of this could be seen in his consistent participation in the Queen's Theological Alumni conferences, especially those of 1898 and 1899. By then, much of his voluminous reading in Kingston was beginning to give definite shape to his thought, and he was nearly ready to give it practical application. 'In Canada as in all English-speaking countries,' he told the 1898 conference, 'social questions are engaging increasing attention. Christianity is becoming primarily sociological, which is a good deal better than if it should be regarded as primarily ecclesiastical or even theological.'[16]

The stamp of Grant, Watson, and Queen's remained on Salem Bland, and no doubt he prized the influence as much as he did the honorary doctorate awarded him by the university in 1900. In the twentieth century the reputations of Bland and Queen's would diverge radically, for by the 1920s Bland was best known as a radical socialist, whereas Queen's under the successors to Grant was gradually to assume an air of academic and humanistic detachment from fundamental social issues, even from Protestantism. Nevertheless, the connection between Bland and the Queen's spirit of the nineties existed and continued to give a philosophical basis for his evolving social views. In 1925 he jotted down some notes on 'A Philosophy of Life,' and they consisted of three propositions: that man is fundamentally good; that there must be fullness of life for everyone; and that there must be a stronger social consciousness. In itself this philosophy was consistent with the Social Gospel in almost any of its derivations, but in the specific ways Bland sought to construct such a philosophy the legacy of his years in Kingston can distinctly be seen.[17]

It would be inaccurate to assume that Bland came away from Kingston with the Social Gospel he was later to preach in full blossom. When in Smiths' Falls in 1899, for example, he still taught that the Kingdom of God could be realized only through individual salvation. At this stage in his career the traditional conception of a transcendent Kingdom held sway, if uneasily. Matters such as minimum wages, municipal ownership of natural monopolies, and more equitable taxation were, in Bland's mind, clearly 'within the range of the gospel, to be manifestly implied in the Kingdom of Heaven which it came to establish. *But these*,' he added emphatically, '*do not make the Kingdom of God*.' At this point in his life, at the age of forty, the essential distinction between sacred and secular still held some meaning for him. 'Knowledge of God is not ... minimum wage of $1.50 a day, not free schools & free rides ... not meat & drink, but *righteousness* & peace & joy in the Holy Ghost.'[18] Yet if these remarks portray a Methodist committed to a traditional conception of righteousness as the main element in the Kingdom of God, they also suggest one who could not see the coming about of such a kingdom without radical measures of social reform. What he had learnt in Kingston suggested that righteousness and an earthly kingdom were far from being incompatible, just as reason and faith were entwined. But for his first twenty years and more, those before his Queen's experience, his conception of the essence of Christianity – particularly on the question of eschatology – had been that of orthodox Methodism.

It took the Kingston experience and its disturbing intellectual adjustments before Bland was able to confront the unexamined convictions of his first twenty years. Late in his life he noted that his career seemed to have fallen neatly into such twenty-year stages. Of the second of these, he wrote: 'Those twenty years to me were the first twenty years of my ministry begun in the devout and untroubled acceptance of traditional orthodoxy in regard to the message and methods of the Evangelical Churches and the slow creeping in in spite of honest and resolute opposition of what at the first were unwelcome and even sinful doubts.'[19] Could it be that by the 1890s Bland had come to believe deep within that he was putting forward from the pulpit a conception of the kingdom he had once accepted, still thought he ought to believe, but no longer did? Could it be that he had not yet quite summoned the courage to give full voice to the range of radical social reforms necessary to bring about the earthly kingdom of Watson and of Grant, a spiritual domain manifested in the secular and material reforms brought about by Christians intent upon a better life for all?

No definitive answer can yet be given to these questions, but it is likely that Bland's admission of spiritual turmoil in the 1890s was, if anything, understated. The fact is that his insistence on individual regeneration and a transcendent kingdom in 1899 was antithetical to his experience at Queen's. Second, within a very few years Bland was to do a complete about face on these very theological matters. In 1903 he moved to Wesley College, Winnipeg, as professor of church history and New Testament exegesis, thereby becoming for a few years a colleague of George Blewett. The complete change of environment, his reading of the works of British and American social reformers, his talks with Blewett, and the fact that life in the boom city of the west involved daily confrontation with the 'social crisis' in its numerous aspects – each undoubtedly contributed to his complete 'conversion' within a few years of his arrival. 'The idea emphasized by Jesus,' he told an overflow interdenominational audience in the Winnipeg City Hall in 1906, 'was that of the kingdom, not of heaven but the kingdom of God on earth. Christianity was not a sort of immigration society to assist us from the hurly burly of this world to heaven; it was to bring the spirit of heaven to earth. ... Christianity,' he went on, 'meant the triumph of public ownership. He believed in public ownership because it is an essential part of the kingdom of God on earth. It meant the substitution of co-operation for competition.'[20]

The radicalization of Salem Bland's social views is well known. What must be noted is simply that the way had been cleared for him on the road to his Damascus. By the time he received his honorary degree from Queen's he had been introduced to the idealist's conception of the essence of Christianity – a religion shorn of traditional doctrine and based on an organic and progressive evolution of society. These assumptions pervaded Bland's writings in the new century. It was also a religion which necessarily had to meet the test of reason; and reason itself was seen as the manifestation of the religious consciousness in thought. In the third place, his had become a faith that separated the concerns of theology from those of ethics, and in so doing clearly subordinated the former to the latter. 'Theology,' Bland told the 1914 Methodist Conference, 'is a very secondary consideration in the Christian life, and it has had too high a place in the Christian church from the beginning.'[21]

Like Watson and Grant, Bland delighted in using dialectical methods to establish dazzling argumentative advantage, and complaints about the alleged 'materialistic society' of the Laurier years furnished one such opportunity. We are told this is a materialistic age, he declared in his column in the 1918 *Grain Growers' Guide*; but it is in fact not materialistic enough. In words that directly echoed those of Principal Grant in the 1880s on the relation of religion to secular life, Bland insisted that Christianity could no longer 'be treated as a distinct realm or department of life ... It has no independent existence ... It is life itself.' Christianity must always, to be vital, be manifested in concrete experience. 'One hears sometimes,' he went on, 'the phrase Applied Christianity. It is only as it is materialized that it reveals itself.' Hence, neither doctrines nor sacred ceremonies constitute part of true religious fellowship. That is 'to be found in the processes of industry and commerce. Co-operation in commerce and industry is the real Holy Communion.'[22]

Thus was the Hegelian dialectic used to a degree and with a confidence that could have been equalled in Canada only by Watson himself. 'Let us not be afraid of materialism,' Bland concluded in triumph. 'We are safe if we materialized everything including our religion. Then the long continued and deadly divorce between the spiritual and the material will be brought to an end. Spirituality will be nowhere because it will be everywhere.'[23]

The social thought of J.S. Woodsworth, perhaps Canada's best known social gospeller, was shaped – like Bland's – by influences as diverse as his reading lists; yet he, too, came under the influence of British idealism. Unsettled after an intellectually disturbing year at Victoria College in 1898, he was persuaded to study at Oxford. His faith already shaken by the forms of 'modernism' taught at Victoria, Woodsworth concentrated at Oxford upon Christian ethics. He found himself even more disturbed with Canadian Methodism in its traditional form, however, after he had read philosophy with Edward Caird and religion with Andrew

Fairbairn. While there, he was also in contact with George Blewett, to whom he was distantly related. At one point he puzzled over the fact that philosophers appeared to be forging a radical separation of ethics from Christian theology, and, in a letter home, noted that 'Blewett, one day speaking of this phase of the work, laughingly described himself as a pagan.' Indeed, Woodsworth added, 'it is true we take no account of the Christian revelation ...' By 1911, upon the publication of his study of urban problems, *My Neighbour*, Woodsworth had largely come to grips with the seemingly pagan implications of Blewett's message, and Blewett could write to him, upon receipt of his book: 'You and Fred Stephenson and men like you and he, are the true light and heart of our church in its work for the country.'[24]

In fact there were good reasons why Blewett should have congratulated Woodsworth, for the latter's new book fully accorded with Blewett's own social teachings. Blewett's *The Study of Nature and the Vision of God*, published four years before *My Neighbour*, had stressed philosophically that Woodsworth's new work stated in practical terms. 'And the truth of the world,' Blewett had concluded, 'the truth both of ourselves and of the world, is God; God, and that 'far-off divine event' which is the purpose of God, are the meaning of the world. And this means that the citizenship to which we are called is a heavenly citizenship; but it also means that that heavenly citizenship must first be fulfilled upon the earth, in the life in which our duties are those of the good neighbour, the honest citizen, the devoted churchman. The perfection of human life lies in being at one with God; but to that oneness with God men can come, not by departure from the world into eternal quietude, but only by flinging themselves into the labours and causes of the history in which God is realizing His eternal purpose.'[25]

These final passages of Blewett's book might well have served as an epitaph to the rest of Woodsworth's life.

How close were the views of the idealists and the social gospellers to the 'mainstream' of opinion in the major Protestant churches? It may be claimed by some that Watson and Blewett were, after all, merely academic philosophers, and that Bland and Woodsworth represented the vanguard rather than the mainstream of religious opinion on social questions. To an extent, of course, this claim is true. Yet even those not technically idealists or social gospellers gradually came to bear the marks of both. We might, by way of conclusion, examine briefly the thought of the man who was to lead Canadian Methodists into Church Union in 1925: S.D. Chown.

Elected general superintendent in 1910, a position he held with Albert Carman until Carman's retirement in 1914, Chown exuded the new liberal and forward-looking spirit. What most strikes one about Chown's views by the second decade of the twentieth century is the complete substitution of sociological concerns for theological ones. His thought suggests in what peculiar terrains of Christian social thought a man could arrive who began his journey working from the inspiration of Canadian idealists. In 1914 Chown gave a lecture on 'Socialism and the Social Teachings of Jesus,' and commenced it by acknowledging his indebtedness to 'Dr Watson.' 'The Sermon on the Mount,' he went on to say, 'which is the very charter of Christianity and the constitution of the Kingdom Christianity came to realize, contemplates society as reorganized, inspired, and upheld by superficial brotherly love. The sayings of Christ therein contained are a picture in outline, and a prophecy of the perfect social state which is to be when Christianity comes into its own.'[26]

For Chown, only the establishment of what he described as a 'systematic sociology' would usher in the perfect social state. Only 'a perfect sociology perfectly applied will result in the establishment of the Kingdom of God,' he once stated in a lecture called 'The Relation of Sociology to the Kingdom of Heaven.' His was the eschatology of a man uncertain as to whether he should be a clergyman or a social scientist (but who saw no reason why he could not simultaneously be both). His lectures on sociology are excellent illustrations of a certain stage in the transmutation of Christian moral philosophy of the nineteenth-century variety into a moralistic, yet essentially secular, study of social relationships. The law upon which this sociology must be based, he insisted, was 'moral laws,' and the culture which arises 'from a well directed study of sociology is not simply intellectual' but 'partakes also of moral discipline.'[7]

The code of conduct that was to give substance to this moral rigour was one centred in the *conduct* of Christ, not in his divinity or in the meaning of his blood sacrifice. 'One of the most extraordinary signs of the times,' noted Chown with obvious approval, 'is that, while many of the doctrines which centre about Christ have to great multitudes almost lost their meaning, his personality and his social teaching have acquired an interest never before felt. This trend of events gives direction to the development of the science of theology to-day, and is giving immense impetus to the coming of the Kingdom.' So it was, and Chown's own views helped channel Canadian Protestantism along this direction. Lacking a systematic program either in theology or in sociology (in fact Chown's sociology was anything but 'systematic' in any meaningful sense), he had been left with a Christ who was, at least in part, 'Hellenized' – a Christ who embodied in his conduct, not only traditional Christian morality but also the standards informing the 'sweetness and light' of Matthew Arnold's conception of culture. Why should the student of the ministry study sociology? asked Chown. 'I should say, firstly, for the sake of culture ... A sociologist who is true to the ideals of his science is particularly inclined to resist the utilitarian and commercial spirit of the times. This is so because he stands for justice; for sweetness and light amongst men rather than for imposing material achievement.'[28]

Here was another point at which speculative idealism and Protestant theology met. Just as the British idealists had seen Kant through evolutionary and progressive Hegelian spectacles, so their vision of Christ was filtered through Hellenistic ones – for after all, Greek evolution marked a later and therefore a higher stage in the evolution of spiritual and intellectual consciousness than did the Judaic. Chown's conceptions of Christ and of culture were similar to those of Arnold (or for that matter Vincent Massey), and they were also a direct legacy of an important element in British idealism: the classical ideal. Having helped strip essential doctrines of much of their traditional import and hence metaphysical authority, they substituted a code of right conduct, of citizenship, which presumed to be Christian but which – at least as Chown gave voice to it – could be reduced to the proposition that 'The Golden Rule' was 'the sum and substance of the sociology of Jesus.'[29]

But was that quite enough to satisfy the spiritual needs and the social consciences of Christians adrift in a twentieth-century world that was not only evolutionary and much older than eighteenth-century cosmology admitted but which also gave rise to a bewildering array of alternatives to traditional religion itself? Those who in 1925 formed the United Church of Canada – Methodists, Congregationalists, and most Presbyterians – apparently thought so, for no church leader more embodied the new ecumenical and forward-looking spirit than did the popular S.D. Chown. It is commonplace in Canadian religious historiography to observe that there was a singular absence of theological discussion during the debates on Church Union. Pressing problems in the west, it is said, created powerful forces for Protestant union that made churchmen set aside their theological and doctrinal differences. Doubtless this was so, but if the influence of philosophical idealism upon Protestant thought in Canada resembled that suggested here, there may not have been many theological questions the advocates of union would have deemed important enough to debate.

In 1925, as one of the consequences of the creation of the United Church of Canada, the venerable Methodist magazine *The Christian Guardian* passed out of existence. Its place was taken by another journal whose very title reflected the profound reorientation of Anglo-Canadian social thought in the previous decades. The new magazine was called the *New Outlook*. Whereas the *Guardian* had been a kind of sentry in its protection of inherited tradition, accepted wisdom, and a closed Anglo-Canadian community, the *New Outlook* was more an advance scout in its orientation towards the contingencies made necessary by social change, shifts in thought, and communities in flux. A critical balance had been tipped.

8

Science, Authority, and
the American Empire

The intellectual and social reorientation of Canada that had begun in the 1870s was by no means complete half a century later. By the 1920s the sense of moral 'rootlessness' found largely in academic circles earlier was coming to be expressed in magazines of general interest to the articulate middle class. One such magazine was the Canadian Forum, *founded in 1920, but inspired by the disintegrating effects of the Great War. By the 1920s however, one could no longer address the question of science without also considering the implications of industrial technology; and technology could not be evaluated apart from the framework of the values associated with the major exporter of modern technology: the United States. Canada's intellectual concerns were necessarily, by the 1920s, also connected with the country's place in North America and the industrial world of modern capitalism. This article was published as 'Science, Values and the American Empire: the* Canadian Forum *in the 1920s' in the* Journal of American Culture 2 (1980): 669–718.*

'At present we are compelled as a nation to concern ourselves rather with the maintenance, than with the reform of the social system.' *Canadian Forum*, 1921

'Surely there has never been a moment in history when the torrent of life has rushed through the rapids at such breakneck speed. Everywhere our inherited institutions, social, moral, and political, are being questioned, criticised, tested, pulled apart, and finally remodelled or thrown aside.' *Canadian Forum*, 1927

Whenever an intelligent undergraduate wishes to improve his prospects for a good grade in post-Confederation Canadian history, he knows that one way of doing so is to construct his assigned essay in such a manner that it contains evidence which not only documents his specific topic but also shows a relevant connection to issues presently deemed of importance. If he is fortunate enough to have a topic which allows him to criticize imperialism, or to deal with movements of social or political protest (and if he has done any secondary reading at all), chances are he knows that the evidence he requires can be found within the pages of the *Canadian Forum* in its first decade of operation. There he can find prophetic critiques of the Versailles Treaty from a refreshingly radical Canadian viewpoint, or an indictment of Canadian corporate capitalism and industrial conditions by the man who (he could cleverly point out) would later be instrumental in founding the CCF. He can find a defence of 'Group Government' by a leading exponent of that concept. He can find all of this, and much more of a similar nature, in the major articles of the *Canadian Forum* during the 1920s.[1] There is, however, another side of the *Forum*, not so well known but no less significant. By reading not only these lead articles but the 'minor' contributions, book reviews, poetry, and 'Science' column as well, one can see a rather different facet of concern on the part of its contributors and staff. There is revealed here a side of the *Forum* decidedly less radical than that which our undergraduate has seen.

As with the Canadian journals of informed opinion on current affairs that had preceded it, the *Canadian Forum* can be seen searching for a means of achieving and maintaining social and cultural stability and direction in a world which seemed to be increasingly without adequate sources of authority. And to a large extent its attention, like theirs, was necessarily drawn towards developments in modern science. The *Canadian Monthly and National Review, Rose-Belford's Canadian Monthly and National Review, Belford's Monthly, The Week*, the *University Magazine* and *Queen's Quarterly* had each been intensely concerned with the impact of 'science' (never really defined) upon human thought and actions, the consequences of scientific thought upon metaphysics, the changing conception of God, the role and survival of 'liberal education,' the nature of 'culture,' and the place of Canada in North America. So, now, did the *Canadian Forum*; and its concern was intensified by the fact that the end of the Great War had meant for many a sharp break with the past and the traditions which were believed to constitute the social bond. Many in Canada may still have given voice to 'the great myths of the nineteenth century,' as W.L. Morton has claimed, but their very reliance upon the shibboleths, the beliefs and heritage of the European community dictated that these same Canadians should also in some measure be, like the rest of the postwar world, 'involuntary bedouins in a desert of the soul.'[2] As one Canadian journalist, whose writings depended heavily upon the vocabulary of the nineteenth century, observed: 'Two years after the Great War finds the world in a state of chaos.' He went on, and his combination of a profound sense of aimless drift with a stock set of Victorian solutions probably mirrored the thoughts of many: 'The swimmer has touched bottom and found its feet, but he is wearied, spent, still half-dazed, half-blinded, and at the mercy of the undertow, which tosses him hither and yon. By and by he will crawl painfully over the hard shingle with bruised and bleeding feet; stretched out on the warm sand and take possession for good, it is to be hoped, of a new continent. And it will be no happy isle ... but a realm demanding all the old qualities of steadfastness, hard work, sacrifice and loyalty to the best that is in the race. The swimmer is the modern man-child; the ocean the tremendous psychological upheaval caused by the war, and the island the changed conditions of human existence on this planet.'[3] Like those who wrote for Canadian periodicals prior to the war, contributors to the *Canadian Forum* during the 1920s were faced with the corrosive presence of modern critical thought and the 'tremendous psychological upheaval' that seemed to follow it; unlike most of their predecessors, however, they could use few shibboleths to evade thinking of the consequences of that thought.

The *Canadian Forum* had evolved from an undergraduate journal, *The Rebel*, begun in 1917 and run by students and faculty members at the University of Toronto. Faculty members on this venture were C.B. Sissons, professor of classics and ancient history, Barker Fairley, who taught German, and S.H. Hooke, professor of Oriental languages. Fairley and Hooke had been recent immigrants from the British Isles. 'We are no believers in the ultimate ability of things to right themselves,' Sissons warned in *The Rebel*'s first issue. But his *caveat* was followed immediately by a qualification. *The Rebel*'s creed was one which stood for 'a progress that is not violently destructive but gradually constructive ... It realizes that existing conditions are themselves the result of previous progress and have their place in society's fabric.'[4] This spirit of cautious liberalism, as much concerned with social stability as with social democracy, continued into the *Canadian Forum* when, in 1920, Sissons, Fairley, and Hooke decided to turn their energies from *The Rebel* in an attempt to create a periodical of national interest and wider scope.

Besides industrial and social unrest, the Great War brought the nineteenth century in Canada to a shattering end. As its historians had chronicled, that century had seen the nation grow immensely in material wealth; physically, politically, and economically its history to 1914 had largely been deemed a success. But Ypres, the Somme, and the horrid, inhuman truth of trench warfare challenged all of this, and questioned the validity of the nineteenth century's major premises: the inevitability of progress and the humanity of man. 'Who shall undo what has been done?' asked one Toronto undergraduate in the pages of *The Rebel*:

> Who shall give back to us yesterday's sun?
> Who shall bring back as it was before
> The light that is quenched and the life that is o'er?

When the sun gladdens after the hail
    The strewn blades do not rise;
When the calm succeeds the gale
    The wreck on the leashore lies;
When the thunderbolts are shed
    The stricken tree no more
Raise her revirescent head –
Nothing shall be as it was before.[5]

In such a world could there be such a thing as 'immutable' values? Was man really by nature a 'moral' being? Were values not subject to the whims and fancies of power-hungry politicians, and likely to be discarded as matters of state dictated? 'One of the most disquieting things about life as it is to-day,' wrote another *Rebel* staff member (probably S.H. Hooke), 'is the way in which values are being hastily jettisoned, relegated to peacetimes; as though life were not a unity ... The only logical issue seems to me to be the acknowledgement either that our values were wrong, were not essential, and have been tried and found wanting ... or that we ourselves have never really held them for values; was only a pose, a garment which was stripped from us.'[6]

In a universe where Albert Einstein had recently (1915) shown even time and space to be relative, was it possible for anything to have absolute value? The Newtonian conception of the universe as a mechanism had been severely tried during the nineteenth century, and had been found seriously wanting; by 1900 the impact of Darwin, Spencer, and Marx was strong enough for most people to have come to view their universe in evolutionary, organic, and material terms. Biblical criticism and the work of natural scientists seemed to undermine the authority of the Pentateuch. Einstein's theories of relativity dictated that the universe must be conceived in terms not of matter but of energy. For a time this had provided room for a renewed debate between the exponents of the authority of science and that of religion, for where there was 'energy' (not yet conceived by all in terms of molecular theory), there might also be room for God. Then, however, came developments in Quantum mechanics and theory, which postulated that even radiant energy itself was finite. Once again, the possibility of a 'life of the spirit' was called into question.

If there were not then any spiritual 'absolutes,' could it be possible to view life in metaphysical terms? In the world of the atom, could there be a domain of the soul? The implications of such questions for orthodox Christianity were obvious. But the threat to the possibility of giving transcendence to any aspect of life posed a problem just as serious to the value-laden concept of 'culture.' 'Culture' and 'faith' had been inseparable for Matthew Arnold, and the fact that his famous definition occurs not only in *Culture and Anarchy* but also in *Literature and Dogma* is proof of this. For Arnold, education and religion were vitally enmeshed, bonded not so much because education was to instill religious values or because religion was to be educative, as for the common element upon which both depended: faith – faith in the essentially supra-rational basis of revealed religion and faith in the ability of men to find valid criteria by which to determine what *was* the best that had been thought and said in the world.[7]

Beyond all else, the Canadian educators and public figures who contributed to Canadian periodicals of informed public opinion in the 1920s were searching for sources of authority upon which to base their own faith in Canada's future development. But faith in what? Faith in the traditional institutions of Christianity, when these institutions were every day being challenged on the basis of failing to 'keep pace' with society? Faith in the liberal arts educational programs, which failed to equip young men and women for life in the commercial and material world of Bay Street? 'Supposing all the inherited theologies were swept out of existence tomorrow what would abide?' asked the editor of *The Onlooker* early in 1921.[8] 'The religion of conduct and the exquisite flower of faith. Faith ... would not die, for faith is just complete and absolute resignation to our final summing up of life.' But again, faith in what? Here he gave an answer which was characteristic of the general response of a growing number of Canadians during the 1920s. 'We may be sure that God is speaking to this age in thunder-tones, and, as never before ... through the method and techniques of science and the final triumph of this method – this law – will mean the uplifting of all mankind to heights of mastery, and power hitherto undreamed of.' Faced with the apparent bankruptcy of political and religious institutions in Canada, Hodgins elevated 'Science' – only an abstraction in his mind – to the level of a metaphysic. Science could solve the ills of society, for it provided a juncture where 'God and man meet ... and mingle, spirit with spirit, in ideals ... The whole fabric of life could fall into ruins if ... no trace of an ideal could be found.'[9] It seems not to have occurred to him that the country whose values he so detested, the United States,[10] led the world in scientific development; that the encroachment of American popular 'culture,' of which he was so afraid, largely meant the increasing impact of American technology; that this technological development, while increasing the nation's productive capacity, also meant the coming of an approach to life which tended to measure success in terms of utility and valued most highly that which was material; and that this approach to life, by elevating its 'means' to the level of ends, threatened the values which he so desperately wished to preserve. It meant, in his own words, 'materialism without a soul.'[11]

One of the main reasons for the relative confidence of the British-Canadian cultural elite prior to the First World War had been, sectarian differences aside, the existence of a firm Protestant conviction.[12] In the years following the war, confidence in such a conviction required more faith than ever. 'The modern man has the scientific temper, and is therefore prepared to welcome all results achieved by the application of scientific methods, whether in the field of biblical scholarship, scientific discovery or in any other legitimate sphere of inquiry,' wrote the principal of Wesleyan Theological College, Montreal. 'In Loyalty to his intellectual integrity he is prepared to follow wherever truth leads, and is not unduly disturbed if this should mean the abandonment of some long cherished assumptions.'[13] Such a man, like his American counterpart, was beginning to develop a 'faith in the efficacy of science to solve all problems' and an essentially anti-historical, 'technical view of Reason' which he felt alone could promote progress.[14]

With regard to the church, 'modern man,' as revealed in the *Canadian Forum*, insisted that in the process of postwar 'reconstruction' the relationship of the church to society be re-examined. One observer wondered whether the church should not properly be regarded as an institution in the same class as a trade union or a university club; or whether it should concentrate on maintaining its 'inherent organic life' and treat problems of polity and structure as matters of minor significance. To follow the latter path meant that the church might possibly be regarded as a relic of the 'age of faith,' more concerned with the perpetuation of dogma than with curing social ills; to follow the former meant social involvement, but the church then ran the risk of losing its theology in order to be 'relevant': 'Many earnest people ... are inclined to make a religion out of the call for social justice. But religion and social reform are not synonymous. More is needed than social enthusiasm to meet permanently the spiritual aspirations of the human heart. Religion in its essence is a response to the ideal and the eternal. It is life in connection with the unseen.'[15] For those whose world outlook precluded the possibility of conceiving of religion purely in terms of a transcendent external authority, such statements held little meaning. The kind of religious sentiment Smyth saw in 'modern man' was merely a vague expression of belief in 'the kingdom of God.' This modern man's conception of salvation was not one in which God saved man from the possibility of hell through an atonement for one's sins; it was, instead, a 'deliverance from all that is opposed to the ideals of the Kingdom and their realization in the life of the individual and in society.'[16] It meant, in short, a social gospel which had as much in common with Auguste Comte as it did with Walter Rauschenbusch.

The *Canadian Forum* quickly picked up the various controversies which divided Christian theologians during the 1920s. In 1923 a vigorous debate took place within its pages concerning the role of the church in society. In 'The Saving of the Church,' S.H. Hooke argued that the true measure of the Kingdom of Heaven depended not upon institutional structures but on the various activities which were fused in religion. 'For true worship is life glorified; it is not merely the assertion that the Kingdom of Heaven exists, but the achieving of it by man.' A month later, Davidson Ketchum countered Hooke's argument by claiming that precisely this frame of mind had helped to produce what now constituted the greatest threat to religion: science; for under the influence of scientific development men tended increasingly to view God as some kind of mystical, pantheistic 'spirit of all life.' This meant the subversion of the Trinitarian conception of God and therefore spelled the coming of His death as the 'personal God' of institutional Christianity. 'That no direct attack is being made upon the Church is no reason for tranquility, for science advances, not by attacking her foes frontally, but by outflanking them.'[17]

These articles provoked a number of letters to the editor. Several claimed that science could not make judgments about ultimate reality, and could not thereby threaten the authority of religion.[18] Another asked: 'what place is left for the affections if we substitute for a personal God a vague, indeterminate, impersonal abstraction called ''the Spirit of all life''? ... If we are going to think of God in terms of energy, are we not likely to be surer of His power than of His holiness? Of His ruthlessness than of His goodness? For do not the ''great processes of nature'' really manifest Him in that moral character?' This correspondent, of St James Cathedral in Toronto, agreed with Ketchum that by explaining Him 'biologically,' as a 'product of evolutionary forces, a manifestation ... of the tendency of the Spirit that is in all life,' the New Theology was undermining the Trinitarian doctrine.[19] Still another wrote that man has for ages been 'searching for God' and added that while 'human scientific research may throw light on historical aspects, God Himself will always remain unknowable. Knowing God – the omniscient – will never be achieved by a simple accumulation of knowledge.'[20] As months passed on, the vigour of the debate was such that Hooke, who had started the controversy within the *Forum*, was moved to write that those who were questioning the church were not trying to make an organized attack on religion, but were merely searching for its true basis: 'the appeal to authority, whether of the Bible or of the Church, has lost its force.'[21] But this remark only provoked a renewed round of letters to the editor by those with similar concerns but different solutions.

The relationship of the church to society was being called into question in part because the discoveries of science (and its handmaiden, 'technology') were making the notion of a spiritual Kingdom of God increasingly untenable as a basis for belief. But this was only one major direction in which science threatened the authority of the church as an institution responsible for the transmission of 'absolute' moral and spiritual values. The postwar world saw the full impact upon intellectual circles not only of the new physics but also of an area of science that was then reaching a maturity of expression not hitherto known. 'Psychology' was coming into its own as an independent branch of science. Canadian theologians, like others around the world, had therefore to contend not only with Albert Einstein but with Sigmund Freud and John B. Watson as well. Just as the spirit in the outside world was being transmuted into 'energy,' so the centuries-old distinction between mind and body, greatly weakened by a century of intensive research in chemistry and physiology, began to dissolve under the impact of psychoanalytic probing and behavioural conditioning. Here again, the response of Canadian theologians and interested laymen was strong, and naturally concerned with the philosophical and theoretical implications for the soul in a body governed not by 'will' but by irrational, primitive desires.[22]

Yet the debate that occurred with the *Canadian Forum* and in the *Canadian Journal of Religious Thought* (which began publication in 1924 and in which several major contributors to the *Forum* placed articles) was a distinctly ambivalent one. While concerned about the 'spirit,' commentators were rarely willing to reject, out of hand, scientific developments in this area. In 1924 Ernest F. Scott, professor of New Testament literature at the Union Theological Seminary in New York (he had occupied the same chair at Queen's Theological College, Kingston, Ontario, for eleven years before that), expressed his concern about psychology because of its assumption that the mind was a mechanism and that understanding mechanical processes constituted knowledge of ultimate reality. What psychology failed to do, he felt, was to question the reality *behind* the mechanism. 'An engine gives you power – but what *is* the power which it calls into action?' Psychology, then, was for Scott a science with severe limitations. Scientists, he noted, observe religious sentiment and think they have *explained* the spiritual facts – yet they only have the *illusion* of knowledge. What they had neglected was the very premise of Scott's philosophy: that 'Life is free and incalculable,' not 'subject to definite laws.'[23]

Scott's article stimulated a reply by G.S. Brett, professor of philosophy at the University of Toronto and, next to John Watson of Queen's, considered to be Canada's leading philosopher.[24] As an historian of psychology from Greek times to the present, Brett was considerably more sympathetic to developments in modern psychology. Indeed, he felt that only by trying to understand the science could Canadians make work a democracy based upon public opinion. Nor was Brett the only academic to find value in the new science. In the *Canadian Forum*, R.M. MacIver (another Toronto staff member) reviewed Carl Jung's book *Psychological Types* (which first put forth the terms 'introvert' and 'extrovert') in a highly favourable vein. Brett himself reviewed, not unfavourably, D.H. Lawrence's *Psychoanalysis and the Unconscious* and *Fantasia of the Unconscious*. Peter

Sandiford, of the *Canadian Forum* editorial staff, assumed the task of reviewing John B. Watson's epoch-making work, *Behaviourism*. As he noted, behaviourism denied any valid meaning for words such as 'mind,' 'mental,' and all other subjective terms, for it meant a view of the human being solely as an organism: as an animal whose every response, mental and physical, was governed by reactions to sensory stimuli. He put the challenge posed by such a psychology in the form of a rhyme: 'First psychology lost its soul, / Then it lost its mind, / Then it lost consciousness; / It still has behaviour, of a kind'.[25]

Altogether, such criticism had important effects upon several of the Protestant churches in Canada. It caused their leadership to submit their creeds to critical questioning at a time when many of their adherents were convinced that an emphasis on 'faith' was needed to combat the influences of materialism and the values it tended to instil. Because of the impact of science and historical criticism upon society, these churches were increasingly forced to defend themselves on grounds that tended to undermine faith in a transcendent God: that is, that they were not inconsistent with 'Reason,' and that they, too, could be made 'relevant.' Most important of all, however, was the fact that as the century progressed and the various debates on theology and sources of morality continued, people seemed to be looking increasingly away from the churches as a pillar upon which to base the new social order. As one theologian noted: 'Many to-day are ready to dismiss religion as a form of culture that has been left behind in the march of the race. It is a survival, we are told ... The field it claims has been taken by science.'[26]

While institutional religion in Canada was being subjected both to external and internal assaults, Canadian higher education during the 1920s was comparatively stable, although itself subject to considerable strain. Its main problem was to justify the role of 'liberal education' in a society which was increasingly business-oriented and whose values were more and more assessed according to their utility. Prior to the Great War, the notion of a 'liberal education' had been a central part of the cultural orthodoxy which had prevailed at the universities.[27] While even then social tendencies had been seen to pose a threat (at least as perceived by the culturally orthodox) to 'liberal education,' the strength of this idealistic tradition[28] was sufficient to make any significant questioning of the actual value of this kind of education for an industrial society tantamount to questioning the institutions of motherhood and the two-party system. (The extent to which this was heretical can be seen by the numerous jeremiads by the contributors to the *University Magazine* on the subject.[29]) By the 1920s, however, it was apparent to most that industrial might, not the power of ideals, had won the war; and Canadian educators in the liberal arts were forced increasingly to define and defend their function and use within society. The defensive posture which they were forced to assume is clearly evident within the pages of the *Canadian Forum*.

Responding to a claim by the secretary of the Civil Service Commission that university education in Canada did not adequately train applicants for positions such as junior trade commissioner, *Forum* contributor J.A. Dale was forced to assess the relationship between industry and education. 'The terms, aims, and products of other industries are definite and realizable ... With education there is no such clearness. The question, What is education? brings many and confusing answers.' Only half aware of the fact that he was doing so, Dale then revealed the dilemma of 'liberal education' in Canada at the time: 'For education is in the apparently paradoxical position of being an instrument both of change and of tradition – at once training in active thinking and a perpetuation of fixed ideas.'[30] Was its purpose to retain a social order based upon the maintenance and passing on of 'the best which has been known and said in the world'? Or was it to precipitate and discover the solution to social ills through the process of trial-and-error? Was its purpose social control or social change? In 1920 the president of the University of Toronto, Sir Robert Falconer, had published a collection of addresses entitled *Idealism in National Character*. In it, he had stated the choice for educators in a different way: 'Our education is twofold, to recall the people to ancient and established truths and to turn their feet through the advance of science into ever-widening paths of liberty. Urbanity is the child of learning and of inherited virtue; science is the product of a brighter day of freedom.'[31] Falconer had seen both elements of education as necessary for the progress towards a national life built upon an 'intellectual and moral idealism.'[32] The relationship of science to technology, of technology to business, and of business to material values which could serve to undermine the kind of 'urbanity' wished by Falconer went largely unnoticed in the depressed conditions which followed on the heels of war's end; but by the mid-1920s it was increasingly obvious that the cultural implications of the advancement of science were far from being entirely consonant with 'liberal education' as certain Canadian educators conceived of that term.

Members of the Canadian academic profession in the liberal arts differed little from each other in their conceptions of the nature of a 'liberal education.' Writing in *The Rebel* in 1918, W.P.M. Kennedy had seen its purpose as 'the building up of character ... "to build up the household of faith"' – in order to make students 'leaders of public opinion, courageous guides to the new Canada, men and women of strong character.' As Arnold had written, students in the arts at Canadian universities were not to be

> ... like the men of the crowd.
> Who all around me to-day
> Bluster or cringe, and make life
> Hideous and arid and vile –

> But souls tempered with fire,
> Fervent, heroic and good,
> Helpers and friends of mankind.[33]

With these lines from 'Rugby Chapel,' Kennedy ended his essay.
In the *Canadian Journal of Religious Thought* seven years later, H.P. Whidden, chancellor of McMaster University, approached the same subject upon somewhat more philosophical grounds. 'Liberal education,' he wrote, 'should seek to relate the individual to his universe.' In doing so, it would be fulfilling Kant's dictum that 'Man's greatest concern is to know how he shall properly fill his place in the universe and understand what he must be in order to be a man.' Science, he felt, would not pose a problem to the values of a liberal education if the student kept in mind that 'the purpose of a truly liberal education should not be to produce scientific expertise, but to fuse knowledge of science and literature in the study of the "universal things in human life."' He added that the student must always recognize that 'man is a spiritual being and that he should live for spiritual ends.' An educated person must not only have knowledge, but have knowledge of a certain type: 'What mankind needs more than anything else is spiritual knowledge. We are getting knowledge fast ... but most of it is applied to material things ... We need an increased power of salvation, and that must be a spiritual power. The mental side of man has been developed ... while his spiritual side has been starved. What is needed now is a development of that spiritual side so that it will hold the rest of the new knowledge and make it safe.'[34] Whidden found in the spiritual resources of a 'liberal education' the authority and security that Canadian imperialists such as Sir Andrew Macphail had found in being part of the British empire, and James Cobourg Hodgins (editor of *The Onlooker*) had sought by extolling the virtues of the Anglo-Saxon race.[35] Each of these rationalizations served as a source of authority that allowed its believer to conceive of himself as more than merely the human animal that modern thought made out he was; it made him part of a seemingly infinite nature of things, part of a social order that had some purpose and direction. Like W.P.M. Kennedy, H.P. Whidden ended his definition and defence of a 'liberal education' with a stanza of verse which embodied, for him, its essence and its aim:

> This, then, is yours: to build exultingly,
> > High and yet more high,
> ...
> That so man's mind, not conquered by his clay,
> > May sit above his fate,
> Inhabiting the purpose of the stars.
> And trade with his eternity.

If the aims and ideals of a 'liberal education' were defined (albeit vaguely) in terms of asserting the supremacy of the 'spiritual' side of life over that of the material and the practical, such definitions were not without their own measure of utility: their purpose was to combat the utilitarian and the material. 'Even before the war, the scientific movement was becoming increasingly strong,' wrote a contributor to *Queen's Quarterly* in 1918, 'in part a natural result of the tremendous industrial development of the last half of the nineteenth century. The discovery by the great mass of the "comforts" of modern civilization, had so emphasized the truth of Herbert Spencer's arguments that even in educational circles the pendulum was swinging more and more to the scientific side. The war has but accelerated this movement.'[36] Exponents of a 'liberal education' frequently felt that this influence tended to confuse the means of education with its ends. 'The Fruits of learning lie in the character formed, not in the prizes won,' warned a *Rebel* contributor. This was important for them, for only by concentrating on the formation of 'character' could they instill in the nation's future leaders the qualities of 'insight, of vision' necessary for the preservation of 'civilization' and 'culture' as they defined these terms. Only then would they know what *was* in fact the best that had been known and said in the world.[37]

The Great War did little, if anything, to make their task easier. Developments in communications and technology made it clear that the major threat to the perpetuation of a system of education (or for that matter a society) with such ideals seemed to be the United States. The decade of the 1920s saw Canada come increasingly under its economic and social influence. By 1922 the Toronto correspondent for the *New York World*, quoting from official Canadian sources, could note that 'at the present time Americans own at least 50% of the total manufacturing capital employed in the Dominion.' Americans, he reported, controlled 61 per cent of the capital in the Canadian motor car industry, 41 per cent in the meatpacking industry, 40 per cent of the rubber, 53.1 per cent of the petroleum, 27 per cent of the lumbering, and 24 per cent of the pulp and paper industry.[38] The Winnipeg-based *Canadian Finance* wondered that 'the surprizing thing is that we were not Americanized generations ago,' especially considering the fact that Canadians 'read American journals; use American machinery and appliances; see American pictures ... listen to American preachers and public men; read news of international events as prepared for the American people and therefore from the American view-point.' By the mid-1920s Gilbert Jackson was to marvel, in his regular *Canadian Forum* column, at the ability of the United States to increase production when the rest of the world seemed in a state of economic stagnation, and declared it natural for Canadians to compare their lot with that of Americans. Another *Canadian Forum* staff member, Richard De Brisay, noted the increasing tendency on the part of Canadians to worry over the economic state of their country. ' "What's wrong with Canada?" is becoming a common question wherever Canadians gather,' he wrote. 'The basic cause of the present stagnation is probably that, in common with most western nations, we are suffering from the fact that we have not yet adjusted our social, financial, and industrial systems to the new conditions which the advances of science have brought about.'[39] Not even the most die-hard opponent of a 'materialistic civilization' desired economic stagnation, however; and the fact that Canadians shared a common border with the main purveyor of the methods and products of modern scientific research only made it easier to accept a way of life not in accordance with professed public standards.

American capital investment in Canada was invisible to all but a few; the presence of products of American technology, however, was an obvious gauge of the state of the country's affluence. As a consequence, the desirability of neither was questioned by Canadians of the 1920s. Indeed, they were welcomed (as in fact they had been in the past) with general delight and increasing purchases. Yet at the same time, those whose beliefs centred on the supremacy of 'spiritual values' even in the secular realm considered the increasing material enticements of the United States to be threats as much to the national 'soul' as to the economic integrity of the country. Again one finds the most extreme statement in the pages of that one-man vigilante committee, *The Onlooker*: 'It is not the cultivated American, half of whose heart and almost the whole of whose culture is in Britain, we dread. It is commercial America we doubt. For commerce is impersonal, without sentiment, and takes no cognizance of those higher things that illuminate and enrich the national life ... Let us look the problem squarely in the face. It is the *soul* of Canada that is involved at the present moment.'[40] While Hodgins directed his attention towards the subversion of Canadian ideals by the influence of America, it will be noted that the objects of his attack were not Americans but Canadians. Here one can see the influence of his strong Calvinist background: 'The danger, in fact, is internal rot, the outcome of a careless espousal of the line of least resistance. Young nations endowed with vast national wealth and consciously on the edge of stupendous material developments are peculiarly liable to this temptation and danger ... The material, and all it stands for, comes in time to overshadow the soul.' Canada, it was clear to him, lacked the moral fiber to resist the temptations of the golden calf. A 'clean, moral race,' he noted, would never read the American cartoons which all Canadian newspapers now carried; they constituted 'a danger to all that is virile, noble, reverential and chaste in our people.' Yet he heard 'not a squeak of protest.'[41]

Hodgins' *Onlooker* marks an attempt to find stability for the social order based upon the past achievements of a race, and in its ability to lead in times of crisis; but that periodical first appeared at a time when the validity of this confidence, at least in the North American context, was questionable to some. 'We need a race of great spiritual interpreters of the order of Thomas Hill Green and Caird,' he implored; yet he could see none in sight, either in Canada or in the Mother Country. And looking aghast at the infiltration of American popular culture he could only wave an admonishing finger, as if at an impertinent child: 'this great country belongs to the descendants of those sturdy British pioneers who felled the forests ... [and] created by their inconquerable faith the beloved Canada we know and love ... an inseparable part of the mightiest and freest confederacy the world has known – the British Empire.'[42]

Hodgins was not the only person to criticize harshly the willingness of Canadians to accept, in a seemingly unquestioning fashion, American ideas, machines, and values; his magazine is remarkable mainly because of the extent to which it insisted that the return of the nineteenth-century conditions could somehow restore Canadian public virtue. Other observers – Canadian, American, and British – noticed equally the ways in which Canada was slowly being transformed, but were for the most part without this backward glance. In the *Empire Review* an observer noted in 1926 how Canada was becoming saturated with American 'ideas' because Canadians daily absorbed the 'comic strips, the full-page illustrations dealing with sex problems and domestic triangles, the silly daily fiction stories, and even the crossword puzzles ... all of American manufacture.' A correspondent for the *National Review*, writing under the significant pseudonym 'Anglo-Canadian,' lamented the fact that Canadians had adopted the 'accent, clothes, customs, and manners, and even the mental processes' of Americans.

Nor was the *Canadian Forum* without similar observations. One editorial commented on the 'booster' mentality of Canadian cities, which it noted was 'strictly in keeping with the modern urban atmosphere,' testimony to a culture the blessings of which consisted 'of Automobiles and Oil, Corsets and BVD's.[43] In 1927 appeared the first full *Forum* article specifically addressed to the American 'invasion' of Canada. As if a barker for the Barnum and Bailey, Robert Ayre began: 'On your left gentlemen – on your right, too; in fact, north, south, east and west of you – you have the great American Empire. There is nothing like it on earth; history cannot show its equal. Its people are not conscious of its greatness, but they do not know the half: it has never occurred to them that they have an empire on their hands; they call it a republic.' Dropping the carney's intonation, Ayre went on to describe the nature of the American empire with a vigour worthy of Baltimore's H.L. Mencken:

the insidious thing about the American civilization is that it is on the surface, free, and the conquered nations are forced into a desire for it ... The real conquest has come about, not with dollars or airplanes or legionaires, but with the great American machine of aggression-standardization. Caesar's methods were childish in comparison with this ... The Roman yoked the people and forced his ideas on them. The result was destruction for Rome. The American sent forth Jiggs and Maggy and Doug and Mary. A puny army to conquer the world for the Empire! But conquer the world it did. As reinforcements, out marched the Rotarian phalanxes, grins unsheathed; and what they didn't do was done by the terrorism of the jazz bands. These, along with the kodak, Christian Science, Singer sewing machines, and the Ford car have swept the world off its feet into the grab bag of the great Empire.[44]

American trade statistics published the next year seemed to lend additional credence to Ayre's assessments. It was reported that 'Canada now buys more goods from us, and sells more to us, than any other nation.'[45]

While Canadians were well aware of the differences which American popular culture and technology were making to their own ways of life, the tumbled-down, postwar world made them value economic stability more than the quality of their cultural life. This was especially true for the man who did not get to university, and probably not to high school, for it was he most of all who was affected by postwar economic fluctuations. It was also this man who sought to raise his own level of existence by seeking to possess the benefits and wonders made possible by American technical genius, and to relieve the monotony of long days at work by the cheap and amusing entertainment which the funny-papers and the corner theatre provided.

Affected, too, was the generation of Canadian intellectuals who had been in their early twenties at the time of the war. Usually at university as students or junior members of staff in 1918, these were the men who were most disenchanted with the inability of traditional political and social structures to solve the ills of postwar society. For most of them, the nineteenth century meant little more than what they learned through their reading; for most of them it was now history. The majority of them who would later reach positions of political influence were well-versed in the past accomplishments of the Anglo-Saxon race; but few drew upon history for constructing the new social order. For most, the past evoked pride, but for few did it promise the key to future stability. It was of men such as these that the staff of the *Canadian Forum* was comprised in its first decade. The majority of them were secular-minded, and of rationalistic inclination. The pride of the rationalist in the twentieth century was science, and to science many of them looked in their search for authority and stability.

'Surely never was the need for the union of science and politics greater than it is to-day,' a *Rebel* contributor had written in 1917. E.E. Braithwaite, president of Western University (later renamed the University of Western Ontario), called for an increase of emphasis in physical and biological sciences, especially with their practical applications to industry and agriculture. Even the cautious *Onlooker* wondered whether the solution to Canada's crisis of faith was not in science: 'it may be that ... the universal spirit of science will gradually permeate our human intelligence and transform us all into the likeness of Truth.' Sir John Willison, too, called for an increase in the pursuit of scientific truth in the face of the problems of reconstruction.[46]

In 1925 the *Canadian Forum* began to run a regular 'Science' column, written by George Hunter. Roughly half of these articles dealt directly with various scientific developments in the areas of hygiene, bacteriology, and so forth. The remainder consisted for the most part of discussions of the relationship between science and society. The latter articles are especially interesting because of the means by which Hunter was forced to defend scientific endeavour and the tremendous expense modern scientific research incurred. 'It is necessary to make clear what is Science and in what way does a scientist differ from what we may call an "ordinary man,"' he wrote in 1926. 'Everybody,' he explained, 'is sometimes a scientist, and ... nobody is always a scientist. Nevertheless some people can more properly be called scientists than others, for the reason that some can keep prejudice out of contact with their logical faculties longer than others. We could deal with many problems more easily if we could only remember that science is knowledge which we possess and adhere to solely on the strength of our reason and logical faculty and not at all according to our will or desire.'[47] In order to defend his position against accusations of some theologians and men of letters that science exalted the cognitive faculty at the expense of one's sentiments, Hunter was often forced to adopt a stance that was a curious reversal from the experiences of American exponents and popularizers of science. During the nineteenth century they had found it necessary to justify expending government funds for 'pure' scientific research on the grounds that it had some 'useful' function in society.[48] Hunter, in contrast, found it necessary to appease Canadian critics of science by the inclusion of quotations such as this one from John Langdon-Davies, *The New Age of Faith*: 'Ninety-five men out of every hundred approach science and its works in the same spirit and through the same gateway as their ancestors approached God and His. This is why we may call the Twentieth century a new age of Faith.'[49] Just as the rhetoric of Social Darwinism in the Canadian context had earlier been used as a foil for putting forth idealist ethics, so Hunter now attempted to forge a similar bond between the pursuits of scientists and the spirit of the humanist.[50] When discussing 'scientific research' in Canada he noted the increasing reliance people were placing on the efficacy of science to cure society's ills, but again tried to allay his critics by declaring that in the end it was essentially lacking any utilitarian value. The scientific researcher was not, he maintained, a rationalistic automaton devoid of feelings, but at one with the poet: 'The curious thing is that his associates are all quite useless people. Some, like the poets, have even the reputation of being sentimental, and that is perhaps the last characteristic we should expect to find in a scientist. Sentiment, it is true, is against the rules of the game in science, yet it is, secretly, the driving force in scientific research.'[51] As the 1920s progressed, Hunter's 'Science' column continued to show the progress being made by 'Science'; but at the same time it consistently stressed its limitations as a basis of belief and the dangers inherent in its abuse.[52] Elsewhere in the *Canadian Forum*, contributors continued to defend 'liberal education' from the seductions of American values; chances were, however, that the same men drove American automobiles and reaped the benefits of American scientific, technological, and industrial research in countless other ways.

In the mid-1930s André Siegfried completed his second major analysis of Canadian life. Its first sentence summed up with precision the country's place in North America: 'At the beginning, in the middle, and in the end of any study of Canada, one must reiterate that Canada is American. History occasionally loses sight of this fact, but at every step geography imperiously recalls it. And yet a political bond does exist with the Old World, and herein lies the novelty and uniqueness of the Canadian problem.'[53] During the 1920s, as at few times before, Canadians seemed to feel the strain of their history and their geography, and part of this tension can be seen in microcosm in the pages of the *Canadian Forum* during the decade which spanned the twin catastrophes of war and depression.

The *Canadian Forum* marked a significant departure from the traditional tone of English-Canadian cultural periodicals in several respects, the most important of which was its steadfast refusal to extol the virtues of the Anglo-Saxon race or to inflate its past accomplishments. It showed, instead, a refreshing willingness to assess the problems of postwar Canada in terms of present realities and future possibilities rather than by an adherence to the dictates of the past. Yet at the same time, it also showed a deep concern for traditions which seemed to be in decline and with sources of individual and social authority that were being eroded. In this respect, the *Canadian Forum* was part of a continuing tradition of responsible and intelligent social commentary in Canadian periodicals already more than half a century old in Canada when the *Forum* was first launched.

For its contributors, the disillusionment resulting from the Great War and its end seemed to have been caused in large measure by the dislocation resulting from the war itself. In reality this was not the case, nor was America and its empire of Jiggs and Maggies to blame for changing beliefs. The real enemy was perhaps what David S. Landes has called 'the Faustian spirit of mastery,' almost as old as Western civilization itself, and reaching its logical conclusion in the late nineteenth and early twentieth centuries.[54] In the areas of religion, morality, and psychology, the decade after the Great War marked in fact only the continuation of an onslaught which perhaps had its greatest impact in Canada in the 1870s and 1880s.

But during the earlier period the sense of inherited cultural tradition had been sufficiently strong to maintain the forms, if not the substance, of cultural orthodoxy and hence stability. By the 1920s, however, this sense of tradition had been significantly shaken, and the decade witnessed as a consequence the attempts of some Canadian leaders to shore up the old cultural institutions, while others searched just as earnestly for ideals with which to build the country along new lines. All were attempting to find sources of social authority and stability; but, as a comparison of the *Canadian Forum* and the *University Magazine* or *The Onlooker* would indicate, the decade nevertheless witnessed a significant shift in the direction towards which Canadian leaders looked. Other writings by Canadians sharing these concerns reveal a similar shift: the 1920s had begun with the appeal of Sir Robert Falconer for a new idealism based upon 'the long process of education of the will rather than of the intellect'; it ended with the appeal of Frank Underhill for a new Benthamism, and the League for Social Reconstruction already in the wind.[55]

Notes

CHAPTER 1:
NATIONALISM, IDENTITY, AND CANADIAN INTELLECTUAL HISTORY

1 Frank Underhill, *The Image of Confederation* (Toronto 1964), 60. An earlier version of
my essay was given, under the title 'Perspectives and Problems in Canadian Intellectual
History,' at the Seventh Queen's Conference for Teachers of History and Social Science. The theme of the conference for 1973 was 'Changing Perspectives on Canada.'
The essay is published here in the spirit in which it was originally presented: to serve as
a basis for discussion and not as a comprehensive historiographical guide to the literature of this growing field. The author is indebted to Professors W.R. Graham and G.A.
Rawlyk, as well as to T.E. Brown and P.G. Reynolds, for suggestions and criticisms.
2 J.M. Bumsted, ed., *Canadian History before Confederation* (Georgetown, Ont. 1972),
253
3 John Higham, 'Intellectual History and its Neighbors,' *Journal of the History of Ideas*
15 (June 1954): 342
4 S.F. Wise, 'Sermon Literature and Canadian Intellectual History,' in Bumsted, *Canadian History*, 254
5 Ramsay Cook, 'Nationalism in Canada or Portnoy's Complaint Revisited,' *South
Atlantic Quarterly* 69 (1970): 2–19. Also reprinted in his *The Maple Leaf Forever*
(Toronto 1972)
6 Wise, 'Sermon Literature,' 255. This conception of identity is explored by J.M.S. Careless in 'Limited Identities in Canada,' *Canadian Historical Review* [CHR] 50 (March
1969), and is implicit in the title of the textbook, *Canada: Unity in Diversity* (Toronto
1967), by P. Cornell et al.
7 There are a few other books in Canadian intellectual history, but not many. Among the
most noteworthy are Richard Allen's study of liberal Protestantism in Canada, *The
Social Passion* (Toronto 1971), and J.A. Irving's *The Social Credit Movement in Alberta*
(Toronto 1959). These works have not been considered here because they do not
address themselves as specifically to the major themes of this essay as do those mentioned above. To have included them would have also made necessary a survey of
articles in Canadian intellectual history, and this would have meant writing an entirely

different kind of essay. Some mention should be made, however, of this article litera- ture, for in so doing the variety of subjects that in one way or another touch upon 'intel- lectual history' may be shown. Pertinent articles include Allan Smith, 'Metaphor and Nationality in North America,' CHR 50 (1970); Gad Horowitz, 'Conservatism, Liberal- ism, and Socialism in Canada: An Interpretation,' in his *Canadian Labour in Politics* (Toronto 1968); David V.J. Bell, 'The Loyalist Tradition in Canada,' *Journal of Cana- dian Studies* [JCS] 5 (1970); Terry Cook, 'John Beverley Robinson and the Conservative Blueprint for the Upper Canadian Community,' *Ontario History* [OH] 64 (1972); V. Nelles, 'Introduction' to T.C. Keefer, *The Philosophy of Railroads* (Toronto 1972); D.P. Gagan, 'The Relevance of "Canada First,"' JCS 5 (1970); Barrie Davies, 'Lampman and Religion,' *Canadian Literature* 56 (spring 1973); M. Bliss, '"Dyspepsia of the Mind": The Canadian Businessman and his Enemies,' in D. Macmillan, ed., *Canadian Busi- ness History* (Toronto 1972); R.J.D. Page, 'Canada and the Imperial Idea in the Boer War Years,' JCS 5 (170); D.L. Cole, 'Canada's "Nationalistic" Imperialists,' JCS 5 (1970), 'The Problem of "Nationalism" and "Imperialism" in British Settlement Colonies,' *Journal of British Studies* (1971), and 'J.S. Ewart and Canadian Nationalism,' Canadian Historical Association [CHA], *Historical Papers* (1969); S.M. Robertson, 'Variations on a Nationalist Theme: Henri Bourassa and Abbé Groulx in the 1920s,' CHA *Historical Papers* (1970); R. Allen, 'The Social Gospel and the Reform Tradition in Canada, 1890–1928,' CHR 49 (1968); M. Horn, 'The League for Social Reconstruction and the Development of a Canadian Socialism, 1932–1936,' JCS 7 (Nov. 1972).

8 J.B. Brebner, *New England's Outpost: Acadia before the British Conquest of Canada* (New York 1927)

9 Gordon Stewart and George Rawlyk, *A People Highly Favoured of God: The Nova Scotia Yankees and the American Revolution* (Toronto 1972), 191–2. See also Gordon Stewart, 'Charisma and Integration: An Eighteenth-Century North American Case,' *Comparative Studies in Society and History* 16, 2 (March 1974): 138–49; and G.A. Rawlyk, *Nova Scotia's Massachusetts* (Montreal 1973), especially chapter 13.

10 S.F. Wise, 'God's Peculiar Peoples,' in W.L. Morton, ed., *The Shield of Achilles* (Toronto 1968), 59. See also the following essays by Wise: 'Sermon Literature and Can- adian Intellectual History,' in ibid.; 'The Conservative Tradition in Upper Canada,' in *Profiles of a Province* (Toronto 1967); 'Colonial Attitudes from the War of 1812 to the Rebellions of 1837' and 'The Annexation Movement and its Effect on Canadian Opin- ion,' in S.F. Wise and R.C. Brown, eds., *Canada Views the United States* (Toronto 1967); and 'The Origins of Anti-Americanism in Canada,' 4th Seminar on Canadian- American Relations, Assumption University of Windsor, 1962.

11 Mircea Eliade, *Myth and Reality* (London 1964), 8

12 See S.F. Wise, 'The Annexation Movement and Its Effect on Canadian Opinion, 1837–67,' in *Canada Views*, 94.

13 See F.H. Underhill, *In Search of Canadian Liberalism* (Toronto 1960), and Donald Creighton, *Canada's First Century* (Toronto 1970).

14 Carl Berger, *The Sense of Power* (Toronto 1970), 9

15 Ramsay Cook, *Canada and the French-Canadian Question* (Toronto 1966), 4

16 G. Parkin, quoted in C. Berger, ed., *Imperialism and Nationalism, 1884–1914: A Conflict in Canadian Thought* (Toronto 1969), 7

17 F.B. Cumberland, quoted in Berger, *The Sense of Power*, 131
18 J.S. Ewart Papers, Public Archives of Manitoba [PAM], box 1, 'Notebook,' nd, 48, 'Sentiment'
19 Andrew Macphail, 'The Conservative,' *University Magazine* 18 (Dec. 1919): 434
20 See J.S. Ewart, *The Kingdom of Canada [and Other Essays]* (Toronto 1908), 53–64.
21 Andrew Macphail, 'A Voice from the East,' *University Magazine* 9 (Dec. 1910), 520; J.S. Ewart to G.M. Grant, 19 Oct. 1891, J.S. Ewart Papers, PAM, Correspondence, 1001–7. Ewart here took exception to certain 'irrational' claims made by Grant in Grant's review of Goldwin Smith's *Canada and the Canadian Question* in *The Week*, 15 May 1891.
22 The influence of evolutionary ideas upon Canadian political thought and assumptions begs to be examined. One example of this influence may suffice. In an address entitled 'The Evolution and Degeneration of Party – A Study in Political History,' Nathanael Burwash stated: 'Our object in this study is ... to treat the party in politics as a species or type, and to determine the forces which contribute to its origin and healthy development. It is to study the laws by which those forces operate, as well as to follow the normal course of the development into the highly complex organism of the modern party.' *Transactions of the Royal Society of Canada*, Section II, 1903, 3
23 'The Annexation Movement,' in *Canada Views*, 94
24 George Grant, *Lament for a Nation* (Toronto 1970), 66
25 Jacques Barzun, 'Cultural History: A Synthesis,' in Fritz Stern, ed., *The Varieties of History* (New York 1956), 397–8
26 Carl Berger, 'The Other Mr. Leacock,' *Canadian Literature* 55 (winter 1973); Ramsay Cook, 'Stephen Leacock and the Age of Plutocracy,' in J. Moir, ed., *Character and Circumstance* (Toronto 1970); J.L. Thompson and J.H. Thompson, 'Ralph Connor and the Canadian Identity,' *Queen's Quarterly* 79 (summer 1972); A.G. Bailey, 'The Historical Setting of Sara Duncan's *The Imperialist*,' *Journal of Canadian Fiction* 2 (summer 1973)
27 D.G. Jones, *Butterfly on Rock* (Toronto 1970), 4. See also Ronald Sutherland, *Second Image* (Toronto 1971); Margaret Atwood, *Survival* (Toronto 1972); and John Moss, *Patterns of Isolation* (Toronto 1974).

CHAPTER 2: SO LITTLE ON THE MIND

1 Robert Darnton, 'Intellectual and Cultural History,' in Michael Kammen, ed., *The Past before Us: Contemporary Historical Writing in the United States* (Ithaca 1980), 327
2 John Higham and Paul K. Conkin, eds., *New Directions in American Intellectual History* (Baltimore 1979)
3 For example, see Perry Miller, *The New England Mind* (2 vols., Boston 1961); Miller, *The Life of the Mind in America* (New York 1965); Merle Curti, *The Growth of American Thought* (3rd ed., New York 1965); Henry F. May, *The End of American Innocence* (Chicago 1964); Morton White, *Social Thought in America* (Boston 1957); Richard Hofstadter, *Social Darwinism in American Thought* (Boston 1955); Hofstadter, *The Age of Reform* (New York 1956).
4 See A.O. Lovejoy, *The Great Chain of Being* (Cambridge, Mass. 1936); Crane Brinton,

English Political Thought in the Nineteenth Century (New York 1963); Basil Willey, *Nineteenth Century Studies: A Group of Honest Doubters* (New York 1956); Gertrude Himmelfarb, *Victorian Minds* (New York 1970); Walter Houghton, *The Victorian Frame of Mind* (New Haven 1957).

5 See W.L. Morton, 'Clio in Canada: The Interpretation of Canadian History,' in A.B. McKillop, ed., *Contexts of Canada's Past: Selected Essays of W.L. Morton* (Toronto 1980), 103–12. D.G. Creighton, 'Macdonald and Canadian Historians,' in Creighton, *Towards the Discovery of Canada* (Toronto 1972), 194–210.

6 Carl Berger, *The Sense of Power: Studies in the Ideas of Canadian Imperialism, 1867–1914* (Toronto 1970); Berger, *The Writing of Canadian History* (Toronto 1976); Ramsay Cook, *The Maple Leaf Forever* (Toronto 1972); Cook, *Canada and the French-Canadian Question* (Toronto 1966)

7 William Westfall, 'Creighton's Tragic Vision,' *Canadian Forum* 50 (Sept. 1970): 200–2

8 See in particular Perry Miller's 'Preface to the Beacon Press Edition' of *The New England Mind: From Colony to Province*, in which he asserts that 'while these kinds of activity [trade routes, currency, property, agriculture, town government and military tactics] require an exercise of a faculty which in ordinary parlance may be called intelligence, such matters are not, and cannot be made, the central theme of a coherent narrative. They furnish forth at their worst mere tables of statistics, on the average meaningless inventories, and at their best only a series of monographs' (vii-viii).

9 The first number of *The Journal of the History of Ideas* appeared in 1940, three years after the publication of Lovejoy's *The Great Chain of Being*. The journal bore the mark of his influence from the outset.

10 John Higham, 'The Rise of American Intellectual History,' *American Historical Review* 61 (April 1951): 453–71; 'Intellectual History and Its Neighbors,' *Journal of the History of Ideas* 15 (June 1954): 339–47; 'American Intellectual History: A Critical Appraisal,' *American Quarterly* 13 (summer supplement 1961): 219–33

11 Henry Nash Smith, *Virgin Land: The American West as Symbol and Myth* (New York 1950); Richard Hofstadter, *The American Political Tradition* (New York 1948)

12 The first number of *American Quarterly* appeared in 1949, on the eve of publication of Smith's *Virgin Land*. If Lovejoy had become the patron saint of the *Journal of the History of Ideas*, that role fell to Smith with respect to *American Quarterly*.

13 Louis Hartz, *The Liberal Tradition in America* (New York 1955). It is ironic that these works of Hofstadter and Hartz should have become central to a celebratory 'consensus' school of historiography since Hofstadter, while stressing 'shared convictions,' was by no means uncritical of them, and Hartz's *tour de force* was a sustained plea for comparative analysis.

14 See the essays in the Higham/Conkin collection, *New Directions in American Intellectual History*, and note the overwhelmingly defensive tone of the volume.

15 Frank Underhill, *The Image of Confederation* (Toronto 1964), 60

16 S.F. Wise, 'Sermon Literature and Canadian Intellectual History,' United Church of Canada, *Bulletin*, 1968; reprinted in J.M. Bumsted, ed., *Canadian History Before Confederation* (2nd ed., Georgetown 1979), 249. Here was an excellent example of the kind of 'externalist' position articulated earlier by John Higham in, for example, 'Intellectual History and Its Neighbors.' See note 10 above.

17 P.B. Waite, 'The Edge of the Forest,' Canadian Historical Association, *Historical Papers*, 1969, 1–13
18 Peter Waite, 'A Point of View,' in John S. Moir, ed., *Character and Circumstance: Essays in Honour of Donald Grant Creighton* (Toronto 1970), 225. See also P.B. Waite, 'Sir Oliver Mowat's Canada: Reflections on an Un-Victorian Society,' in Donald Swainson, ed., *Oliver Mowat's Ontario* (Toronto 1972), 12–32.
19 Ramsay Cook, *Canada and the French-Canadian Question* (Toronto 1966)
20 For the range of this debate see Carl Berger, ed., *Imperialism and Nationalism, 1884–1914: A Conflict in Canadian Thought* (Toronto 1969). See also chapter 1, above.
21 More than a decade after its publication it remains one of the most frequently cited monographs in English-Canadian historical scholarship.
22 See A.B. McKillop, 'Carl Berger and Canada's Pastmasters,' *Queen's Quarterly* 84 (winter 1977): 621–6.
23 André Siegfried, *The Race Question in Canada* (Toronto 1966) [1907]; Frank Underhill, *In Search of Canadian Liberalism* (Toronto 1960)
24 For Berger and Cook, see above. Richard Allen, *The Social Passion: Religion and Social Reform in Canada, 1914–28* (Toronto 1970); Michiel Horn, *The League for Social Reconstruction: Intellectual Origins of the Democratic Left in Canada, 1930–1942* (Toronto 1980); William Westfall, 'The Dominion of the Lord: An Introduction to the Cultural History of Protestant Ontario in the Victorian Period,' *Queen's Quarterly* 83 (spring 1976): 47–70; Allan Smith, 'American Culture and the Concept of Mission in 19th Century English Canada,' Canadian Historical Association, *Historical Papers*, 1971, 169–82; S.E.D. Shortt, *The Search for an Ideal: Six Canadian Intellectuals and Their Convictions in an Age of Transition 1890–1930* (Toronto 1976); Douglas Owram, *Promise of Eden: The Canadian Expansionist Movement and the Idea of the West 1856–1900* (Toronto 1980)
25 Michael Bliss, *A Living Profit: Studies in the Social History of Canadian Business, 1883–1911* (Toronto 1974); Eli Mandel, 'Images of Prairie Man,' in Richard Allen, ed., *A Region of the Mind: Interpreting the Western Canadian Plains* (Regina 1973), 201–9; D.G. Jones, *Butterfly on Rock: A Study of Themes and Images in Canadian Literature* (Toronto 1970)
26 John English, *The Decline of Politics: The Conservatives and the Party System 1901–20* (Toronto 1977), esp. chap. 6, 'The Ideology of Service,' 106–22; Mandel, 'Images of Prairie Man'; Underhill, *In Search of Canadian Liberalism*
27 In this sense the term 'social thought' is a fiction, for although all thought is arguably social in purpose and must be viewed in a social context, it is nevertheless the product of individual experience. Committees, as such, cannot 'think.'
28 A.B. McKillop, *A Disciplined Intelligence: Critical Inquiry and Canadian Thought in the Victorian Era* (Montreal 1979)
29 See ibid., 5–9.
30 William Westfall, 'On the Concept of Region in Canadian History and Literature,' *Journal of Canadian Studies* 15 (summer 1980), 11
31 Westfall develops this theme at some length in 'The Sacred and the Secular: Studies in the Cultural History of Protestant Ontario in the Victorian Period,' unpublished PHD thesis, University of Toronto, 1976

32 Ibid., 11
33 See H. Stuart Hughes, *Consciousness and Society: The Reorientation of European Social Thought 1890–1930* (New York 1958), 3–7, 24–5.
34 Ibid., 24–5
35 See Robert Allen Skotheim, *American Intellectual Histories and Historians* (Princeton 1966), 256–88.
36 McKillop, *A Disciplined Intelligence*, 229–32
37 Donald Swainson, 'Tribal Drummers,' *Books in Canada* (March 1980), 3–6
38 Ibid., 6
39 *Queen's Quarterly* 87 (autumn 1980): 505
40 Fernand Ouellet's *Economic and Social History of Quebec 1760–1850* (Toronto 1980), especially his 'Conclusion: The Slowness of Socio-Economic Changes and the Enduring Mentalities of the "Ancien Régime," ' 547–609, is the most sustained attempt in Canadian historiography to relate social structure and economic conditions to consciousness. This product of the 'Annales School' of historical analysis poses a challenge to conventional forms of intellectual history which no intellectual historian can afford to ignore. One historian has described the Annales approach as follows: 'The particular ideas of a Locke or a Rousseau are less important for these historians than the accumulated thoughts and feelings of great masses of people. What counts (and is countable) are not the particular creations by a few thinkers working on the conscious surface of life, but the replicated series and rhythms of thoughts – regularities and patterns – that lie beneath that surface and over long periods of time give form to the symbols and myths of social life – what the French call *mentalités*. Man has a consciousness of sorts, but it is a collective one of long duration; particular reason, momentary purpose, and individual volition count no more in its formation than they do in the formation of a demographic profile or an economic cycle. Unique events are swallowed up in a repetitive series of actions or ideas.' Gordon S. Wood, 'Intellectual History and the Social Sciences,' in Higham and Conkin, eds., *New Directions in American Intellectual History*, 30
41 See Arthur Schlesinger, Jr, 'Review Essay/Intellectual History: A Time for Despair?' *Journal of American History* 66 (March 1980): 888–93.
42 For an excellent discussion of the emergence of 'voluntarism' and its subsequent influence on American social science see Thomas L. Haskell, *The Emergence of Professional Social Science: The American Social Science Association and the Nineteenth-Century Crisis of Authority* (Urbana 1977).
43 Wood, 'Intellectual History and the Social Sciences,' 33
44 Ibid., 34, 38
45 Ibid., 33
46 See Antonio Gramsci, *The Modern Prince and Other Writings* (New York 1975), 118–32; Raymond Williams, *Marxism and Literature* (Oxford 1977). For a recent Canadian study that uses Gramscian insights into the formulation of intellectuals see Paul Craven, *'An Impartial Umpire': Industrial Relations and the Canadian State 1900–1911* (Toronto 1980), esp. 3–73.
47 Quoted in Williams, *Marxism and Literature*, 79–80
48 Ibid., 80

CHAPTER 3: SCIENCE, HUMANISM, AND THE ONTARIO UNIVERSITY

1 Carl Berger has treated the major Anglo-Canadian historians in *The Writing of Canadian History* (Toronto 1976); Leslie Armour and Elizabeth Trott have examined the most prominent Canadian philosophers in *The Faces of Reason: An Essay on Philosophy and Culture in English Canada, 1850–1950* (Waterloo 1981). The paucity of scholarship on the history of science in Canada is partially explained by Richard A. Jarrell in 'Why Do Many Canadians Know Nothing of Canadian Science?' *Science Forum* 10 (1977): 23–6.

2 See Hilda Neatby, *Queen's University, I: 1841–1917: To Strive, to Seek, to Find, and Not to Yield* (Montreal 1978); Frederick W. Gibson, *Queen's University, II: 1917–1961: To Serve and Yet Be Free* (Montreal 1983); Charles M. Johnston, *McMaster University, I: The Toronto Years* (Toronto 1979) and *McMaster University, II: The Early Years in Hamilton, 1930–1957* (Toronto 1981); John R.W. Gwynne-Timothy, *Western's First Century* ([London] 1978).

3 Laurence Veysey, 'The Plural Organized Worlds of the Humanities,' in Alexandra Oleson and John Voss, eds., *The Organization of Knowledge in Modern America, 1860–1920* (Baltimore 1979), 51–106

4 See David R. Keane, 'Rediscovering Ontario University Students of the Mid-Nineteenth Century: Sources For and Approaches To the Study of the Experience of Going to College and Personal, Family and Social Backgrounds of Students,' PHD thesis, University of Toronto, 1981.

5 The late Frank H. Underhill once told me, for example, that during his years as a student at the University of Toronto, shortly before the First World War, the names of Marx and Freud were not mentioned (at least in his presence). See also A.B. McKillop, *A Disciplined Intelligence: Critical Inquiry and Canadian Thought in the Victorian Era* (Montreal 1979).

6 See McKillop, *A Disciplined Intelligence*, and 'Science, Authority, and the American Empire,' chapter eight, below.

7 See Mel Thistle, *The Inner Ring: The Early History of the National Research Council of Canada* (Toronto 1966); Peter Oliver, 'Government, Industry and Science in Ontario: The Case of the Ontario Research Foundation,' in Oliver, *Public and Private Persons: The Ontario Political Culture 1914–1934* (Toronto 1975), 157–78; Vittorio Maria Giuseppe de Vecchi, 'Science and Government in Nineteenth-Century Canada,' PHD thesis, University of Toronto, 1978; Paul Axelrod, *Scholars and Dollars: Politics, Economics, and the Universities of Ontario, 1945–1980* (Toronto 1982); Philip C. Enros, 'The "Bureau of Scientific and Industrial Research and School of Specific Industries": The Royal Canadian Institute's Attempt at Organizing Industrial Research in Toronto, 1914–1918,' *HSTC Bulletin* 1 (1983): 14–26; and Enros, 'The University of Toronto and Industrial Research in the Early Twentieth Century,' in Richard Jarrell and Arnold Roos, eds., *Critical Issues in the History of Canadian Science, Technology, and Medicine* (Thornhill, Ont.), 155–66; B. Sinclair, N.R. Ball, and J.O. Petersen, eds., *Let us be Honest and Modest: Technology and Society in Canadian History* (Toronto 1974); T.H. Levere and R.A. Jarrell, eds., *A Curious Field-book: Science and Society in Canadian History* (Toronto 1974); Richard A. Jarrell, 'The Social Functions of the Scientific

Society in Nineteenth-Century Canada,' in Jarrell and Roos, eds., *Critical Issues*, 31–44; C.M. Johnston, 'Aspects of Science and Technology at McMaster University with Special Reference to Chemistry and Physics 1939–1959,' Ibid., 3–15.

8 See Berger, *Writing of Canadian History*; Margerie Fee, 'English-Canadian Literary Criticism, 1890–1950: Defining and Establishing a National Literature,' PHD thesis, University of Toronto, 1981; Armour and Trott, *Faces of Reason*.

9 S.E.D. Shortt, *The Search for an Ideal* (Toronto 1976); Alan Franklin Bowker, 'Truly Useful Men: Maurice Hutton, George Wrong, James Mavor and the University of Toronto, 1880–1927,' PHD thesis, University of Toronto, 1975; Bruce Bowden, 'Adam Shortt,' PHD thesis, University of Toronto, 1979

10 Erna Buffie, 'The Massey Report and the Intellectuals: Tory Cultural Nationalism in the 1950s,' MA thesis, University of Manitoba, 1982; Pat Jasen, '"Knowledge for What?" The Liberal Arts in the English-Canadian University since World War II,' paper given to the Department of History Colloquium, University of Manitoba, October 1983. I am grateful to Ms Jasen for sending me a copy of this paper, a prospectus of her forthcoming PHD thesis in the Department of History at the University of Manitoba.

11 'The Humanities and Modern Science: Two Cultures or One?' Symposium II, National Council of Colleges and Universities of Canada, *Proceedings*, 1960, 39–65

12 Ibid, 64–5

13 David F. Noble, *America by Design: Science, Technology and the Rise of Corporate Capitalism* (New York 1977); Paul Starr, *The Social Transformation of American Medicine* (New York 1983)

14 Bryan R. Wilson, ed., *Patterns of Sectarianism: Organisation and Ideology in Social and Religious Movements* (London 1967), 2

15 See especially James R. Moore, *The Post-Darwinian Controversies: A Study of the Protestant Struggle to Come to Terms with Darwin in Great Britain and America 1870–1900* (London 1979). For the specifically Canadian context see McKillop, *A Disciplined Intelligence*; Carl Berger, *Science, God, and Nature in Victorian Canada* (Toronto 1983); Robert Taylor, 'The Darwinian Revolution: The Responses of Four Canadian Scholars,' PHD thesis, McMaster University, 1976; see also chapters 5 and 7, below.

16 McKillop, 'Science, Authority, and the American Empire,' chapter 8, below

17 Watson Kirkconnell and A.S.P. Woodhouse, *The Humanities in Canada* (Ottawa 1947); *Royal Commission on National Development in the Arts, Letters, and Sciences* (Ottawa 1951); T. Symons, *To Know Ourselves: The Report of the Commission on Canadian Studies* (Ottawa 1975)

18 See, for example, Harold Innis, *Empire and Communications* (rev. ed., Mary Quayle Innis, Toronto 1972); Donald Creighton, *The Forked Road: Canada 1939–1957* (Toronto 1976); Marshall McLuhan, *Understanding Media: The Extensions of Man* (New York 1964); George Grant, *Technology and Empire: Perspectives on North America* (Toronto 1969); Northrop Frye, *Divisions on a Ground: Essays on Canadian Culture* (Toronto 1982). See also Arthur Kroker, *Technology and the Canadian Mind: Innis/McLuhan/Grant* (Montreal 1984).

19 Veysey, 'Plural Organized Worlds of the Humanities,' 57

20 Derek de Solla Price, quoted in 'The Breakthroughs: They Were Caused by Advancing Technology, Not Great Minds, Historian has Theorized,' *Globe and Mail*, 3 Sept. 1984. Much of the controversy that surrounds Price's assertions was derived from reaction to his George B. Sarton Memorial Lecture, 'Sealing Wax and String: A Philosophy of the Experimenter's Craft and its Role in the Genesis of High Technology,' given at the 1983 meetings of the American Association for the Advancement of Science. I am grateful to Craig Fraser of the Institute for the History and Philosophy of Science and Technology at the University of Toronto for supplying me with a copy of this unpublished paper. I am especially grateful to Philip Enros, also of the institute, for sharing his time and knowledge with me.

21 E.H. Gombrich, 'Focus on the Arts and Humanities,' in Gombrich, *Tributes: Interpreters of Our Cultural Tradition* (Ithaca 1984), 11–12

22 John Metcalf, *General Ludd* (Downsview, Ont. 1980)

CHAPTER 4: EVOLUTION, ETHNOLOGY, AND POETIC FANCY

1 George Basalla, William Coleman, and Robert H. Kargon, eds., *Victorian Science: A Self-Portrait from the Presidential Addresses to the British Association for the Advancement of Science* (New York 1970), 48

2 'British Association for the Advancement of Science,' *Canadian Journal* [CJ], series 2, 5 (March 1860): 66–7

3 Ibid., 67–8

4 Basalla et al., *Victorian Science*, 19–20, 132, 400, 412–13, 415–16; George H. Daniels, *Science in American Society* (New York 1971), 45–6; George H. Daniels, *American Science in the Age of Jackson* (New York 1968)

5 See Daniels, *American Science*, 66, for a short but apt description of the 'Baconian method.'

6 Francis Bacon, *The Works of Francis Bacon*, ed. James Spedding et al. (London 1883), IV, 32–3. I am indebted to Dr Graham Reynolds for this reference.

7 Daniel Wilson, 'The President's Address' (read before the Canadian Institute, 7 Jan. 1860), [CJ], series 2 5 (March 1860), 127

8 He had also written pieces for *Tait's Magazine*, *Chambers' Information for the People*, and *The Scotsman*, among others. Further information on Wilson may be obtained from these sources: H.H. Langton, *Sir Daniel Wilson: A Memoir* (Toronto 1929); Jessie Aitken Wilson, *Memoir of George Wilson* (Edinburgh 1860) (George Wilson was Daniel Wilson's young brother, who was Regius Professor of Technology at Edinburgh University and director of the Industrial Museum of Scotland until his death in 1859); G.M. Adam, 'Daniel Wilson,' *The Week* (6 Oct. 1887): 726–7; T.F. McIlwraith, 'Sir Daniel Wilson: A Canadian Antrhopologist of One Hundred Years Ago,' *Transactions of the Royal Society of Canada*, section II, series 4 (1964): 129–36; Bruce G. Trigger, 'Sir Daniel Wilson: Canada's First Anthropologist,' *Anthropologica*, ns 8 (1966): 3–28.

9 Daniel Wilson, *Prehistoric Annals of Scotland* (2nd ed., London 1863), I, xvii

10 Ibid., 119

11 Daniel Wilson, 'Sonnet – from "Spring Wild Flowers,"' *Canadian Monthly and National Review* 8 (July 1875): 8
12 Quoted in a review (anonymous) of *Prehistoric Man: Researches into the Origin of Civilization in the Old and New Worlds,* in *British American Magazine* 1 (1863): 92. The fact that the reviewer chose this passage from the many other quotable ones in Wilson's book illustrates the hold of the metaphor of the veil upon at least one person other than Wilson and myself.
13 James Bovell, *Outlines of Natural Theology, for the Use of the Canadian Student* (Toronto 1859), iii
14 Basalla et al., *Victorian Science,* 48, 53
15 Editorial, *Dalhousie Gazette* 4 (27 April 1872), 10–11
16 John C. Greene, *Darwin and the Modern World View* (Baton Rouge 1973), 4 passim. The historiography of nineteenth-century science is both brilliant and fascinating. See, for example, Loren Eiseley, *Darwin's Century* (New York 1961); John C. Greene, *The Death of Adam* (Ames, Iowa 1959); Cecil J. Schneer, *Mind and Matter* (New York 1970)
17 G. Mercer Adam, 'Prominent Canadians. II: Daniel Wilson,' *The Week* 4 (6 Oct. 1887): 727
18 William Nesbitt Ponton, 'Lecture Notes – Professor Wilson's Lectures – 1873 – 1st year,' notebook, 13, 15; 'Rhetoric,' 63–4, University of Toronto Archives, University of Toronto. Emphasis in original
19 Wilson, 'President's Address,' 1860, 115–16
20 See Michael T. Ghiselin, *The Triumph of the Darwinian Method* (Berkeley 1972). Ghiselin provides a remarkably brief but accurate description of the theory of natural selection as put forward by Darwin: 'Organisms differ from one another. They produce more young than the available resources can sustain. Those best suited to survive pass on the expedient properties to their offspring, while inferior forms are eliminated. Subsequent generations therefore are more like the better adapted ancestors, and the result is a gradual modification, or evolution. Thus the cause of evolutionary adaptation is differential reproductive success' (46).
21 The very characteristics rejected by Wilson constituted the essence of the Darwinian 'revolution' in scientific method. See ibid., 63. It must be stressed that these reactions by Dawson and Wilson were by no means unique or uncommon. Similar objections were voiced by the most prominent British and American scientists of the day. See Sir William Armstrong's presidential address to the British Association for the Advancement of Science: 'But when natural selection is adduced as a cause adequate to explain the production of a new organ not provided for in original creation, the hypothesis must appear to common apprehensions, to be pushed beyond the limits of reasonable conjecture' (reproduced in CJ, series 2, 9 [1864]: 37). See also the presidential address several years later to the American Association for the Advancement of Science by J. Lawrence Smith. Darwin, said Smith, 'is to be regarded more as a metaphysician with a highly wrought imagination than as a scientist ... He is not satisfied to leave the laws of life where he finds them, or to pursue their study by logical and inductive reasoning. His method of reasoning will not allow him to remain at rest; he must be moving onward in his unification of the universe' (reproduced in the *Canadian Naturalist and Quarterly Journal of Science,* ns 7 [1875], 184–55).

22 J.W. Dawson, 'Review of "Darwin on the Origin of Species by Natural Selection,"'
Canadian Naturalist and Geologist 5 (1860): 100
23 Ghiselin, Darwinian Method, 63, 76–7
24 Wilson, 'President's Address,' 1860, 116
25 Ibid., 116, 117. Emphasis in original
26 Ibid., 118. Emphasis in original
27 Ibid., 120, 121
28 Ibid., 119
29 Ibid., 122
30 Ibid., 1861, 114
31 See, for example, W.H.W., 'Darwinism and Christianity,' Christian Guardian 41 (28 Dec. 1870): 204.
32 'Darwinism and Christianity'
33 G. Mercer Adam, 'Daniel Wilson,' The Week 4 (6 Oct. 1887): 726
34 Daniel Wilson, Caliban: The Missing Link (London 1873), xi–xii
35 Ibid., 2–4
36 Ibid., 8, 11
37 Ponton, 'Lecture Notes,' 26: 'Literature,' University of Toronto Archives
38 Wilson, Caliban, 78
39 Ibid., 20–1, 90–1
40 Ibid., 93
41 Ibid., 101, 113
42 H. Alleyne Nicholson, 'Man's Place in Nature,' Canadian Monthly and National Review 1 (Jan. 1872): 35–7
43 Quoted in Tibor R. Machan, The Pseudo-Science of B.F. Skinner (New Rochelle, NY 1974). A more thorough discussion of the Darwinian 'debate' in Canada may be found in A.B. McKillop, A Disciplined Intelligence: Critical Inquiry and Canadian Thought in the Victorian Era (Montreal 1979).

CHAPTER 5: SCIENCE, ETHICS, AND 'MODERN THOUGHT'

1 'Ste-Beuve,' Westminster Review (April 1871): 216. All quotations by LeSueur lacking references are from essays reproduced in A.B. McKillop, ed., A Critical Spirit: The Thought of William Dawson LeSueur (Toronto 1977).
2 Ibid., 213. The best short treatment of Ste-Beuve's place in French letters is probably in Roger L. Williams, The World of Napoleon III (New York 1957), 113–31. See also Irving Babbitt, The Masters of Modern French Criticism (New York 1912), 97–188, and C.K. Trueblood, 'Sainte-Beuve and the Psychology of Personality,' Character and Personality 8 (1939–40): 120–43.
3 Transactions of the Ottawa Literary and Scientific Society (1897–98): 12
4 Biographical materials on the life of W.D. LeSueur are scarce. Those provided here are mainly from standard sources: John Reade, 'William Dawson LeSueur,' Proceedings of the Royal Society of Canada (1918): iv–vi; P.G. Roy, Fils de Quebec, vol. 4 (Quebec 1933), 173–4; Henry James Morgan, eds., The Canadian Men and Women of the Time, 2nd ed. (Toronto 1912), 654; University of Toronto Calendar, 1891–92 (Toronto 1892),

Appendix 1, 34; Norah Story, *The Oxford Companion to Canadian History and Literature* (Toronto 1967), 453. See also Clifford G. Holland, 'The Sage of Ottawa: William Dawson LeSueur,' *Canadian Literature* 96 (spring 1983): 167–81.

5 *Transactions ... Ottawa ... Society*, 17–20, contains a list of the Ottawa Literary and Scientific Society's officers from its beginnings in 1869 (as an outgrowth of the Ottawa Natural History Society) to 1898.

6 Sara Jeannette Duncan, 'Saunterings – The Age,' *The Week* 4 (3 March 1887): 216–17

7 Prior to 1872 Canadian periodicals were generally of a local nature and often experienced only a brief existence owing to a number of publishing difficulties. The periodical press from the publication of the *Canadian Monthly and National Review* (1872–8) on was of a more national scope and, while these periodicals suffered no few publishing problems, throughout the rest of the nineteenth century one such journal or another was in existence. *Belford's Monthly Magazine* (1876–8), *Rose Belford's Canadian Monthly and National Review* (1878–82), *The Bystander* (1880 – intermittently to 1890), and *The Week* (1883–96). See R.L. McDougall, 'A Study of Canadian Periodical Literature of the Nineteenth Century' (PHD thesis, University of Toronto, 1950), 4–5.

8 W.J.R., 'Man Here and Hereafter,' *Belford's Monthly Magazine* 3 (May 1878), 757

9 Fidelis, 'The Seen and the Unseen,' *Canadian Monthly and National Review* 9 (June 1876), 495. 'Fidelis' was the pseudonym that Miss Machar (the daughter of a principal of Queen's University) used throughout her life. See Norah Story, *The Oxford Companion to Canadian History and Literature* (Toronto 1967), 188, for biographical information.

10 Goldwin Smith, 'The Immortality of the Soul,' *Canadian Monthly and National Review* 9 (May 1876): 408

11 James DeKoven, 'The Gates of the Invisible,' quoted in Paul A. Carter, *The Spiritual Crisis of the Gilded Age* (DeKalb, Ill. 1971), 16

12 'H.' 'A Few Words About Nature,' *Dalhousie Gazette* 7 (3) (19 Dec. 1874): 17–19

13 Carl Berger, 'The Vision of Grandeur' (PHD thesis, University of Toronto, 1966), 434. LeSueur believed that Fiske's attempts at such a reconciliation were wholly inadequate. See W.L. LeSueur, 'Evolution and the Destiny of Man,' *Popular Science Monthly* 26 (Feb. 1885), 456–68.

14 I., 'Science,' *Dalhousie Gazette*, ns 4 (5) (25 Jan. 1879): 50–2

15 [anon.], 'Is a Belief in Darwinism Consistent with a Teleological View of the Natural World?' *Dalhousie Gazette* 18 (11) (April 1886), 141–3

16 J.E. Creighton, 'The Age and Its Tendencies,' ibid. (10), (27 March 1886): 123

17 Berger, 'Vision of Grandeur'

18 M.A. Jevons, 'One Faith in Many Forms,' *Rose-Belford's Canadian Monthly* 4 (Oct. 1884): 344

19 'Morality and Religion' [unsigned editorial], Toronto *Mail*, 10 Jan. 1880, 2

20 For an indication of the international debate see note 30, below.

21 See Herbert Spencer, *The Data of Ethics* (New York 1883), chap. II, 'The Evolution of Conduct,' 8–20, and passim; J.D.Y. Peel, *Herbert Spencer: The Evolution of a Sociologist* (New York: 1971), 84. LeSueur's representation of Spencer's philosophy, in his article 'Mr. Spencer and His Critics'/'A Vindication of Scientific Ethics,' may be seen

as accurate. Spencer, having read the article, wrote to the author: 'You have not only given a very admirable exposition of certain of the cardinal principles contained in that work but have very effectively enforced them by arguments of your own.' Herbert Spencer to W.D. LeSueur, 27 April 1880, W.D. LeSueur Papers, 1, file 4, PAC.

22 See D.H. MacVicar, 'Recent Aspects of Materialism: Being a Lecture delivered at the Opening of the Session of 1871–72, of the Presbyterian College, Montreal' (Montreal 1871), 1–11; Rev. James Carmichael, 'Design and Darwinism' (Toronto 1880), 5; Surena, 'Modern Scepticism,' *Canadian Monthly and National Review* 2 (Aug. 1872): 173; 'Round the Table,' ibid. 11 (May 1877): 547–8. 'G.,' ' ' 'The Marvels of Scientific Logic,' ' ' *Rose-Belford's Canadian Monthly* 5 (Oct. 1880): 361–71. For an indication of the plight in which men suspended between the worlds of religion and science could find themselves see these articles on W.H. Mallock by R.W. Boodle: 'Modern Pessimism,' *Rose-Belford's Canadian Monthly* 3 (June 1879): 591–601; 'Mr. Mallock: A Retrospect,' ibid. 6 (Feb. 1881): 195–203; 'Mr. Mallock's ''Romance of the 19th C'' – Review,' ibid. 7 (Sept. 1881): 322–7.

23 Each of these examples is drawn from MacVicar, 'Recent Aspects,' 3–4. In a 'Prefatory Note' to this pamphlet, MacVicar noted that 'the arguments advanced against Materialism were delivered *in substance* in the Class-room three years ago, and in several respects more fully developed than in their present form.'

24 For Tyndall's address and a discussion of the context in which it was delivered see George Basalla, William Coleman, and Robert H. Kargon, eds., *Victorian Science: A Self-Portrait from the Presidential Addresses to the British Association for the Advancement of Science* (New York 1970), 136–78. The quotation from Tyndall is drawn from 474–5.

25 Ibid., 137

26 Alexander Johnson, *Science and Religion: An Address Delivered at the Convocation of McGill University, May 1st, 1876, to the Bachelors of Applied Science* (Montreal 1876), 6–7. The address was originally published in the Montreal press at the request of the students.

27 Ibid., 7

28 A Canadian by birth (he was born in Kingston in 1848, the son of Queen's College's professor of Greek), G.J. Romanes was raised in England, to which his family returned when the father came into an inheritance. Although his many biological writings gave him a reputation as one of the leading scientific naturalists of his day (the *Times* stated in 1886 that 'Mr. George Romanes appears to be the biological investigator upon whom in England the mantle of Mr. Darwin has most conspicuously descended'), he has, perhaps more accurately, been described as one of those men whose philosophies of life hovered 'between science and religion': 'Romanes was ... clearly a man of unsettled intellectual conviction who throughout life kept hoping to discover a single set of principles that would satisfy all conditions.' Hence his book *A Candid Examination of Theism* (1878), published under the pseudonym 'Physicus,' saw no validity in the orthodox arguments for natural religion, while his posthumously published *Thoughts on Religion* revealed that he refused to give up the possibility of a religious interpretation of man and nature. *Christian Prayer and Natural Laws* (1873), written while Romanes was still

a student at Cambridge, was an essay which sought a middle way between science and religion. 'The essay, though clearly favouring the possibility of answered prayer,' wrote F.M. Turner, 'revealed neither zeal for orthodoxy nor firm adherence to naturalistic opinion. Rather, it sought to fend off the dogmatic claims of both positions.' The above biographical information and quotations are drawn from 'George John Romanes: From Faith to Faith,' chap. 6 in F.M. Turner, *Between Science and Religion* (New Haven 1974), 134–63.

29 Other articles which bear directly on the controversy are John Tyndall, 'Reply to the Critics of the Belfast Address,' *Canadian Monthly and National Review* 7 (Feb. 1875): 183–95; 'Current Literature' [an editorial note], ibid., 8 (Dec. 1875): 549–551; John Tyndall, '"Materialism" and Its Opponents,' ibid. (Jan. 1876): 56–68; Rev. James Martineau, 'Modern Materialism: Its Attitude Towards Theology,' ibid. 9 (March 1876): 223–37; John Watson, 'Science and Religion: A Reply to Prof. Tyndall on Materialism and Its Opponents,' 9 (May 1876): 384–97; John Watson, 'Professor Tyndall's "Materialism,"' *Rose-Belford's Canadian Monthly* 1 (1878): 282–8. It must be stressed that almost every article or pamphlet published in Canada during the 1870s which discussed the relationship between science and religion referred, either directly or obliquely, to Tyndall and the 'materialism' question.

30 The debate was heralded by a detailed review of Romanes's book in the *Canadian Monthly and National Review* 7 (March 1875): 284–6. It was launched, however, by an article by Agnes Maule Machar which reviewed the 'Prayer Question' as it had evolved in England (and as set forth in an appendix to Romanes's book entitled 'The Physical Efficacy of Prayer'); see A.M. Machar, 'Prayer for Daily Bread,' ibid. (May 1875): 415–25. This was followed by LeSueur's rebuttal, 'Prayer and Modern Thought,' ibid. 8 (Aug. 1875): 145–55. After the publication of these two articles the debates proceeded apace: Fidelis, 'Prayer and Modern Doubt,' ibid. (Sept. 1875): 224–36; Fidelis, 'Prayer and Christian Belief,' ibid. (Oct. 1875): 328–34; S.E. Dawson, 'Prayer and Modern Science,' ibid. (Dec. 1875): 512–22; George J. Romanes, 'The Physical Efficacy of Prayer,' ibid. 9 (March 1876): 211–21; Fidelis, 'The Divine Law of Prayer,' ibid. 10 (Aug. 1876): 144–55.

31 See Goldwin Smith, 'The Immortality of the Soul,' ibid., 9 (May 1876): 408–16; Fidelis, 'The Seen and the Unseen,' ibid. (June 1876): 495–508; Professor J.E. Wells, 'Evolution and Immortality,' ibid. 10 (Oct. 1876): 291–8; John Watson, 'Darwinism and Morality,' ibid. (Oct. 1876): 319–26; J.A. Allen, 'The Evolution of Morality: A Reply,' ibid. 11 (May 1877): 490–501; John Watson, 'The Ethical Aspect of Darwinism: A Rejoinder, ibid. (June 1877): 638–44; W.J.R. [W.J. Rattray], 'Man Here and Hereafter,' *Belford's Monthly Magazine* 3 (May 1878): 757–78; A.W. Gundry, 'Spencer's "Data of Ethics,"' *Rose-Belford's Canadian Monthly* 3 (Dec. 1879): 646–50; Goldwin Smith, 'The Prospects of a Moral Interregnum' [a revised version of an article published slightly earlier in *Atlantic Monthly*], ibid. (Dec. 1879): 651–63; G.A.M., 'Mr. Goldwin Smith's *Atlantic Monthly* Articles,' ibid. (Dec. 1879): 663–5; W.D. LeSueur, 'The Future of Morality,' ibid., 4 (Jan. 1880), 74–82; W.D. LeSueur, 'Morality and Religion,' ibid. 4 (Feb. 1880): 166–71; Rev. J.F. Stevenson, 'Morality and the Gospel,' ibid. (April 1880): 335–42; Fidelis, 'The Source of Moral Life,' ibid., 343–51; W.D. LeSueur, 'Mr. Spencer and His

Critics,' ibid. 413–22; W.D. LeSueur, 'Morality and Religion Again – A Word With My Critics,' ibid. (June 1880): 642–55; W.D. LeSueur, 'Mr. Goldwin Smith on "The Data of Ethics,"' *Popular Science Monthly* 22 (Dec. 1882): 145–56.

32 One such exception was Allen, 'The Evolution of Morality.'

33 See Watson's essays, above, but especially his essay 'A Phase of Modern Thought,' *Rose-Belford's Canadian Monthly*, ns 3 (Nov. 1879): 457–72.

34 See G.J. Romanes's critique of LeSueur's first article on the 'Prayer Question,' in 'The Physical Efficacy of Prayer.'

35 LeSueur's essay criticizing Fiske was 'Evolution and the Destiny of Man,' *Popular Science Monthly* 26 (Feb. 1885): 456–68; his essay on Lyman Abbott was 'Evolution Bounded by Theology,' ibid. 29 (June 1886): 145–53; on Porter, 'Ex-President Porter on Evolution,' ibid. (Sept. 1886): 577–94. LeSueur's debate with G.M. Grant began with a discussion of the merits of the theological claims made by the American evangelists Dwight L. Moody and Ira Sankey, but soon broadened to a full discussion of the place of Christianity itself in 'modern culture.' LeSueur wrote under the pseudonym, 'Laon,' but by 1885 Laon had been identified in print: see William Cushing, ed., *Initials and Pseudonyms*, rev. ed., 1st series (New York 1885), 165. I am indebted to Marilyn G. Flitton for this reference. The 'Laon'-Grant debate consisted of the following pieces: Laon, 'Messrs. Moody and Sankey and Revivalism,' *Canadian Monthly and National Review* 7 (June 1875): 510–13; Rev. G.M. Grant, 'Laon on "Messrs Moody and Sankey and Revivalism,"' ibid. 8 (Sept. 1875): 250–5; Laon, 'Proofs and Disproofs,' ibid. (Oct. 1875): 339–48; Grant, 'Christianity and Modern Thought,' ibid. (Nov. 1875): 437–41; Laon, 'Modern Culture and Christianity,' ibid. (Dec. 1875): 523–33. For the debate with Bishop John Travers Lewis see 'Agnosticism – A Lecture Delivered in St George's Hall, Kingston, on the Occasion of the Meeting of the Synod of the Diocese, June 12, 1883, by the Lord Bishop of Ontario' (Kingston 1883), 32; W.D. LeSueur, 'A Defence of Modern Thought' (Toronto 1884), 40; Vindex, 'A Criticism of Mr. LeSueur's Pamphlet, entitled "Defence of Modern Thought"' (np, nd) 16; W.D. LeSueur, 'Evolution and the Positive Aspects of Modern Thought. In Reply to the Bishop of Ontario's Second Lecture on "Agnosticism"' (Ottawa 1884), 43. The author has been unable to locate a copy of Lewis's second lecture.

36 W.D. LeSueur, 'Science and Its Accusers,' *Popular Science Monthly* 34 (Jan. 1889): 379, 375

37 'G.' 'The Marvels of Scientific Logic,' 361

38 Ibid., 371

39 LeSueur, 'Ex-President Porter on Evolution,' 577

40 Ibid.

41 C.W. Parkin, 'Diderot and Materialism,' *Rose-Belford's Canadian Monthly* 7 (Dec. 1881): 642

42 Alfred North Whitehead, *Science and the Modern World* (New York 1967), 57

43 Robert M. Young, *Mind, Brain and Adaptation in the Nineteenth Century* (Oxford 1970), 2

44 It was Vogt who had pronounced, in his *Physiological Epistles* (1847), that 'the brain secretes thought, just as the liver secretes bile.' See chap. 2, 'Materialism, Naturalism

and Agnosticism,' in John Passmore, *A Hundred Years of Philosophy* (Harmondsworth, Eng. 1970), 35–47, for background and context.

45 See Daniel Clark, 'Physiology in Thought, Conduct, and Belief,' *Rose-Belford's Canadian Monthly* 6 (April 1881): 363–77; R.M. Bucke, 'The Correlation of the Vital and Physical Force,' *British American Journal* 3 (May, June, July 1862): 161–7, 225–38; R.M. Bucke, 'The Moral Nature and the Great Sympathetic,' *American Journal of Insanity* 35 (Oct. 1878): 229–53; James Horne, 'R.M. Bucke: Pioneer Psychiatrist, Practical Mystic,' *Ontario History* 59 (1967): 197–208.

46 W.D. LeSueur, 'The Moral Nature and Intellectual Power,' *Rose-Belford's Canadian Monthly* 3 (July 1879): 104–5

47 Ibid., 105

48 Ibid., LeSueur's italics

49 Richard Hofstadter, *Social Darwinism in American Thought* (Boston 1970), 32

50 See ibid., chap. 2, 'The Vogue of Spencer,' 31–50, and passim. For a more recent estimate of the rise and decline of Spencer's reputation see Peel, *Spencer*, chap. 1, 'The Man and His Work,' 1–32, and chap. 9, 'History's Revenge,' 224–48.

51 From William Graham Sumner, *The Challenge of Facts*, quoted in Hofstadter, *Social Darwinism*, 59. See Richard D. Altick, *Victorian People and Ideas* (New York 1973), 232, for an equation of 'Social Darwinism' (in this sense) with the philosophy of Herbert Spencer.

52 LeSueur, 'Evolution and the Destiny of Man,' 467

53 Ibid., 467–8. Italics in original

54 LeSueur, 'Ex-President Porter on Evolution,' 589–90

55 Ibid., 591

56 Ibid.

57 The substance of this paragraph is drawn from Peel, *Spencer*, chap. 7: 'The Organic Analogy,' 166–91.

CHAPTER 6: THE RESEARCH IDEAL AND THE UNIVERSITY OF TORONTO

1 This is examined in my book, *A Disciplined Intelligence: Critical Inquiry and Canadian Thought in the Victorian era* (Montreal 1979). See also Fred D. Schneider, 'The Habit of Deference: The Imperial Factor and the "University Question" in Upper Canada,' *Journal of British Studies* 17 (fall 1977): 82–104.

2 Sir Daniel Wilson, *Address at the Convocation of University College, 1890* (Toronto 1890), 16. Quoted in Peter N. Ross, 'The Establishment of the PHD at Toronto: A Case of American Influence,' *History of Education Quarterly* 12 (fall 1972), 371

3 See *A Disciplined Intelligence*, 110–16, passim.

4 Daniel Wilson, 'The President's Address,' *Canadian Journal*, series II, 6 (March 1861): 119

5 Ibid., 120

6 'Extract from Exhibition Lectures,' *Canadian Journal*, series I, 7 (1853): 158–9

7 Richard Pomfret, *The Economic Development of Canada* (Toronto 1981), 132–55

8 See *Canada Investigates Industrialism*, ed. Greg Kealey (Toronto 1973).

9 C.R. Young, *Early Engineering Education at Toronto, 1851–1919* (Toronto 1958), 19–88
10 See T.C. Keefer, *Philosophy of Railroads*, ed. H.V. Nelles (Toronto 1972); Pierre Berton, *The National Dream* (Toronto 1970).
11 See *A Disciplined Intelligence*, 95–8, 105–10.
12 Daniel Wilson, 'Address at the Convocation of University College, 1884,' *Canada Educational Monthly* (11) (Nov. 1884): 418–19
13 Senate Reform Act, April 1873, 36 Vict., chap. 29. See also 'Minutes of the University Senate,' University of Toronto, 15 Sept. 1873, 3.
14 Frank Underhill, *The Image of Confederation* (Toronto 1963)
15 For the origins and nature of 'Canada First' see Carl Berger, *The Sense of Power* (Toronto 1970).
16 See A.B. Macallum, 'Huxley and Tyndall and the University of Toronto,' *University of Toronto Monthly* 2 (Dec. 1901).
17 'Journal of Daniel Wilson,' Part 1, 56, 6 Oct. 1881, University of Toronto Archives
18 W.J. Loudon, *Sir William Mulock: A Short Biography* (Toronto 1932), 64
19 Hon. J.M. Gibson to G.W. Ross, 21 June 1887, Department of Education Correspondence, box 4, Public Archives of Ontario, RG2 D7
20 See, for example, another letter by Hon. J.M. Gibson to George Ross, concerning the appointment in Latin mentioned above: 'It is true his political leanings have been very decidedly the other way – the wrong way – but you will acknowledge that an appointment of that kind would go a long way to silence any suggestion of a political favouritism in these matters.' J.M. Gibson to G.W. Ross, 10 May 1887, ibid.
21 James Reaney, *The Dismissal; or Twisted Beards & Tangled Whiskers* (Erin 1978)
22 William Dale to G.W. Ross, 9 Dec. 1890, Department of Education Correspondence, box 2, Public Archives of Ontario RG2 D7
23 'Memoirs of James Loudon,' 5–6, University of Toronto Archives
24 James Loudon, 'The President's Address,' *Canadian Journal*, ns 94 (April 1877): 376–7
25 William Hincks, 'The Sensationalist Philosophy,' *Canadian Journal* 4 (Sept. 1859): 399
26 The years 1914–18 were not easy ones for professors of German. See Barbara M. Wilson, ed., *Ontario and the First World War 1914–1918* (Toronto 1977), 162–4.
27 E.E. Stewart, 'The Role of the Provincial Government in the Development of Universities in Ontario' (EDD thesis, University of Toronto, 1970), 255–6
28 Ibid., 263
29 Legislative Assembly of Ontario, *Sessional Papers*, no. 74, vol. XXVII, part IX, First Session of the Eighth Legislature, Toronto 1895
30 Toronto *Globe*, 2 April 1897
31 See Peter N. Ross, 'The Establishment of the PHD at Toronto: A Case of American Influence,' *History of Education Quarterly* 12 (fall 1972): 364–6.
32 The generalizations that follow concerning this controversy are based on the findings of Tory Hoff, in his 'The Controversial Appointment of James Mark Baldwin to the University of Toronto in 1889' (MA thesis, Carleton University, 1980). Mr. Hoff's study is a model of meticulous research.
33 'Journal,' 22 March 1889, 149

34 See Toronto *World*, 26, 27 Sept. 1889.
35 'Journal,' 21 Oct. 1889
36 James Mark Baldwin, *Philosophy: Its Relation to Life and Education* (Toronto 1890)
37 See R. Jackson Wilson, *In Quest of Community* (New York 1968); Anne Ashley, *William James Ashley* (London 1932).
38 See, for example, 'Technical Education,' *Industrial Canada* 2 (4) (30 Nov. 1901): 154–6.
39 Quoted in Stewart, 'The Role of the Provincial Government,' 143
40 Peter N. Ross, 'The Origins and Development of the PHD Degree at the University of Toronto, 1871–1932' (ED D thesis, University of Toronto, 1972), 372
41 See Stewart, 'The Role of Provincial Government,' Table 2, 'Provincial Assistance to Higher Education in Ontario, 1891–1916,' 556.
42 James Loudon, *Convocation Address, October 1, 1900* (Toronto 1900)
43 James Loudon, 'Convocation Address, October 2, 1899,' in Loudon Papers, file c22, 7, University of Toronto Archives
44 See Vittorio M.G. De Vecchi, 'Science and Government in Nineteenth-Century Canada' (PHD thesis, University of Toronto, 1978), 257–9.
45 James Loudon, 'The Universities in Relation to Research,' *Proceedings of the Royal Society of Canada, 1902*, Appendix A, xlix
46 Charles W. Humphries, 'James P. Whitney and the University of Toronto,' in *Profiles of a Province: Studies in the History of Ontario* (Toronto 1967), 118
47 *Report of the Royal Commission on the University of Toronto* (Toronto 1906), lx
48 Claude Bissell, *Halfway Up Parnassus* (Toronto 1974), 3–16

CHAPTER 7: THE IDEALIST LEGACY

1 See A.B. McKillop, *A Disciplined Intelligence: Critical Inquiry and Canadian Thought in the Victorian Era* (Montreal 1979).
2 The series is entitled 'The Philosophy of Immanuel Kant: A collection of eleven of the most important books on Kant's philosophy reprinted in 14 volumes,' selected by Lewis White Beck. The Watson volumes selected are *Kant and His English Critics* (New York 1881) and *The Philosophy of Kant Explained* (Glasgow 1908).
3 John Watson, *The Relation of Philosphy to Science* (Kingston 1872), 18. For social and political context of the transformation of Canada see R.C. Brown and Ramsay Cook, *Canada 1896–1921: A Nation Transformed* (Toronto 1974).
4 For the influence of idealism on, for example, a Canadian imperialist and a Canadian poet see Terry Cook, 'George R. Parkin and the Concept of Britannic Idealism,' in *Journal of Canadian Studies* 10 (1975); and John Robert Sorfleet, 'Transcendentalist, Mystic, Evolutionary Idealist: Bliss Carman, 1886–1894,' in George Woodcock, ed., *Colony and Confederation* (Vancouver 1974).
5 John Watson, 'The Sadness and Joy of Knowledge,' part II, *Queen's Journal* (29 March 1901), 260
6 The Editors, 'Salutatory,' *Queen's Quarterly* 1 (July 1893): 1–2
7 John Watson, 'The Middle Ages and the Reformation,' ibid., 6–11
8 Ibid., 88–91

9 Albert Carman Papers, United Church Archives, Toronto, vol. 18, no 123. Rev. C.T. Scott to Carman, 28 Feb. 1906

10 George John Blewett, *The Study of Nature and the Vision of God: with other Essays in Philosophy* (Toronto 1907), viii

11 John Watson Papers, Queen's University Archives, Kingston, J.M. Grant to John Watson, 20 Nov. 1911; Watson to Grant, 17 May 1914

12 John Passmore, 'Darwin's Impact on British Metaphysics,' *Victorian Studies* (1959–60): 52–3

13 Watson Papers, Watson to Grant, 17 May 1914; Grant to Watson, 7 June 1914. See also Watson to Grant, 13 March 1917; Grant to Watson, 16 March 1917; Grant to Watson 16 April 1916; Watson to grant, 22 April 1916; Grant to Watson, 7 March 1917; Grant to Watson, 6 April 1918; Watson to Grant, 10, 19 April 1918. By 1918 Watson's patience had worn thin. His last letter to Grant was short: 'Dear Mr. Grant ... I don't think I care to say any more about Christian Science, which to my mind is based upon indefinite thinking.'

14 The scope of this paper precludes treatment of many individuals. Yet another, very much infected by the Queen's spirit of the 1880s and 1890s was Alfred Fitzpatrick, the founder of Frontier College. Fitzpatrick had taken a BA there in 1889 and attended its Theological College from 1889 to 1892. During this time he became dedicated to the proposition that education and everyday life, thought and action, must not be separated; hence he sought throughout his life to make the sacred and the secular meet. G.M. Grant was the greatest influence on his life, and when he wrote a book (never published) entitled 'Schools and Other Penitentiaries,' he dedicated it to 'the memory of George Monro Grant, Canada's Greatest Force and Personality in Education and Statesmanship.' Frontier College Papers, vol. 194, Public Archives of Canada

15 The Toronto *Daily Star*, 24 June 1930. See also Salem Bland, 'Memories of Old Kingston,' ibid., 30 July, 2, 4 Aug. 1938. Bland's notes from Watson's courses are in the Salem Bland Papers, vol. 9, no 811, United Church Archives

16 Quoted in Richard Allen, 'Salem Bland and the Social Gospel in Canada,' (MA thesis, University of Saskatchewan, 1961), 52

17 Salem Bland, 'A Philosophy of Life,' 26 Nov. 1925, Salem Bland Papers, vol. 2, no 158

18 Salem Bland, 'The Kingdom of God realized only in Individual Regeneration,' 18 Jan. 1899, ibid., vol. 4, no 356. Bland's early years are treated in detail in Richard Allen, 'Salem Bland: The Young Preacher,' *Bulletin* of the Committee on Archives of the United Church of Canada 26 (1977): 75–93.

19 Salem Bland, 'A Contribution to a Possible Sketch of My Life,' nd, Bland Papers, vol. 9, no 726

20 Salem Bland, 'The Place of the Kingdom of God in the Preaching of Today,' unidentified newspaper clipping, 12 Feb. 1906, ibid., vol. 3, no 235. See also Richard Allen, 'Children of Prophecy: Wesley College Students in an Age of Reform,' *Red River Valley Historian* (1974): 15–20.

21 See Salem Bland, 'A Faith Rational But Not Rationalistic,' sermon, 22 Oct. 1921, Bland Papers, vol. 6, no 544; 'The Religiousness of Reason,' nd, ibid., vol. 9, no 810; 'Pre-eminence of Christ and Theology. Lecture III,' 30 May 1914, ibid., vol. 3, no 232.

22 Salem Bland, 'The Deeper Life – Not Materialistic Enough,' *Grain Growers' Guide*, 5

June 1918. Bland's statement echoed the 1913 comment of a Presbyterian clergyman, who began a Presbyterian Assembly address on 'The Messenger' by saying: 'The task assigned to a Canadian preacher resembles nothing so much as the general managership of a big department store.' Rev. G.B. Wilson, in *Pre-Assembly Congress: Addresses delivered at the Presbyterian Pre-Assembly Congress, Held in Massey Hall* (Toronto 1913), 32

23 Bland, 'The Deeper Life'

24 Quoted in K.W. McNaught, *A Prophet in Politics* (Toronto 1963), 10, 14–16, 48n. See also William H. Brooks, 'The Uniqueness of Western Canadian Methodism 1840–1925,' *Bulletin* 26 (1977): 68–9, 73n; J. Warren Caldwell, 'The Unification of Methodism in Canada, 1865–1884,' *Bulletin* 19 (1967); William H. Magney, 'The Methodist Church and the National Gospel,' ibid. 20 (1968); Burkhard Kiesekamp, 'Presbyterian and Methodist Divines: Their Case for a National Church in Canada, 1875–1900,' *Studies in Religion* 2 (1973).

25 George John Blewett, *The Study of Nature and the Vision of God* (Toronto 1907), 354. For a description of Woodsworth's view of the nature of religion by 1920 see Richard Allen, *The Social Passion* (Toronto 1971), 101–2. For a comprehensive summary of the origins and course of the Social Gospel movement in Canada see George N. Emory, 'The Origins of Canadian Methodist Involvement in the Social Gospel Movement 1890–1914,' *Bulletin* 26 (1977): 104–19, or the full treatment in *The Social Passion*.

26 S.D. Chown, 'Socialism & The Social Teachings of Jesus, Vanc. Feb. 14, 1914,' 6, S.D. Chown Papers, United Church Archives, vol. 2, no 58b

27 S.D. Chown, 'Sociological Course. Lecture I. Importance of the Study of Sociology,' 1–2, ibid., no 50b

28 D.S. Chown, 'Sociological Course. Lecture II. The Relation of Sociology to the Kingdom of Heaven,' 1–2, ibid., no 51a; 'Lecture I,' 2

29 'Sociological Course. Lecture II,' 12. For an examination of the classical ideal and its relationship to philosophical idealism see S.E.D. Shortt, *The Search for an Ideal* (Toronto 1977), 59–76. See also H. Richard Niebuhr, *Christ and Culture* (New York 1956), 1–115, for theological background and implications.

CHAPTER 8: SCIENCE, AUTHORITY, AND THE AMERICAN EMPIRE

1 See, for example, C.B. Sissons, 'The Rise of Co-operation in Canada,' *Canadian Forum* 1 (1) (Oct. 1920): 8; J.S. Woodsworth, 'Unemployment,' 1 (6) (April 1921): 200–2; Ernest Thomas, 'Social Reform and the Methodist Church,' 1 (9) (June 1921): 264–6; J.S. Woodsworth, 'The Labour Movement in the West,' 2 (19) (April 1922): 585–7; H.W. Wood, 'In Defense of Group Politics,' 3 (27) (Dec. 1922): 72–4; J.S. Woodsworth, 'Mobilizing Progressive Opinion in Canada,' 5 (5) (Nov. 1924): 40–1. For writings on the *Canadian Forum* which have stressed its progressive inclinations see Margaret Prang, 'Some Opinions of Political Radicalism in Canada between the Two World Wars' (MA thesis, University of Toronto, 1953); F.W. Watt, 'Radicalism in English-Canadian Literature since Confederation' (PHD thesis, University of Toronto 1957); Ramsay Cook, 'A Peculiarly Canadian Experience,' *Canadian Forum* 50 (1970): 36–7;

Frank H. Underhill, 'The First Generation,' ibid., 32–3. Several other articles in this
fiftieth anniversary issue of the *Canadian Forum* deal with its early years.
2 W.L. Morton, 'The 1920s,' in J.M.S. Careless and R.C. Brown, eds., *The Canadians*
(Toronto 1967), 205
3 *The Onlooker* 1 (7) (Nov. 1920): 1. See also *Canadian Forum* 1 (3) (dec. 1920): 67; 'The
New Year' [editorial by E.H. Blake] ibid., 1 (4) (Jan. 1921): 102–4; '[The postwar] world
... is something strange and unexpected; neither what was promised, nor yet what is
familiar. Many of the idols of the nineteenth century have been pulled off their pedes-
tals.' The notion of the inevitability of 'progress' was by 1920 no longer accepted, at
least by some, as a truism: see the review of J.B. Bury's *The Idea of Progress*, ibid. 1 (3)
(Dec. 1920): 86–7: 'Progress and civilization – our civilization – became [by the nineteenth century] synonymous terms; it was a comfortable doctrine for, on the whole, a
comfortable world ... But will it last?' R.M. MacIver, then a staff member at the University of Toronto, also questioned 'progress': ibid. 3 (31) (April 1923): 216–18. See also
G.H. [George Hunter], 'Scientific Research,' 6 (71) (Aug. 1926): 340–1; George Hunter,
'Meditations,' 7 (84) (Sept. 1927): 364–6.
4 *The Rebel* 3 (5) (March 1919): 216; see also 1 (1) (Feb. 1917): 3.
5 Ibid., 2 (1) (Oct. 1917): 21; from 'A Mood Sequence in Time of War,' by M
6 Ibid., 2 (5) (Feb. 1918): 200
7 Matthew Arnold, *Culture and Anarchy* (Cambridge 1948), 6, 37, 44–5, 70; *Literature
and Dogma* (New York 1899), xi. Arnold's debt to Bishop Thomas Wilson and his *Max-
ims of Piety and Christianity* (c 1781) merits investigation. Arnold attempted in the
above writings to reconcile an increasingly secularistic rationalism with religious inspiration and perfectionism: 'To make,' in Bishop Wilson's words, 'reason and the will of
God prevail!' (quoted in *Culture and Anarchy*, 45). Despite this attempt, Arnold was
desperately afraid of 'the critical intellect' and its effect upon the creative imagination.
See Lionel Trilling, *Matthew Arnold* (New York 1965), 24–5, 241–2.
8 As a celebration of the sixtieth anniversary of the Canadian publishing house Hunter-
Rose Co, the firm decided to revive Goldwin Smith's *The Bystander* (which George
Maclean Rose had published) under a new title; it did so 'in the belief that an organ of
independent criticism is sadly needed at this particular time.' Foreword to the first number, *The Onlooker* 1 (1) (April 1920): 1. The man chosen to follow in Smith's shoes as
editor was James Cobourg Hodgins, a Presbyterian with experience both in journalism
and the mission field. He also tried his hand occasionally at poetry. Hodgins hoped that
The Onlooker, like *The Bystander* before it, would exercise a 'restraining force' and be
'a great power for righteousness,' ibid., 1.
9 Ibid. (9) (Jan. 1921): 23–4
10 Ibid. 1 (11) (March 1921): 'A Word to the Protectionist Liberals,' 3. Also 1 (8) (Dec.
1920): 21–2; 1 (12) (April 1921): 26–8; 1 (6) (Oct. 1920): 6
11 Ibid. 1 (11) (March 1921): 4
12 This is not to say that the nature of that conviction remained static; on the contrary, the
period of the 1870s to the 1920s marked on one hand an attempt to bolster Christianity
both in the universities (Nathanael Burwash, Sir William Dawson, Daniel Wilson, D.H.
MacVicar, John Watson) and within the institutional churches (Albert Carman); on the

other hand, liberal Protestantism made very strong inroads (Salem Bland, D.H. Macdonnell, A.P. Coleman, J.S. Woodsworth, S.D. Chown, G.M. Grant, Daniel M. Gordon). This shift within Canadian Protestantism meant a significant reorientation of Christian ethics, but scarcely touched the conviction, held by all, that Protestantism (in its various denominations) was the only *true* means by which one could lead a righteous and sanctified life. The result of this conviction, which sometimes bordered upon outright bigotry (the line between conviction and prejudice being a very fine one), can be seen in the social sphere by the assimilationist policies of J.T.M. Anderson, *The Education of the New Canadian* (Toronto 1918) and J.S. Woodsworth, *Strangers Within Our Gates* (Toronto 1909). The Manitoba Schools Question of the 1890s, the debate over Laurier's Autonomy Bills in 1905, and later over Regulation 17 in Ontario, were largely enflamed by a combination of Anglo-Saxon ethnocentricity and an outraged Protestantism then under seige.

13 James Smyth, 'The Faith of the Modern Man,' *Canadian Journal of Religious Thought* [CJRT] 1 (Feb. 1924): 61. For similar views by *Forum* contributors see H.S. Patten, 'Progress and Measurement,' 2 (15) (Dec. 1921): 456–9; GH, 'What Is Science?' 7 (73) (Oct. 1926): 402; and GH, 'Science and Religion,' 7 (77) (Feb. 1927): 142–3.

14 Cushing Strout, 'The Twentieth Century Enlightenment,' *American Political Science Review* 49 (2) (June 1955): 328. That this 'enlightenment' was received favourably by at least some in Canada may be seen in the favourable reviews which the books by some of Strout's twentieth-century technocratic 'philosophers' (Carl Becker, Charles Beard, James Harvey Robinson, Harry Elmer Barnes, Thorstein Veblen), received in the *Canadian Forum* during the 1920s. *Social Planning for Canada*, it might be added, was a work with which any of the above would have been proud to be associated. Indeed, Barnes contributed an article to the *Forum*: 'Dynamic History and Social Reform,' 4 (47) (Aug. 1924): 331–3.

15 Smyth, 'The Faith of the Modern Man,' 68. Men such as Smyth were in an increasingly minoritarian position, however. One exponent of 'Social Service' in the 1920s insisted that social workers could not make progress 'so long as the search for truth' was 'hindered by taboos; whether these are connected with supposed political expediency or theological conceptions, or merely with social customs which were developed in more primitive environments and have lost their validity to-day.' *Canadian Forum* 4 (46) (July 1924): 293. See also 3 (25) (Nov. 1922): 54–6; 5 (58) (July 1925): 293.

16 Smyth, 'The Faith of the Modern Man,' 69–70

17 S.H. Hooke, 'The Saving of the Church,' *Canadian Forum* 3 (30) (March 1923): 168–70; Davidson Ketchum, 'The Saving of God,' 3 (31) (April 1923): 204–6

18 Donald D. McKay to the editor, ibid. 3 (32) (May 1923): 237–8; F.J. Moore to the editor, ibid., 237; H.J. Davis, 'The Saving of Man,' ibid., 238–9; see also Irene Moore, 'The Duty of the Christian Church,' ibid., 3 (33) (June 1923): 272–2. Hooke in fact applauded modern developments in science. Science was coming to recognize that man has both spiritual and purely naturalistic qualities. The resolution of this old antagonism between man 'as the substance of God' and man 'of the substance of man' meant for Hooke that 'there seems no limit to the ultimate possibilities, for the individual and for society, of the development of these forces.' 'That One Force,' ibid. 3 (27) (Dec. 1922): 76–8

19 F.J. Moore to the editor, ibid. 3 (35) (Aug. 1923): 334
20 W.A. Robinson to the editor, ibid.
21 S.H. Hooke, 'A Modern Lay Apologia,' ibid. 335–6. Other correspondence concerning the subject includes J. Duff to the editor, 4 (37) (Oct. 1923): 13–14; W.A. Langton to the editor, ibid., 14.
22 One regular contributor to the *Canadian Forum*, especially affected by the impact of Freudian theory, was Edward Sapir, then in Ottawa as head of the Anthropological Section of the Geological Survey of Canada. Elected to Section II of the Royal Society of Canada in 1922, Sapir later moved to the University of Chicago. It was while he was in Canada, however, that his major works were published, including 'Culture, Genuine and Spurious,' *American Journal of Sociology* 29 (Jan. 1924): 401–29; and *Language* (New York 1921), a pioneering work in linguistics and cultural anthropology. It is still considered a classic in both fields.

As well as contributing articles and reviewing books, Sapir wrote several poems for the *Forum*. It is in these highly personal contributions that the impact of Freudianism can especially be seen. From 'The Dispossessed Philistine (an Interlude)': 'Wild visitors make havoc in the brain,/Possess, harass, leave all bewilderment/When Bacchanalian music's blown and spent/And Bacchanals have frenzied out in vain,/The demon comes, the Philistine is slain,' 3 (36) (Sept. 1923): 367. Or, even more overtly, in 'This Age': 'They say this age is subtle, swift, and dark,/And headstrong with an infinite disgust,/Saying to Live, "We know you for the lust/You are. Cease strumming in the moony park!"'/They say this age is like a frantic shark/That snaps his rapid psychological jaws/Upon those hoary sentimental laws/That still come floating down from Noah's Ark,' ibid., 366. For other poems by Sapir see ibid., 2 (24) (Sept. 1922): 753, and 6 (61) (Oct. 1925): 13. For a review of Sapir's *Language* see ibid., 2 (24) (Sept. 1922): 762–3.
23 Ernest F. Scott, 'Some Doubts About Psychology,' CJRT 1 (2) (April 1924): 98–100
24 G.S. Brett, 'Some Beliefs About Psychology,' *Canadian Forum* 4 (6) (Dec. 1924): 463–72. Among Brett's numerous publications (he was the first editor of the *University of Toronto Quarterly*) are *The Philosophy of Gassendi* (London 1908); *A History of Psychology*, 3 vols. (London 1912–21); and *Psychology, Ancient and Modern* (New York 1928). Both authors' titles give a good indication of the shift of philosophical thought in Canada from the 1870s to the 1920s. For good examples of Brett's attitude towards philosophical idealism, and his position within the philosophical spectrum, see G.S. Brett, 'A Woman in Philosophy,' *Canadian Forum* 3 (31) (April 1923): 212–14; and 'The Philosopher's Stone,' ibid., 6 (72) (Sept. 1926): 370–2.
25 *Canadian Forum* 6 (70) (July 1926): 306–8; 4 (39) (Dec. 1923): 5 (60) (Sept. 1925): 371–2
26 W. Morgan, 'Religion's Right and Value,' CJRT 3 (4) (July-Aug. 1926): 268. Morgan was a well-known theologian and professor of theology at Queen's Theological College. For two studies which reveal both the conflict within the major Protestant denominations over organic union and the debate between traditionalists and 'Moderns' see E.L. Morrow, *Church Union in Canada* (Toronto 1923), and C.E. Silcox, *Church Union in Canada* (Toronto 1933). D.C. Masters, *Protestant Church Colleges in Canada* (Toronto 1966), 133–206, and H.H. Walsh, *The Christian Church in Canada* (Toronto 1968),

288–307, discuss the impact of Liberal Protestantism (Biblical Criticism and the Social Gospel) upon Canadian churches during the period 1890–1930.

27 For an early, yet characteristic, elaboration see Rev. Egerton Ryerson, *Inaugural Address on the Nature and Advantages of an English and Liberal Education ... at the Opening of Victoria College, June 21, 1842* (Toronto 1842); see also [Principal] William Leitch, *Introductory Address at the Opening of the University of Queen's College, November 8, 1860* (Montreal 1860); James George, *The Relation Between Piety and Intellectual Labour* (Kingston 1855); Principal [J.W.] Dawson, *The Duties of Educated Young Men of British North America* (Montreal 1863); Principal [G.M.] Grant, 'Education and Co-Education,' *Rose-Belford's Canadian Monthly and National Review* 3 (5) (Nov. 1879): 509–18; John Watson, *Education and Life* (Kingston 1873) and 'The Higher Life of the Scholar' [university sermon], *Queen's College Journal* 27 (5) (21 Dec. 1899); 88–92; D.M. Gordon, 'Education and Culture' (c 1903) and 'Principles of Education,' (c 1912), Gordon Papers, Queen's University, Kingston; R.A. Falconer, *Idealism in National Character* (Toronto 1920), especially chap. 1: 'The Education of National Character,' 9–38; Rev. Thomas W. Morton, 'Rough-Hewing the Mind,' [Convocation Address, University of Manitoba] (Winnipeg 1926); R.A. Falconer, 'The Tradition of Liberal Education in Canada,' *Canadian Historical Review* 8 (1927): 99–118.

28 By 'idealism' here is meant 'the view that mind and spiritual values are fundamental in the world as a whole,' Paul Edwards, ed., *The Encyclopedia of Philosophy*, vol. IV (New York 1967), 110. This, in Edward's view, is the essence of 'idealism' as a philosophical creed. Upon this basic assumption all idealist philosophers agree; they differ, of course, over the means by which spiritual values can be maintained and over the power of mind for perceiving the real.

The combination of religious and philosophical heritages which went into the making of Canadian institutions of higher learning in the nineteenth century (at least those which were English-speaking) served to reinforce this idealistic position and to see Canadian educators attempting to elevate 'cultural life' by idealist social ethics. The tradition is by no means dead at mid-twentieth century. In Canadian writings since 1950 it may be seen in the work of Northrop Frye, George P. Grant, Hilda Neatby, and especially in the *Report* of the Royal Commission on National Development in the Arts, Letters and Sciences (Ottawa 1951). For example, the commissioners state: 'Physical links are essential to the unifying process but true unity belongs to the realm of ideas. It is a matter for men's minds and hearts.' And elsewhere they note: 'The work with which we have been entrusted is concerned with nothing less than the spiritual foundations of our national life.' Perhaps convictions of this kind are to be expected from a royal commission which prefaced its *Report* from Saint Augustine's *City of God*.

29 For example R.E. Macnaghten, 'The Future of Latin,' *University Magazine* 7 (Feb. 1908): 90–101; A. Macphail, 'Oxford and Working-Class Education,' ibid. 9 (Feb. 1910): 36–50; A. Macphail, 'An Obverse View of Education,' 10 (April 1910): 192–204; Norman W. De Witt, 'The Educated Layman,' 9 (Feb. 1910): 18–19. Articles dealing implicitly with the issue may be found as follows: 7 (Feb. 1908): 4; 8 (Feb. 1909): 4; 8 (April 1909): 304–8.

30 J.A. Dale, 'A Challenge to Education,' *Canadian Forum* 2 (16) (Jan. 1922): 488–9
31 R.A. Falconer, *Idealism in National Character*, 82–83
32 Ibid., 194–5
33 *The Rebel* 1 (1) (Feb. 1917), 14–18. For similar views by *Forum* contributors see the letter to the editor by IAI), *Canadian Forum* 1 (5) (Feb. 1921): 150–1; and, surprisingly, Douglas Bush, 'Young Canada,' ibid. 3 (36) (Sept. 1923): 372–3. Bush here chides Canadian students for no longer searching for 'the "larger" vision,' and for 'replacing idealism with utility' (373).
34 H.P. Whidden, 'What Is a Liberal Education?' CJRT 1 (1) (Feb. 1924): 36–9. Similar concerns may be found in *Canadian Forum* 1 (1) (Oct. 1920): 3; 1 (3) (Dec. 1920): 70–2; 1 (8) (May 1921): 235–7; 4 (8) (May 1921): 228.
35 For example, [Andrew Macphail], 'A Voice from the East,' *University Magazine* 9 (Dec. 1910): 518–21; *The Onlooker* 1 (1) (April 1920): 15; 1 (9) (Jan. 1921): 3–4
36 J.K. Robertson, 'Pure Science and the Humanities,' *Queen's Quarterly* 26 (1) (Aug. 1918): 54
37 HB, 'Leadership and the Universities,' *The Rebel* 3 (3) (Jan. 1919): 103–5; Falconer, *Idealism in National Character*, 9–93
38 'American Capital Buying Canada,' *Literary Digest* 73 (6 May 1922): 89–90
39 *Canadian Finance* quoted in *Literary Digest* 71 (26 Nov. 1921): 20; G.E. Jackson, 'Trade and Industry,' *Canadian Forum* 6 (65) (Feb. 1926): 161; Richard De Brisay, 'The Opportunity of the City,' ibid. 5 (60) (Sept. 1925): 364–6
40 *The Onlooker* 1 (11) (March 1921): 3. A *Canadian Forum* editorial half a year earlier had said virtually the same thing: 'Real independence is not the product of tariffs and treaties. It is a spiritual thing,' 1 (1) (Oct. 1920): 3.
41 'The Plague of the American Cartoon,' *The Onlooker* 1 (8) (Dec. 1920): 20–2; 'The Invasion of American Literary Slush,' ibid. 1 (6) (Oct. 1920): 6–11. For another, equally vitriolic, attack on Americans while at the same time voicing a vigorous defence of the British empire and 'sound British stock' see the article by Hodgins quoted in 'Canadian Literary Declaration of Independence,' *Literary Digest* 67 (Dec. 1920): 35.
42 'The Invasion of American Literary Slush,' 7, 10–11
43 *The Empire Review* article was by R.S. Somerville: 'Canada and Jonathan and John,' quoted in *The Living Age* 330 (July 1926): 227–32; the *National Review* article was quoted in 'Why England Must Save Canada,' *Literary Digest* 19 (27 Nov. 1923): 19–20; *Canadian Forum* 3 (35) (Aug. 1923): 325–6; 6 (67) (April 1926): 217–18.
44 Robert Ayre, 'The American Empire,' *Canadian Forum* 7 (76) (Jan. 1927): 105–6. In connection with 'Jiggs and Maggy, Doug and Mary' (from the comic strip 'Bringing up Father') it is interesting, and not a little pathetic, to note a comment made by the editor of *The Onlooker*: 'Whoever saw a father like him? He is dwarfed, mis-shapen, ugly. He has the prognathism of a savage and cranium of an ape. He is a drunkard, a gambler, a libertine ... As for the creature his wife, she is the last word in repulsiveness.' 'The Plague of the American Cartoon,' 21
45 'Canada Our Best Customer,' *Literary Digest* 99 (20 Oct. 1928): 14–15
46 *The Rebel* 1 (2) (March 1917): 16; E.E. Braithwaite, 'New Era for Canada,' *Canadian*

Monthly 53 (June 1919): 92–3; editorial comment on Willison's speech, *Vancouver Province* (24 Sept. 1918), quoted in J.S. Willison, 'New Problems of a New Era' (Canadian Reconstruction Assocation, nd), 18

47 GH, 'Popular Science – A Contradiction in Terms,' *Canadian Forum* 6 (68) (May 1926): 245. For other *Forum* articles which also show this insistence that 'Scientific Knowledge' (and its pursuit) does not constitute the only means of perceiving reality, and does not eliminate notions such as 'will' or 'desire' see H.S. Patten, 'Progress and Measurement,' 2 (15) (Dec. 1921): 456–9; Hartley Munroe Thomas, 'The Saving Symbol,' 3 (34) (July 1923): 302–4; S.H. Hooke, 'The Religion of a Scientist: I,' 5 (51) (dec. 1924): 81–2; S.H. Hooke, 'The Religion of a Scientist: II,' 5 (52) (Jan. 1925): 110–12; 'Pestle,' 'Concerning the Nature of Things' 5 (58) (July 1925): 306; Peter Sandiford, (77) (Feb. 1927): 142–3; GH,' 'Meditations,' 7 (84) (Sept. 1927): 364–6.

48 See George H. Daniels, *The Pursuit of Science in Jacksonian America* (New York 1968), 20–31; George H. Daniels, *Science in American Society* (New York 1971), 281.

49 GH, 'Popular Science,' 245–6

50 The most forceful attempt in Canada to utilize evolutionary theory to buttress cultural orthodoxy was made by John Watson of Queen's; Watson, like other Hegelian idealists of his day, attempted to incorporate scientific evolutionary thought within the idealist schema. At a more popular level, the turning of Herbert Spencer and William Graham Sumner on their heads, through the use of Darwinian terminology, to combat 'materialist' ethics may be seen in a speech given by Rudyard Kipling to the students of McGill University in 1907: 'When ... you go out into the battle of life you will be confronted by an organized conspiracy which will try to make you believe that the world is governed by the idea of wealth for wealth's sake, and that all means which lead to the acquisition of that wealth are, if not laudable, at least expedient. Those of you who have fitly imbibed the spirit of your university ... will violently resent that thought, but you will live and eat and move and have your being in a world dominated by that thought. Some of you will probably succumb to the poison of it.' Rudyard Kipling, 'Ad Universitatem,' *University Magazine* 6 (1907): 450–1. The *Canadian Annual Review* selected Kipling as Canada's 'Outstanding Visitor' for that year.

51 GH, 'Scientific Research,' *Canadian Forum* (71) (Aug. 1926): 340-1

52 See the articles by 'GH' above (note 47).

53 André Siegfried, *Canada: An International Power*, trans. Doris Hemming (London 1949), 13. Originally published in 1937 as *Canada*

54 David S. Landes, *The Unbound Prometheus: Technological Change and Industrial Development in Western Europe from 1750 to the Present* (Cambridge 1969), 24

55 Falconer, *Idealism in National Character*, 12–13; F.H. Underhill, 'Bentham and Benthamism,' *Queen's Quarterly* 39 (4) (Nov. 1932): 668. Underhill moved to Toronto in 1927.

Index